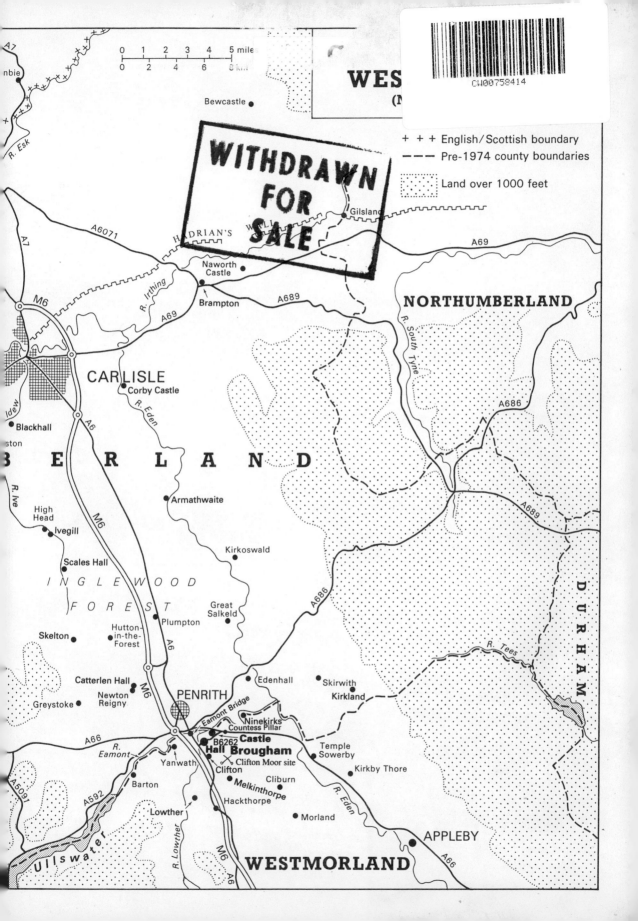

A HISTORY OF
Brougham Hall
and
High Head Castle

Brougham Hall, 1876, by John Dobbin (1815-88). Dobbin, a Darlington-born watercolour artist exhibited at the Royal Academy between 1842-75 and at the Society of British Artists. He specialised in architectural paintings.

A HISTORY OF
Brougham Hall
and
High Head Castle

MARK THOMAS

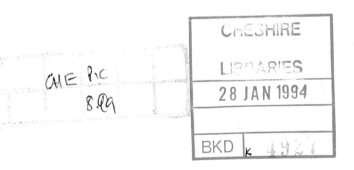

Phillimore

1992

Published by
PHILLIMORE & CO. LTD
Shopwyke Hall, Chichester, Sussex

ISBN0 85033 845 X

Printed and bound in Great Britain by
BIDDLES LTD.,
Guildford, Surrey

To Peter Brougham Wyly for his tireless and invaluable help and advice, Miss Marjorie (Peggy) Stacey for all her assistance and research and to Christopher and Alison Terry for their kindness, help and encouragement during the research and writing of this book.

'Unless the Lord builds the house, its builders labour in vain.'

Psalm 127, Verse 1

Contents

List of Illustrations

Frontispiece: Watercolour of Brougham Hall, 1876

Illustration Acknowledgements

I would like to thank everyone who has helped me with the illustrations in this book: Alisdair Aynscough, 2-3, 8, 57-58, 61; Lord Brougham, 50, 52; The Brougham Hall Charitable Trust (for allowing me to reproduce 13, 32, 59; Charles Fearnsides photographs, 36, 44; Jameson's photograph, 52; John Valentine photographs, 37-39) Mark Fiennes, 55; Fitzwilliam Museum, Cambridge, 46; Sam Gardener Photography, 5, 16-18, 20-21, 27-28, 33-34; Andrew Humphries, 11-12, 15, 47-49; Kendal Record Office for the reproduction of L. Benson's print in Hutchinson's *History of Cumberland*, 22; MacAteer Evans, 1, 7-8, 60; Mr. Freddy Markham/MacAteer Evans, 40-2, 45; Mr. Tom Marshall, 26; National Portrait Gallery, 6, 23-24, 31; Geoff Nelson, 54; The RIBA Library/Geremy Butler Photography, 30; Martin Rice/Downing Street Studios, 10, 18-19; Anthony Sharp, 14; Quentin Simpson/Studio 7, Carlisle, 4; The Tank Museum, Bovington, 53; Deborah Thomas, 56; University College, London (for E. Fowler Richard's of Penrith's photograph, 25, 43, and Herbert Watkins' photograph, 35; Peter Brougham Wyly, 29. Many thanks are also extended to the various private collections from which the following pictures have been loaned: 10, 12, 16, 17, 18, 19, 20, 21, 27, 33, 34.

Lastly, I would like to thank the Christopher Wood Gallery of 15, Motcombe Street, London, SW1 for permission to reproduce the John Dobbin watercolour of Brougham Hall that is the frontispiece of the book, and Mr. Paul Smith of Paul Smith Outfitters Ltd., 41-44 Floral Street, Covent Garden, London for courteously allowing me to reproduce the Neville Lytton oil painting of the Dower family on the back cover.

Foreword by Lord Hailsham of St Marylebone

My own connexion with Brougham Hall, which I have never visited, is necessarily limited to the respect I continue to feel for the memory of my eminent predecessor, the first Lord Brougham and 35 Vaux whose family home it was. In doing so I commend this scholarly collection of essays relating to a unique and historically most interesting part of our national heritage.

Brougham was one of the most talented and many-sided of his ancient office, reformer, educator, good European, innovative administrator, resolute and fearless defender of Queen Caroline and unlike most Lord Chancellors, the scion of an ancient family of landowners which is what gives a special cachet to the house in which his family had lived for generations, and of which he was legitimately, and intensely proud.

I was delighted when I discovered some years ago that this ancient edifice had acquired a Society of Friends to protect and improve its environment. I hope this volume, well worth the study, will enlarge many libraries, serve to increase the number of and prestige of the Friends and to keep bright and respected the memory of one of the most versatile and, in 18th-century parlance, ingenious of its former residents.

Hailsham of St Marylebone

Preface

This has been a hard but rewarding book to write. In it I have told the story of Brougham Hall and High Head Castle and how their owners, architects and builders shaped them from medieval times to the present day. Though many families figure in these two inter-linked stories, I have devoted much space to the Brougham family in my account because they dominate the narrative and are the connecting link between its two strands.

In this book, Peter Brougham Wyly (who drew up the Brougham genealogical charts) and I have tried to dissect and dispel some of the many historical myths which have developed about the Broughams. These (like the inventions William Brougham introduced into the family pedigree) have too often appeared in the work of some professional historians. At the same time, any errors which appear are my own, and I take full responsibility for them. Much new material, a great deal of it from previously unpublished sources has been uncovered and used in this account. This material often sheds new light on various aspects of the family, such as its work in the exise service in the 18th century, on the private life of Henry, 1st Lord Brougham, the fraught purchase of half of High Head in 1854, and the sad, devastating collapse of the family's status and finances under the 4th Lord Brougham's control in the early 1930s. The result is, I feel an interesting and revealing story. It fascinated me as I researched it, and as it had not been told in one account before I enjoyed the challenge of writing it.

The book is not a complete history of the Brougham family, or a life of the 1st Lord Brougham. Rather it aims to tell the history of the Hall and Castle and of the Broughams and other owners who were closely associated with them. Thus Broughams who were part of or sprang directly from the Brougham Hall branch of the family are mentioned in the text or shown in the seven charts at the back of the book. The narrative also mentions families like the Birds and Carletons at Brougham, and the Richmond, Richmond-Gale-Braddyll, Hills and Dower families at High Head.

The book's narrative is in eleven chapters. The first of these takes Brougham Hall's story from 1066 (when Wilfred de Burgham probably held it) through its division into three shares after the Broughams died out in the male line in 1276 up to the extinction of the first Broughams of Brougham in 1608. The second chapter traces the Hall's story from 1609 to 1726. This period saw its re-uniting under one owner c.1676 by James Bird, steward to the redoubtable Lady Anne Clifford, and its purchase from Bird's heirs by the dynamic John, Commissioner Brougham of Scales in 1726. John, son of the first Brougham squire, Henry Brougham of Scales (c.1638-98), was the most successful Brougham of the 18th century. His career as landowner, barrister and excise com-missioner is described in Chapter Three, along with that of his nephew, Henry Richard Brougham. Henry Richard Brougham, who inherited both the Richmond and Brougham family lands built High Head Castle, a magnificent Gibbs-style mansion on the site of a ruinous pele he had inherited from his grandmother, Mrs. Isabella Miller. Sadly when he died the Castle was unfinished, and this led to a period of decline for the family which is described in Chapter Four. This covers the years 1749-1810, when the Brougham squires, John, Henry the Elder, and Henry the Younger struggled with a much reduced estate and legal and financial problems. However, when Henry the Younger's eldest son, Henry Peter, inherited the estate in 1810 he transformed both it and his family's standing, helped by his brothers, James and William. Henry Peter's public career as barrister, M.P., journalist, inventor, legal reformer and Lord Chancellor (1830-34) is outlined in Chapter Five. The subsequent development of the Brougham family, and Brougham Hall's striking transformation between 1829-47, by the Gothic architect, L. N. Cottingham, is described in Chapter Six. Chapter Seven (1847-68) tells of the later years of Henry, 1st Lord Brougham and the increasing dominance of his brother, William, who had R. C. Hussey rebuild part of the Hall between 1862-65. The story of the stewardship of William, 2nd Lord Brougham and his son, Henry Charles, is told in Chapter Eight (1868-1927). Chapter Nine takes the history of High Head Castle from 1820 to 1956. It describes how the Castle, which had been split in two by the feuding Gale and Baynes families, following Henry Richmond Brougham's death, were acquired in 1820 and 1854 by the Broughams. They in turn sold it as a farmhouse to the Hills family in 1902. The Hills family restored it as a country house but misfortune intervened. After being sold twice more it was burnt down in 1956. Chapter Ten, (1927-67) returns to Brougham and the devastation that both the Hall and the Brougham family experienced under the control of Victor, the 4th Lord Brougham. For the Hall, partial demolition, use in the Second World War as a secret tank development area, then as a camp for Polish displaced persons, was followed by its purchase by Beacon Builders of Penrith in 1967. Chapter Eleven traces both mansions' history from that date, following Brougham's pillage and subsequent regeneration and High Head's recent history (despite being saved from demolition in 1986) as one of the north-west's melancholy shells.

Acknowledgements

I would like to thank everyone who has helped me with this book. So many have done so that it seems arbitrary to select a few whose great help (and patience!) stand out. However, Peter Brougham Wyly has been a staunch friend and provided constant encouragement in the face of many obstacles. He shared with me any information he uncovered and very generously devised the fine Brougham genealogical trees for the book. I have also been helped by another Brougham genealogist, Miss Peggy Stacey, who has given a plethora of information, particularly on less well known Broughams. Christopher and Alison Terry have been very hospitable, and helpful and supportive of the project, despite having to bear many other burdens of their own. I would also like to acknowledge the help of Miss Gillian Furlong, the Manuscript Room archivist at University College, London, for answering my enquiries kindly and patiently. I would like to thank Mr. Andrew Humphries of the Cumbria College of Agriculture for telling me much I did not know about the history of High Head Castle, and for lending me items from his large collection of High Head related material for reproduction. I am very grateful, too, to Dr. Janet Myles of Leicester Polytechnic for lending me part of her Ph.D thesis on L. N. Cottingham and correcting errors in Chapter Six. I would also like to thank Lord Hailsham for the Foreword to the book. I would also like to say a special thank-you to Mr. Alasdair Aynscough for lending me his vast run of site news-sheets on the Brougham Hall restoration project and his avalanche of photographic negatives of the Hall site from which to choose some illustrations. Lord Brougham also deserves mention for being unfailingly helpful in many ways. I would also like to thank the staff of libraries and record offices I have used for their help. Others who have kindly provided me with information include: Mr. Roger Bird, Mr. Michael Maclagan, the late Mr. C. Roy Hudleston, Prof. Gerald Aylmer, Dr. S. T. Chapman of Penrith Museum, Dalemain Estate Office, Mr. M. Dennett (Hon. Archivist, Saddleworth Museum, Oldham), Lt. Col. J. J. Dingwall, D.S.O., Mrs. A. L. G. Dower, Dr. Kenneth Garlick, Mr. Richard Mounsey, Mr. Keith Richmond, Mrs. Dorothy Snell, Dr. R. T. Spence, Mr. B. Stacey and various members and relations of the Hills family. Last, but not least I would like to thank my parents for the help they have given me, especially with proof-reading, and also my sister, Dr. Rosalind Thomas, for her constructive criticism of parts of the book. Getting a family history with only specialist appeal published is no easy task. It is inevitably a non-commercial venture which needs people to buy a 'pre-publication' copy and to supply generous grant aid. The project has been fortunate enough to receive enough of both to meet its costs. I would like to thank everyone who bought a copy of the book in advance. In particular I would like to thank those who gave grants to meet the cost of publishing the book, especially the Curwen Archives Trust, for their handsome generosity, British Nuclear Fuels plc and Mr. Christopher Brougham Q.C., for their very kind and substantial donations. I would also like to thank an anonymous charitable trustee and the Brougham Hall Charitable Trust for their quite substantial financial support. Lastly I would like to thank Miss Mary Burkett O.B.E. for her help, enthusiasm and advice and the Friend of Brougham who almost single-handedly kept this project afloat with a large interest-free loan, which met much of the cost. Thanks are also due to Miss Cathleen Blackburn of solicitors Morrell, Peel and Gamlen of Oxford for swiftly devising a contract for this book. I would like to end this list by thanking Mr. Noel Osborne, Mr. Simon Fletcher and Miss Helen Chadwick, of Phillimore and Co. Ltd. for all their assistance with this book and forebearance, despite the delays and difficulties in researching, writing and correcting it.

Chapter One

Genesis: Brougham Hall to 1608 and the Rise of the Broughams of Blackhall and Scales in the 17th Century

In the Eden Valley's rolling hills, on the B6262 two miles south of Penrith, is Brougham Hall. It is just east of the village of Eamont Bridge and bounded west and north by the A6 and the A66. Near the River Eamont, it is some 437 ft. above sea level. It is easy to see what drew medieval knights to this site. It had some obvious advantages. These included a natural defensive position on the brow of a hill, and water. This came from an artesian well in the courtyard (which still rises summer and winter), a spring on the Hall's west side (now in a grotto) and to the north-west another spring, which once came up through the floor of neighbouring St Wilfred's chapel.

When Brougham became settled and fortified is unclear. There are other very early fortifications in the immediate area, one dominated by border conflict until the early 17th century. Mayburgh Henge (a massive circular fort built *c.*2500 B.C.), King Arthur's Round Table (*c.*1800 B.C.), and the Roman fort Brocavum are but three. Brocavum (just south of Brougham Castle) has the closest connection with Brougham. In A.D. 76, the Roman army of Petillius Cerialis arrived in the Eden Valley. They constructed roads east of what is now Penrith, from north to south and east to west. One, called High Street, probably ran through the Hall's site. The routes all intersected at the Roman fort of Brocavum, whose civilian population seems to have lived outside the walls. Shown on the third-century Antonine Itinerary, Brocavum was five stations away from York, after Veteris (Brough) and before Lugavalio (Carlisle), 21 miles away. It was probably visited by the Emperor Hadrian in A.D. 122 and occupied (on the evidence of recovered pottery) by the Romans in the third and fourth centuries. By the year 400 the Romans had abandoned it, leaving a Romano-British settlement by the fort. Unfortunately Danish and Norwegian raiders attacked along the Roman roads, forcing the villagers to move to a spot near Ninekirks by the Eden River.

Information about Brougham Hall in early medieval times is scarce. Firstly, there is the problem of the derivation of the name 'Brougham'. The English Place Name Society's volume for Westmorland (1967) lists more than 10 different spellings of it: Bruham, Burgham, Broham, Brouham, Brougham, Browgham, Broweham, Brugham, Burham, Browham, Browgam and Browhame. A. L. F. Rivet and Colin Smith's *The Place-Names of Roman Britain* (Batsford, 1979) says that it might derive from 'Brocavum' (meaning either place of badgers, pointed place, or heathery place). This seems unlikely. The more convincing explanations put forward by Rivet and Smith are that the Old English words 'bru' (brow of a hill) and 'ham' (homestead) became fused together or that the word is a metathesised form of the Old English word 'Burh-ham' (meaning homestead near the fortification). The site's first recorded probable owners are equally obscure. The de Burgham lords (who probably held it in Edward the Confessor's reign) were, unusually, allowed by William the Conqueror to keep their lands. The first of this family to be recorded is Wilfred de Burgham in Henry I's reign (1100-35). The de Burghams retained their lands by drengage (military service) to the de Veteriponts, who lived at nearby Brougham Castle.

Not surveyed for Domesday Book and under Scottish rule, Cumberland and Westmorland only became permanently part of England in 1157. As a result, their early medieval landowners are poorly documented. Odard de Burgham (1140-85), the probable owner of Brougham Hall, appears however in unflattering references in English records of 1176/7. In 1173-4 William the Lion, King of Scotland, invaded England with an army of 80,000 men. He failed to take Carlisle, but then took Appleby very easily and, after some effort, Brough. Odard de Burgham, something of a rogue, was third-in-command at Appleby under its Constable, Gospatric, son of Orme. Odard and others quickly gave up the castle to the Scots. After this, fearing the wrath of Henry II on the latter's return from France, Odard escaped on the Second Crusade. For surrendering Appleby, Gospatric was fined 500 marks and Odard 20 marks by the king.

Undaunted, Odard later bore arms against the king. The Pipe Roll for 1176 (22 Henry II), (in the Chapel of Rolls) records: 'Udardus de Browham renders account for 80 marks (four times 20) because he was with the King's enemies. In the Treasury 40 marks – and he owes 40 marks'. Though in the mid-19th century the Broughams proudly displayed Odard's alleged sword, shirt of chain-mail and hauberk in the Hall, he was clearly a far from heroic figure. What drew the family to him was the discovery in October 1846 of his grave in Ninekirks church. Under a grave slab carved with a cross flory with a shield on one side and sword on the other, was a complete skeleton, an iron prick spur and an interesting elliptical piece of glass, later called the Brougham Cup-Mount, decorated with metal ornament. In an article in the journal *Medieval Archaeology* in 1977, 'A Cup-mount from Brougham, Cumbria', Mr. Richard Bailey concluded that it was an example of eighth-century insular metalwork, possibly of Pictish manufacture and perhaps originally buried in the Viking period.

The next recorded de Burgham is Gilbert de Burgham. Perhaps Odard's son, he was definitely lord of the manor of Brougham. Gilbert believed discretion the better part of valour. Anxious to avoid going to Normandy with King John's army, he incurred a 50

1.   The tomb of Odard de Burgham (1140-85) in Ninekirks church.

mark fine in 1201-2 for not appearing for military service. An entry in the Rolls reads: 'Seventeen drengi of Westmorland whose names Symon of Pategil has, give to our Lord the King, Fifty Marks that they may remain and not cross the seas, at the passage of our Lord the King'. Between 1216 and 1218, Gilbert concluded an agreement with his over-lord, Robert de Veteripont. He granted Robert rights over half the village of Brougham and its advowson, agreeing to pay for holding the rest with cornage (payment with produce) rather than drengage. As a direct result of the deal, the de Veteriponts could enlarge their hunting grounds in Whinfell Forest, moving the inhabitants to Brougham from the village of Ninekirks, which was then flattened.

Gilbert de Burgham's life is poorly documented, but we know he was buried at Ninekirks in 1230. In 1846, his 6 ft. 2 in. skeleton was discovered in the chancel of Ninekirks church under a slab carved with three sword shapes. After his death there is something of a gap in Brougham's history until 1272, when the de Burghams ran out of male heirs. As a result the estate was divided into three, its parts being held by Christiana de Burgham, William de Crackenthorpe and Henry Rydin. The last two may have mar-ried sisters of Christiana. This was a very important change for the Hall. The 'domus de Bruhame' was then in a dilapidated state.[1] Until 1676 the Hall was to be held in divided ownership.

From now on there are scattered references to the holders of Brougham Hall. In 1286 (14 Edward I), Idonea de Veteripont (Robert's younger daughter) had assigned to her the homage and service of the holders of the three shares of the manor of Brough-am, Christiana de Burgham, William de Crackenthorpe, and Henry Rydin (or Reddings). In 1315-16 (8 Edward II), John Godberd, William de Crack-enthorpe and Henry de Red-dings held the manor. Its ward-ship was valued at £3 6s. 8d., and its cornage at 13s. 6d. In 1338-9 John de Reddings and Agnes his wife suf-fered a recovery of land at Brougham (that is, they were forced by court ruling to give up the land). However, in 1345

2.   Brougham Hall: the 13th-century gateway.

(18 Edward III) a new set of holders appear in the shape of William de Crackenthorpe, John Tyndal and John Trotter. How had Tyndal and Trotter gained shares? The situation had altered by 1370-1 when one John Cuthberd (or Godberd) died, his inquisition post mortem showing that he was possessed of one third of the Manor. He paid for this and 40 acres by cornage. He also paid 2s. every year and provided three quarters and three bushels of oats for the 'puture' of the foresters of Roger de Clifford, Lord of Westmorland. Cuthberd also paid 10d. to the maintenance of the king's bailiff.

John Cuthberd's will named one John Fernesyde (of whom little is recorded) as his heir. In 1379 (2 Richard II), however, there is a record of the bounder roll of the manor being agreed between Roger de Clifford and John de Burgham. This, however, does not mean that John de Burgham (Sheriff of Westmorland in 1351 and 1362) held any of the manor. Records of 1392-3 (15 Richard II) mention John de Tyndal and William de Crackenthorpe as holding two shares of the manor. It is likely that the third part was held by Thomas Redin, Rydin or Reddings, lord of the manor in 1394-5. In 1393 he agreed with the rector of Brougham, Edward Skelling, that 'all manners of sacraments of the Church' were to be said in the chapel at Brougham except burials. There was to be song and mass on Christmas morning, and high mass and 'offering' later at the church. Easter would be celebrated with 'mattins with resurrection and soling mass for servants and old aged persons and sick persons' at the chapel, the rest going to high mass at the church. Redin granted the rector and his successors a tenement and one acre in return for finding 'two seargies[2] afore St Wilfrey, on his own proper costs'.

After Thomas Reding comes another puzzling gap in the records. In 1423, however, on the death of John de Clifford, an inquisition found that two parts of the manor of Brougham were held by John de Lancaster and Katherine, his wife, and by John de Crackenthorpe. The first part was held in the right of Katherine de Lancaster. This situation was unchanged in 1425. The de Lancaster family, according to Hugh Owen, traced their recorded ancestry back to the 12th century and had in 1319 acquired the manors of Hartsop and Sockbridge in the parish of Barton.[3] It is, however, a mystery how Katherine acquired her right to a part of the manor of Brougham. The third part was held by Johan Teasdale. In 1435 the de Lancaster moiety was held by William Thorneburgh. The Teasdales' part in 1438-9 (16 Henry VI) was given by Johan (or Joan) Teasdale to Henry Bird when he married her daughter, another Johan. According to C. Roy Hudleston, the pedigree of 18 generations of the Bird family made by Gregory King, Rouge Dragon in 1681 and certified by Sir William Dugdale, says this Joan was John Teasdale of Walton's daughter.[4] Her mother, the elder Joan, was the daughter and heiress of Richard Tyndale. Both Hudleston and Nicholson and Burn agree that this marriage resulted in Henry Bird acquiring a third of the manor.

The second quarter of the 15th century marked Brougham's first connection with the Bird family. Some accounts say that the Bird family originated from Little Croglin in the 12th century, others that they came from Birdoswald, Gillesland on the Roman wall and took their name from it. Henry Bird is supposed to have died 'before 1463'. In 1453 John Bird, John Crackenthorpe de Newbiggin and John Burgham held the manor. But the ownership of the manor was unstable. The Calendar of Patent Rolls shows that on 11 July 1471, William and John Parre, knights (and the heirs male of their bodies), were granted the manors and lordships of 'Pendrageon (*sic*), Burgh, Appilby (*sic*), Burgham Maller-stang and Whynfell', with their members and knight's fees, advowsons and services of free tenants and still held them in 1474-5. However, in 1475 William Parre received a licence to grant 'Pendragon, Burgh and Appulby, Burgham' to the king's kinsman, George, Archbishop of York, John Conyers, knight, John Whelpdale, clerk, and Richard Glebra, chaplain and their heirs without fine or fee according to the form of the act in Parliament at Westminster, 6 October (12 Edward 4). He was going to cross the sea with the king.

It is impossible to draw a genealogical chart linking the medieval de Burghams with the Burghams and the two Brougham families of Brougham Hall because, unfortunately, there is little information to indicate how or if successive Burgham or Brougham holders of the Hall and manor were related. In 1440, Thomas Brougham (called 'the Elder' on his coming to an agreement with Henry Bird on 10 July 1439) and his wife Joan bought half Brougham manor from William and Eleanor Thornburgh. In 1482 John Burgham held the moiety. In 1495-6 (10 Henry VII), John Burgham died seised of one third of the manor of Brougham. He may have held two-thirds and was succeeded by his son, another John. This John, 10 years later in 1505-6, is recorded as one of three holders of the manor, and he, John Crackenthorpe and William Bird each paid 11s. per annum. Almost a generation later in 1526 (18 Henry VIII), Christopher Burgham, John Crackenthorpe and William Bird held the manor, paying cornage of 13s. 6d. each to the Clifford family. Christopher Burgham also bought an estate in Brougham from Thomas Sandforth and Christopher Crackenthorpe. It is not clear what relation Christopher was to the second John Burgham. Perhaps either or both had a hand in constructing the Tudor Hall and byre of c.1480-1520 at Brougham.

Christopher Burgham (perhaps the Christopher Brugham named in legal documents as a 'gentleman of Westmorland' in 1539) may have been the father of John Brougham. John (who died on 18 November 1552) held one third of the manor of Brougham in 1552. According to Bellasis (*Westmorland Church Notes*) he married Elizabeth Seymour, daughter of Lancelot Seymour of Armathwaite. Their children were Henry (b. 20 January 1539), Thomas, Christopher, John, Agnes and Jane. Henry Brougham, the eldest of these

3. Brougham Hall: the Tudor Hall (*c*.1480-1520).

children occurs in records of Brougham Hall. Henry was a ward of Reynold Warcopp, a local landowner. According to the Calendar of Patent Rolls, on 8 April 1554 Reynold Warcopp held one third of the manor of Brougham as guardian of Henry, then fourteen. Warcopp also had to decide whom Henry should marry, a problem he solved by marrying his charge to Dorothy Warcop (possibly his own daughter). The other two thirds of the manor were held by Margaret, wife of William Crackenthorpe and John their son, and the widow of Henry Bird in 1552-60.

Sometime before 1563, John Crackenthorpe's mother sold his third of the manor to James Bird. A licence for Henry Brougham to enter on his land on reaching his 21st birthday (his majority) is dated 28 May 1561. In 1563 (5 Elizabeth I), Henry Brougham was in possession of the family share of Brougham. The same year he had a suit in chancery against Thomas Bird concerning some land called Newlands. This suit may not have succeeded since in 1568 he is recorded as conveying some land to Thomas Bird. He died the next year, in 1569. His will is dated 1565.

Henry and Dorothy Brougham had five children: Thomas (the eldest), Edward, Elizabeth, Margaret and Katherine. In 1581 Thomas was ward to Thomas Warcop, but later that year was in possession of part of the manor of Brougham. Three years later, in 1586, he was selling some land to James Bird. According to Brougham genealogist, Peter Brougham Wyly, Thomas got married before 1593 to a woman whose first name was Agnes. Her surname is unknown. In August 1604 Thomas Brougham bought the manor of Kirkland. On 7 January 1608, however, he died, leaving no male heirs. His sisters, Elizabeth, Margaret and Katherine, transferred their shares in a deed of 29 March that year to Agnes (alive in 1609). A summary of this deed (produced in court proceedings in 1843) says that it transferred 'all that manor capital messuage and demesne lands called Brougham Hall with appurtenances To hold to the said Agnes and her assigns during her life'. This arrangement was short-lived, though. The Brougham third was eventually sold to a local farmer, William Wright. One third was sold to Agnes, widow of William Fleming of Rydal, while another third remained the Birds'. No Brougham held an interest in the Hall for more than 100 years afterwards.

The extinction of the 16th-and 17th-century Broughams of Brougham did not mean the family's extinction in Cumberland and Westmorland. The will of John Brougham (d. 1552) mentions one Peter Brougham without, unfortunately, saying what relation he was to John. When Peter Brougham died in 1581 he was living in Eamont Bridge. His house, he claimed, 'these manie years hath not bene spoiled nor devided'. His will mentions his wife Jane (possibly a Dudley), his son Henry Brougham (born in 1560 or before: he had reached his majority by 1581), his nephew Roger Salkeld and members of the Dudley family of Yanwath, just south of Penrith. Peter Brougham had founded a new branch of the Brougham family, which was to reach gentry rank by the 1660s, eclipsing its ancestors' achievements.

Henry Brougham proved his father, Peter's, will in 1581. By the early 1600s he was living at Blackhall, in St Cuthbert's parish, Carlisle. His first marriage was to Jane Wharton of Kirkby Thore. This produced a daughter Jane, who married Edward Aglionby. Henry Brougham's second marriage was to Katherine, daughter of Thomas Fallowfield of Melkinthorpe Hall, at Morland on 21 October 1602. According to Peter Brougham Wyly, Katherine may have been a distant relation. Jane Brougham (possibly daughter of John Brougham, d. 1552) had married a Thomas Fallowfield at St James' church, Garlickhithe, London, on 27 November 1569. Was Katherine their daughter? Whatever the relationship, Katherine Fallowfield's husband was clearly a reasonably well-off yeoman farmer. Wyly estimates that their son and heir, Thomas Brougham, was born c.1619 when his father would have been about sixty. Around this time Henry made an important purchase. On 28 July 1619, an indenture was drawn up '... BETWEEN Robert Southwycke of Skelton Skailes ... John Southwycke eldest sonne of the sd. Robt. ... and Christopher Harrison of Brignoll in the Cty. of Yorke ... of the one part and Henry Browgham of Bleckhall ... and John Aglionby of Carlisle' for Scales Farm and Michael Field. The price Henry Brougham paid was £550.

Henry Brougham did not long enjoy his new property, dying in 1622. At Carlisle on 17 January that year his wife Katherine proved his will. This, made on 10 February 1621/2, shows that Henry died the owner of the mill and demesne of Blackhall, land at Penrith ('Peareth'), at Carleton, of King meadow near Carlisle, a house and garth at Botchardgate, Hodge Close in Carlisle, a tenement at 'Banckend' and one at Eamont Bridge. Henry appointed as 'supervisors of my last will and testament' John Lowther, Thomas and Richard Fallowfield and John Dudley. He made his son Thomas Brougham his sole executor. But, as Thomas was a minor on his father's death, his wife Katherine applied for and received letters of administration over his estate.

Thomas Brougham's life is hardly documented. It is known that he entered St John's College, Cambridge, as a Fellow Commoner on 13 May 1637, aged 18, and would have dined at high table with the dons. He left without taking a degree after not more than a year. On 28 January 1638 he married Mary Fleming at Kirkland while still the ward of his uncle, John Fleming. His bride was the youngest daughter of local squire Daniel Fleming of Skirwith. The couple produced six sons and a daughter: Henry (b. *c*.1638), Toby (b. *c*.1640, alive in 1658), William (b. *c*.1640), Christopher (b. *c*.1645), Thomas (baptised at Penrith in 1643, buried in 1663), John (*c*.1645-1730) and Agnes. She married Anthony Wybergh of Clifton Hall. Toby, William, and Thomas are shadowy figures. The other three male children, however, are better documented. Christopher, who died before 18 October 1671, may have been an apothecary. He and his son, Dudley, founded a new family branch: the Broughams of Askrigg. They attained gentry rank through his descendant, Dr. James Brougham (1775-1845) who built Stobars Hall near Kirkby Stephen around 1825. Another of Thomas Brougham's sons, John Brougham, left descendants who became a Cockermouth branch.

The most interesting of Thomas Brougham's sons was Henry of Scales. In 1648, when he was about ten, his father died intestate. On 6 July 1655, administration of 'the goods of Thomas Browham late of Eamondbrigg, co Westm'land' was 'granted to John Fleeming the curator lawfully assigned to Toby, Thomas, Christopher, Agnes, William and John Browham natural and lawful children of afsd decd.'.[5] On 27 November 1656 Henry entered Queen's College, Oxford as a commoner at the age of eighteen. Like many well-heeled students, he left without taking a degree. But he seems to have been diligent in his studies and to have written dutifully to his 'honourd Unckle' and guardian, John Fleming of Skirwith, who was paying for his tuition. In August 1659 Henry was still in Oxford. However, on 25 November 1660, he married Mary Slee at St Mary's, Carlisle.

Henry's genealogy was enveloped by a whole series of myths. Recent genealogical research (described in *Chapter Eight* and the *appendix*) has stripped these away, revealing a more simple picture. Mary, Henry's bride, was the daughter of William Slee of Fisher Street, Carlisle, a grocer who kept a shop with his wife and had 'some small parcels of land of no great value'. He was neither rich, not it seems, entirely sane. According to one account, 'he was brought up a singing man in the Cathedral Church at Carlisle and did constantly attend that service, when he had his lucid intervals, for ... he was often very melancholick even unto lunacy'. Though it may have contributed genetically to the mental instability evident in some later Broughams, Mary's marriage was a success. It lasted 37 years and produced nine sons and three daughters.

Henry Brougham was the first of his branch of the Broughams to attain gentry rank. He transformed the farmhouse at Scales into a gentleman's residence, Scales Hall. At the same time, his income was not great. Sandford's *A Cursory Relation of all the Antiquities & Familyes in Cumberland* estimated it at £300 a year in 1676. He was 27 at the time of Sir William Dugdale's 'Visitation of Westmorland', on 25 March 1665, when he certified his pedigree. This began with Peter Brougham of Eamont Bridge, his great-grandfather. He encountered some difficulty with his coat of arms (the three lucies), however. This, once that of the Redding and Lucy families, Dugdale respited 'for want of proof', and it was not presented.

At Dugdale's 'Visitation', Henry already had four children. These were Agnes (baptised 16 September 1661), Thomas (baptised 18 May 1663), Henry (baptised in March 1664), and Jane (who probably died young). There followed William (whose date of birth is unknown), Bernard (baptised 23 June 1670), Mathias (baptised 22 March 1675), John (baptised 5 February 1677), Peter (baptised 16 May 1675), George (baptised 14 August 1680), Samuel (baptised 23 July 1681) and Mary, whose dates of birth and baptism are unknown. Of these William and George probably died in infancy, and Mathias sometime before 1698. Henry, who was admitted to Queen's College as a 'poor serving child', eventually becoming a Fellow in 1690 and later Pro-Proctor, died in 1696. The most important of the sons were Thomas, John and Peter. They, and Samuel (from whom descended seven owners of Brougham Hall) appear in *Chapters Three* and *Four*.

Henry Brougham of Scales was clearly a man of some distinction. On 11 November 1693 he was chosen to serve as sheriff of Cumberland, his tenure of office lasting until 19 December 1694. He was helped in his shrievalty by one Mr. Charles Smithson, attorney-at-law, to whom he left 20s. in his will. Henry's will (dated 16 December 1697) shows that he had enlarged the family's holdings considerably. Apart from the land at Scales, he now possessed 'freehold messuages tenements and lands in Skelton Sebergham Carlisle Ireby Routhwaite and Applethwaite in Cumberland', left to his eldest son Thomas. It also provided generous bequests for his daughter Mary (£400), his sons John (£500), Peter (£150), Samuel (£150), the rents from his lands and tenements (£60 per annum) to his

4.   Scales Hall, Calthwaite.

wife for life, along with £40 and all the household goods at their house in Carlisle. There were also some smaller bequests to other relatives, and £5 for a large Bible and Book of Common Prayer for Skelton parish church, the residue from which was to go to 'poor housekeepers in the parish'.

5. Mary Brougham (d. 1754), daughter of Henry Brougham of Scales, by an unknown artist.

By the time Henry Brougham of Scales made his will, his eldest son, Thomas, had become Receiver of Aids and other taxes in Cumberland and Westmorland, on 22 February 1697.[6] When Henry died in 1698, he was succeeded by Thomas, who proved his will at Carlisle on 11 June 1698. Henry's sons, Thomas, John and Peter Brougham, were to further increase the family's fortunes.

1. A. H. Smith 'The Place-Names of Westmorland' Pts. 1 & II, Vols. XLII and XLIII, English Place-Name Society, (Cambridge University Press 1967).
2. Woollen fabrics, used for clothing. The chapel was standing by 1377, according to Dr. Markhouse, Prebendary of Carlisle, writing in 1690.
3. Hugh Owen, *The Lowther Family* (Phillimore, 1990).
4. C. Roy Hudleston, R. S. Boumphrey and J. Hughes, *An Armorial For Westmorland and Lonsdale* (1975). The 1681 Bird pedigree, however, has John Bird of Penrith (Henry's father) marrying Jane, daughter of (...) Redding or Ryddings of Brougham in 1430 and so acquiring a third of Brougham then.
5. The Brougham Family, C. Roy Hudleston, F.S.A. (1960).
6. His appointment (he succeeded his cousin, Andrew Hudleston of Hutton John) was made on the recommendation of Sir John Lowther and Sir George Fletcher. Previously, Henry Brougham (d. 1622) had appointed John Lowther as one of the supervisors of his will. These good relations between the Broughams and Lowthers continued under Thomas Brougham of Scales. He appointed William, Viscount Lonsdale and three others to determine any subsequent lawsuits arising from his own will of 1716.

Chapter Two

Brougham Hall to Bird's Nest (1609-1726)

The Broughams of Brougham Hall became extinct on the death of Thomas Brougham of Brougham in 1608, still only possessing a third of the manor and Hall. On the death of Thomas' widow, Agnes, it passed out of the Brougham family, to her sister-in-law, Elizabeth, Thomas Brougham's married sister. She had married William Hudson of Barton Kirk. Her ownership, however, was brief. On 16 July 1611, she sold the third to Rowland Hodgson of Surrey, husband of her youngest sister, Katherine.

Hodgson did not own the third of the manor he had purchased for long. Soon it was sold to a local farmer, William Wright. On William's death it passed to his son Alexander. It is unlikely that either Hodgson or the Wrights would have spent much money on the Hall. It probably consisted of the Tudor Hall or bire, an 'ancient chamber' and a square pele-like tower resembling nearby Clifton Hall. There may have been a wall interlinking these and forming an oval courtyard. Archaeological evidence suggests some building may have been done in the first half of the 17th century. A beam felled between 1609 and 1627 was discovered on the site of Bird's Tower. Unfortunately no record of what, if any, part the Hall played in the Civil War has emerged.

Brougham Hall probably saw no service. Cumberland and Westmorland were largely Royalist counties in the conflict. Nearby Brougham Castle was garrisoned, with Sir John Lowther II of Lowther (1606-75) as its governor. But the response of the local gentry was cautious to say the least. Some argued that they should not fight outside the counties' boundaries. In autumn 1644, when the Scots invaded, many submitted, later taking the covenant, and suffering fines and sequestration in December 1645. They had to pay these despite the considerable looting they had already borne. In the second Civil War of 1648 the Royalists held the two counties and Carlisle and Appleby for six months until they had to surrender to Cromwell's army. But neither county played much part in the third Civil War. It is not clear what Alexander Wright did in any of these conflicts. Could he have been one of those fined by the victors? For whatever reason, in the late 1640s or in 1650 he sold his share of the manor of Brougham to one of them. Its new owner was one of Cromwell's captains, James Browne of Martindale (a village south-west of Pooley Bridge, near Ullswater).

James and his wife Elizabeth did not retain Brougham for long. In 1654 they sold it to the owner of nearby Brougham Castle, Lady Anne Clifford, Countess of Dorset, Pembroke and Montgomery (1590-1676). Lady Anne Clifford was by any standards a great figure, a territorial magnate who behaved like a conservationist or architectural restorer. Despite a period at Queen Elizabeth's court when young, her world view was in some ways that of a medieval noble. She journeyed around the country between her numerous castles: in Westmorland, Brougham, Brough, Appleby, Pendragon; and in Yorkshire, Skipton and Barden Tower (a fortified hunting lodge). She carried with her a retinue of courtiers and administrators. Servants left in charge of her properties provided for their own upkeep and were later repaid on production of their accounts. Lady Anne herself led a life free of self-indulgence, never drinking wine and dressing after her second widowhood in black serge. From her castles, however, she dispensed largesse in the grand medieval manner to local people.

Lady Anne's vigour and success contrasted starkly with a sad private life. She had lost her mother when she was 26, her father in 1605 and had two unhappy marriages. In 1609

6. Lady Anne Clifford, Countess of Pembroke and Montgomery, *c.*1646, by an unknown artist.

she had married Richard Sackville, Lord Buckhurst, later 3rd Earl of Dorset, who died in 1624. They had produced three sons (all of whom died young) and two daughters. After her first husband's death she had suffered a severe attack of smallpox which, on her own account, wrecked her face. Six years later she had begun a childless marriage to Philip Herbert, 4th Earl of Pembroke and Montgomery. After they had been estranged for some time, the Earl (who had received Charles I from the Scots in 1647) died on 23 January 1650.

Lady Anne's wealth and beneficence compensated for her personal hurts. On the death of Henry Clifford, the 5th and last Earl of Cumberland, on 11 December 1643, the Clifford estates reverted to her under the will of her father, George Clifford, the 3rd Earl. Anne was now able to satisfy a passion for building. Her castle restorations must have appeared doggedly unfashionable. In addition Anne, a Royalist, aroused the suspicions of the parliamentary authorities and Cromwell. She also worked against the grain of fashion and military science. Since the 16th century the gentry had been leaving often inhospitable castles for more comfortable, airy mansions or manor houses. Cannon had begun to make castles militarily obsolete even in Henry VI's time. In 1464, after the Battle of Hexham, the Yorkists' cannon-fire had reduced the modern, massive fortifications of Bamburgh Castle to rubble before the eyes of its Lancastrian defenders. But Lady Anne's determination has to be admired. She restored the castles of Appleby

(1651), Brough (1659-62), Brougham, Pendragon, and Barden Tower (1659). Her energy also extended to churches at Appleby, Skipton and Bongate. She rebuilt or constructed chapels at Mallerstang, Barden, and Ninekirks, and almshouses at Bethmesley and Appleby.

In Westmorland, Lady Anne was aided by her chief secretary, local squire Sir Edward Hassel of Dalemain (1642-1707). He joined her service in 1668, remaining with her until her death in 1676.[1] Before this, however, she had not only purchased a third of the manor of Brougham in 1654 but also paid £4 a year in alms to the local poor of Brougham parish. She left other lasting memorials in the area. The first was the Hospital at Brougham, now called Hospital Farm, for the local people, built in 1654. The second, built in 1656, was an eccentric monument, the Countess Pillar. This she erected (by what is now the A66, just east of Brougham Castle) in honour of her mother, Margaret, dowager Countess of Cumberland. Born Lady Margaret Russell, third daughter of Francis, 2nd Earl of Bedford, she had died aged 55, on 24 May 1616. Lady Anne selected the place she had said goodbye to her mother for the last time on 2 April 1616 for the monument. On it she had inscribed:

> This pillar was erected, A.D. 1656, by the right honourable Anne Countess dowager of Pembroke, and sole heir of the right honourable George Earl of Cumberland, for a memorial of her last parting in this place with her good and pious mother, the right honourable Margaret Countess dowager of Cumberland, the 2d of April 1616. In memory whereof, she also left an annuity of £4, to be distributed to the poor within this parish of Brougham, every 2nd day of April, upon the stone here by. Laus Deo.

This and the St Anne's Hospital in Appleby were, according to Dawn Tyler, financed with the money produced by James Browne's portion of the manor of Brougham.

Lady Anne also repaired a third building, St Wilfred's chapel at Brougham. This building she had pulled down and rebuilt at her own expense. According to her diary, it was '... wholly finished about the latter end of April 1659 ...'. It is still largely Lady Anne's creation and has suffered a better fate than some of Lady Anne's castles. All bar Appleby and Skipton are now ruins.

One of the most significant acts of Lady Anne at Brougham was to appoint James Bird as her attorney-at-law. Bird was ambitious and keen to increase his family's standing. The Birds were small, but rising, gentry. Their ancestry and genealogy is problematic. No complete genealogical tree or history of the family exists. The selling of the historically valuable records and pictures of the Birds of Birdby (another Cumbrian branch of the family probably related to those of Brougham) three generations ago does not help. As a result there are conflicting and sometimes erroneous accounts of it. So I am indebted to Mr. Roger Bird of Birdby for sharing his knowledge with me and to the late Mr. Roy Hudleston's fascinating two-part article: 'The Birds of Bird's Nest' (*Newsletter of the Cumbria Family History Society* nos. 32 and 33, November 1984) for my account below.

The Bird family first held part of Brougham in the 15th century, when Henry Bird (who died before 1463) married Joan, daughter of John Teasdale of Walton and his wife, Joan, daughter and heiress of Richard Tyndale. Henry received a third of the manor of Brougham from his mother-in-law, Joan Teasdale. This third passed down to James Bird.

James Bird's considerable achievements were undermined by malign fate. He took the Birds of Brougham to greater wealth and standing than ever but was denied by a series of family tragedies a single heir amongst his 13 children. Born in 1637, James Bird was a man of some standing in the Penrith area by 1665 when he certified his pedigree and arms for the King of Arms Sir William Dugdale's 'Visitation'. Bird was an antiquarian

7. The Birds of Brougham pewter platter of 1660 in Kirkby Thore church (detail).

The Birds of Brougham's coat-of-arms in a stained ᴀss window of Crossby Garrett church.

who made a considerable but now vanished collection of family records. These, according to Nicholson and Burn, were a collection of papers of the lords of the manors of Westmorland taken from material at Appleby Castle, and also included other antiquarian papers. Bird later had Dugdale's secretary, Gregory King, Rouge Dragon, produce a Bird family pedigree of 18 generations with beautifully produced coloured coats of arms in 1681. It was updated in 1688. By this time Bird had become an influential local squire. Sometime before 1676 he had bought the Crackenthorpe family's share of Brougham Manor, while around 1674 he had become steward to Lady Anne Clifford.

For small landowners there were considerable benefits in serving great families: public office, land, property, advantageous marriage alliances and the family's friendship. For James Bird the rewards were good. He was made Under-Sheriff of Westmorland. Lady Anne trusted and respected him, giving him gifts which included the splendid Bird Chalice made in Nuremburg in 1598, and, less impressively, a lock inscribed 'A.P.' (for Anne, Countess of Pembroke). But, most importantly, he was able to purchase the last remaining third of Brougham (the Brougham family's old third) from Lady Anne's grandson, John, Lord Tufton after her death in 1676. Bird was now the first person to own the whole manor since the de Burgham family in 1272.

A 1672 map of Brougham shows a 'hall, fyne house, byre and maldoer' at Brougham Hall. James Bird now decided to transform this. John, Lord Tufton had made him his steward after Lady Anne's death and his prosperity continued. Bird now built Hill House, an impressive rectangular block which jutted out into what is now the Terrace. The tower, perhaps a rebuilt pele tower, was retained next to it, as was the 'ancient chamber', and a medieval tower further along against the road leading to Lowther Bridge. Bird also built a gatehouse adjoining the byre or Tudor Hall, and now called the Guard House. Like subsequent Cumbrians, Bird did not shrink from using architectural salvage. He removed part of the ruinous Brougham Castle around 1685, and re-erected it along with its oak doors. He may also have 'salvaged' from there the traceried windows at the front of Bird's Tower.

Brougham Hall, now called Hill House, was regarded as one of the area's big houses, and worth recording. On 12 March 1685, cartographer John Adams wrote to Sir Daniel Le Fleming: 'Brougham is near perfect and I intend to print'. In Volume II of his *North Country Life In The Eighteenth Century*, Edward Hughes says that in Cumberland and Westmorland society, squire land tenure was remarkably stable until the 18th century. Bird stressed his family's medieval origins with his genealogical tree and by making Hill House look more ancient.

In the grounds of Hill House and in the village of Brougham, Bird was equally energetic. He may have introduced the sundial of 1660 with a Latin inscription which stood near the West Wall until 1934. But he had more the attitude of a ruthless improver than a benevolent squire. In 1679 he argued with Nicholson, Bishop of Carlisle, over the poor condition of St Wilfred's chapel, then used as a school for the children of 20 families in Brougham. Each thought the other should pay for its repair. After 1686, despite a pledge on buying the last third of the manor of Brougham to continue paying the sum of £4 a year, Bird shifted the entire medieval village of Brougham (from what is now the avenue) into Eamont Bridge and removed at least nine households and tenements. He used their stone to make the park walls. He also planted a great double avenue of oaks (two deep each side of the road) and firs, walnuts and ashes. The park created was the habitat of fallow deer who lived in some 2,000 acres of the Whinfell Forest.

A brief account of Bird's alterations was written by the Rev. Thomas Machell (1647-98), second son of Lancelot Machell of nearby Crackenthorpe Hall and rector of Kirkby Thore from 1677 to 1698. An antiquarian and amateur architect, Machell and his friend,

9. The 17th-century guardhouse at Brougham Hall, built by James Bird.

influential master-mason Edward Addison (b. 1656) brought classical architecture to Cumbria, producing work like Appleby Castle's east range for the 6th Earl of Thanet in 1686-8. An acute observer, Machell commented sharply that Bird had 'made a great improvement: but is become like a pelican or an owle in the desert'.

In 1663, James Bird had married Dorothy, daughter of John Sanderson of Penrith. Hudleston says that Dorothy (christened at Penrith on 22 May 1650) may have only been 15 when she married. Between 1666 and 1688 Dorothy bore James 13 children, 14 if one counts a daughter 'still born' in 1679. Hudleston writes: 'Dorothy's sorrow was to see every one of her children die, several in their twenties and thirties'. Of the eight sons, one, Thomas (b. 1672) died aged two, while another, Mark (b. 1680) lived less than a day. Of the rest, William (the first child, born in 1666) and Oswald (b. 1684) never reached their majority. Those who did showed promise but died prematurely. James (b. 1668) matriculated at Oxford in 1687 and was called to the Bar in 1699. He was, it seems, later hanged for his wife's murder. Henry (b. 1676), matriculated at Oxford in 1693, becoming a Fellow of Queen's College there in 1703. He died from alcoholism in 1705. John (b. 1674) who matriculated at Oxford in 1691, was called to the Bar in 1699, married and had three children but died in 1704. Emmanuel (b. 1677) matriculated at Oxford in 1695 but was dead before 1713. Of the five daughters, Dorothy (b. 1679), Sizericia (b. 1681), and Manuella (b. 1688) died before they were one, and, even more heart-breakingly, Johanna (b. 1683) died aged 24. In 1713, the one surviving child was Isabella (b.1685). The Brougham parish registers record the burials of Sizericia, William, John, Oswald, Henry and Johanna.

On 9 April 1713 Isabella Bird married Thomas Carleton junior, of Appleby, at St Wilfred's chapel, Brougham. On 10-11 March, Bird had settled the lands of the manor of Brougham, Brougham Hall, and his lands in Brougham and Clifton on the couple with remainder to their male and female heirs. This settlement allowed Bird to make another remainder of the property in his will. This he did on 13 November that year. Bird wrote that, if Isabella died childless, after her husband's death, if he survived her, the properties were to go to his granddaughters. These were the daughters of his son John Bird (d. 1704): Ann Dorothy, Sizericia and Margaret Bird.

James Bird had one more grief to endure: Isabella died after eight months of marriage. This may well have contributed to his death soon after. On 6 February 1714 he was buried. Like many rich self-made men, Bird left no dynamic successor to bear the family flag. Instead he left rather ineffectual relations who let things at Brougham Hall stand still.

On James Bird's death, Thomas Carleton now owned the Hall. But James Bird's widow, Dorothy maintained a life-interest in the property. Its future now depended on her granddaughters. One, Ann Dorothy Bird married the Rev. Carleton Atkinson, rector of Brougham and a cousin of Thomas Carleton, at Kirkby Thore on 5 May 1716. Another, Sizericia Bird of Penrith, died unmarried, and was buried at Penrith on 2 April 1724. The third granddaughter, Margaret Bird, seems to have been unmarried. This complex situation was resolved after old Dorothy Bird, their grandmother, died around June 1724. In her will, she left her life interest in the estate to her son-in-law Thomas Carleton. She also made a provision for the settlement of the estate after Carleton's death. As Carleton's wife had had no issue, Dorothy provided for the estate and Hall to pass on to her remaining granddaughters: Ann Dorothy Atkinson (née Bird) and Margaret Bird.

Thomas Carleton, however, had other ideas. Divided possession of the property for 10 years perhaps dulled his interest in Brougham Hall and he resolved to be rid of it. In 1726, he secured agreement with Dorothy Atkinson and Margaret Bird to convey the property to a prospective buyer: the dynamic Commissioner John Brougham of Scales. Paying £5,000 to Thomas Carleton, Ann Dorothy Atkinson and Margaret Bird for the Hall and estate on 9 November 1726, John Brougham now bought both.

The sale of Brougham Hall and the extinction of the Birds of Brougham on the death of the childless Ann Dorothy Atkinson in 1740 did not mark the end of the Bird family in Cumberland and Westmorland. The Rev. William Bird, who had been born at Brougham, went on to found a new branch of Birds, squire-rectors at Crossby Garrett in 1719. It is not clear what relation he was to the Birds of Brougham. Holding the lordship of the manor there for more than a century, these Birds died out in the male line in 1831. Another surviving branch of the family became established at Birdby, one of whose family traditions is that they are related to the Birds of Brougham. Mr. Roger Bird of Birdby, son of Birdby's present owner, Mr. Arthur Bird, D.F.C., has patiently traced these back to Christopher Bird of Birdby (1726-1814), who was buried at Morland.

A bizarre footnote to the saga of the Birds of Brougham is that their extinction and the 1726 sale did not deter other Birds from trying to take control of Brougham Hall. Claiming they were its rightful owners, Birds from Eamont Bridge in July 1785 and from Ashton-under Lyme in May 1843 forcibly entered the Hall to assert their 'rights'. As late as September 1852 some Birds were still trying to claim legal right to it. These manoeuvres all met predictable and deserved failure.

1. Son of the Rev. Edward Hasell, Fellow of Clare Hall, Cambridge, Senior Taxor of Cambridge University and Rector of Middleton Cheyne, Northamptonshire (d. 1642), Hasell purchased the Dalemain estate from the trustees of Sir William Layton with monies left him by Lady Anne Clifford. Appointed a J.P., D.L. for Cumberland and High Sheriff in 1682, he was knighted in 1699 and made a Knight of the Shire (M.P.) in 1701.

Chapter Three

The Commissioner and his Nephew 1726-1749

... the estate which I now enjoy shall go entire to my brother John Brougham after my decease without issue and out of the love and affection I have for him and for the great trouble I gave him and the signal services he did me when I was Receiver-General of the counties of Cumberland and Westmorland I make and constitute him my heir and sole executor ...

Extract from the will of Thomas Brougham of Scales Hall (1716), in Carlisle Probate Registry.

John Brougham of Scales (1677-1741) was the sixth son of Henry Brougham of Scales (d. 1698). He was the most successful member of the Brougham family in the 18th century. A lifelong bachelor, dynamic and benevolent, he did what he could to help a large number of Brougham relatives. According to Peter Brougham Wyly, Commissioner Brougham was baptised at Skelton 'on or about 5th February 1677'. His early career took a route common for the sons of gentry – the law. On 16 July 1691, at the tender age of 14 he was admitted to Staple Inn; on 26 January 1695, when 18, to Gray's Inn. In December 1702 he was made secretary to the Commissioners of Excise. Next year, on 11 June 1703, he was called to the Bar at the seasoned age of twenty-six.

On 29 November 1715, John Brougham was made a commissioner for England in the excise service, at a salary of £800, an income as great as that of some country squires. This was later increased to £1,000 per annum. The Scales Hall estate was then held by his eldest brother, Thomas Brougham (baptised 1663). A distinguished man in his own right, Thomas had been made Receiver of Aids and other taxes in Cumberland and Westmorland in 1697, Mayor of Carlisle in 1709 and Sheriff of Cumberland in December 1715. In June 1716, however, Thomas died. On 4 August John proved his brother's will. By the entail of their father, Henry Brougham of Scales, he inherited the Scales Hall estate. The fourth son, the Rev. Bernard Brougham (baptised 1670, d. 1750) was missed out, receiving an annuity.

It is not clear how John Brougham combined the jobs of excise commissioner, barrister and squire. As commissioner he seems to have had considerable power in the excise service. In the Excise Minute Books at Kew Record Office (CUST.47) are records of his being entrusted with surveying large areas of England. On 26 April 1716 he is recorded as having just returned from surveying Hertfordshire, Cambridgeshire, Lincolnshire, Yorkshire, Derbyshire, Oxfordshire and Surrey. On 23 May 1718 his recent return from surveying Surrey, Wiltshire, Hampshire, Dorset, Somerset and Devon is noted. These sources show that the job also gave John Brougham the power to help less fortunate relatives. In January 1705/6 it was decided, on John Brougham's motion, that Henry Brougham (c.1670-1718), possibly a nephew of Henry of Scales, was to be instructed by Thomas Gargett, officer at Penrith. In November 1718, John helped to get Michael Brougham (d. 1771 and eldest son of Edward Brougham of Barns, d. 1725, a distant relative) made a supernumerary in the service.

Despite being renewed as a commissioner of excise in June 1720, John Brougham resigned the post on 20 May 1724. Whether this was to concentrate on his legal career or

JOHN BROUGHAM
of SCALES
"COMMISSIONER"
OB.T 1741.

10. John, Commissioner Brougham (1677-1741).

his estates is not quite clear. He is said to have gone on the Grand Tour, and one unsubstantiated family legend says that he lived for some time in Florence. It is clear, however, that John assiduously acquired land and houses, a hobby he indulged like many well-off single people. Apart from purchasing Brougham Hall in 1726, he also bought New Hall, at Fairbank, Nether Staveley, near Windermere from his uncle, another John Brougham.[1] In addition, Jackson (*Papers and Pedigrees* Vol. 1) says that Commissioner Brougham owned the Moresby estate and Distington, a coalmine.[2] Well-respected in Cumberland and Westmorland, he was made a Freeman of Appleby in July 1723. He turned down the Shrievalty of Cumberland as being incompatible with his position: as one of the attorneys of the Pipe attending the Court of Exchequer he had to pass the sheriffs' accounts in the Pipe rolls and give them their *quietus*.

Along with his gifts for administration and acquiring property, Commissioner Brougham clearly took a close interest in his family. An agreement of 4 June 1727 between him, his brother the Rev. Bernard Brougham and Thomas Stevens, a lieutenant and adjutant in Major-General Lord Gore's Regiment of Dragoons, shows this. Stevens had then just married Catherine Forrester, the Commissioner's niece. Accordingly, the Commissioner settled £200 on Catherine, invested £100 he had received from Stevens towards her provision and undertook to pay the interest on these two sums to Stevens.[3]

However, it is clear that the Commissioner's anger was not to be taken lightly, as his nephew, the Rev. Thomas Brougham, discovered in early 1740. Thomas had been thoughtless on the death of his brother James that year and during the ill-health of his mother Mary Brougham (the Commissioner's sister), not writing to her or answering the Commissioner's letters. In a letter of 5 February 1740 Thomas' brother, John Brougham of Cockermouth, informed him that 'Uncle Brougham' was 'highly provoked':

> He complains too of yr. not vouchsafing him yr. answer to his letters & calls it a family failing, I wish you may not bring yourself under his Displeasure, who has done much, to put us under no Difficulty to Behave so as to deserve his doing more for us, He hates indolence, & it gives him reason to censure the guilty.[4]

One assumes that Thomas took note of these repeated warnings.

As 18th-century novels like Richardson's *Clarissa* and Fielding's *Tom Jones* make clear, it was vital to the gentry that sons and daughters who stood to inherit, married people of equivalent or greater social rank. Ostracism, even disinheritance, often awaited those who did not. Once thus married, sons and daughters consolidated the family's properties and also its social and political standing. Though small gentry, like the Broughams, were somewhat overshadowed in Cumberland and Westmorland by big families like the Howards and the Lowthers, considerable holdings could be built up through wise marriages, judicious purchases and the rewards for loyal service to local magnates. So it was fortunate for the Broughams that Commissioner Brougham's brother, Peter Brougham (baptised 1677, d. 1732), seventh son of Henry Brougham of Scales, married Elizabeth Richmond in 1718.

Peter's marriage turned out to be astute. He was originally apprenticed to a mercer, Edward Parkinson of Newcastle-upon-Tyne, in 1695, later developing a career in excise in the north-east and Cumberland. The Kew Excise Minute Books reveal that he had, in March 1705/6, been lately appointed Collector for Northumberland, Thomas Brougham of Scales and two others being named as sureties for him in the penalty of £4,000. In June 1707 it was decided he was to be Collector of Cumberland. He was later elected a Freeman of Newcastle-upon-Tyne in 1708. In 1709 he was admitted to the Tanners' Guild of Carlisle. In November 1711, Peter Brougham was taking out a fresh bond in the penalty of £5,000, and in March 1717 he was made a Freeman of Appleby. So, on marrying, Peter was already a prosperous, rising man both in Newcastle-upon-Tyne and Cumberland. His bride, Elizabeth Richmond (1680-1729) was the daughter of Christopher Richmond of High Head Castle (nine miles from Scales Hall) and Catterlen Hall (three-and-a-half miles north-west of Penrith). Elizabeth was 38 and Peter was 41 when they married.

The couple produced three children, Henry Richmond (b. 1719), John (b. 1724), and Mary (d. before 1737). Their marriage eventually drew more land into the Brougham family and may well have increased Peter Brougham's standing amongst his fellow gentry. The Richmonds were an old established Cumberland family. Hereditary Constables of Richmond Castle in medieval times, they had changed their name from Musard to Richmond. On 14 December 1722 Peter was made Sheriff of Cumberland, and in May 1724 it was decided he was to be Collector of Durham. In December 1729 Elizabeth died, but Peter Brougham's prosperity and good standing continued. In June 1730 Peter was made Collector of Cumberland, remaining so until his death, intestate at an early age. He was buried on 5 August 1732 at Skelton. His eldest son, Henry Richmond Brougham, was only thirteen.

Henry was fortunate to inherit High Head. In 1676 Christopher Richmond (baptised 1641) had inherited High Head Castle. He had four children from his first wife, Mary, daughter of Sir Wilfred Lawson of Isel Hall. She died in 1672. In 1678 Christopher married a second wife, Isabella Towerson, daughter of Thomas Reynolds. They produced another 11 children (eight daughters, three sons). When Christopher Richmond died in 1693, the castle passed to a son of his first marriage, another Christopher Richmond (b. 1675). When this Christopher Richmond died in 1702, High Head and Catterlen Hall passed to his stepbrother Henry Richmond (b. 1690), one of his father's children by Isabella Towerson.

In 1702 Henry Richmond inherited High Head, then being lived in by his mother Isabella and her husband Mathias Miller of Whitehaven. Miller was probably comptroller of the Customs House there and had married Isabella in 1696. He died in 1705. When Henry Richmond died childless in 1716, he left High Head to his mother, Isabella Miller. In 1719, Isabella Miller acquired a grandson when Henry Richmond Brougham, the eldest son of her daughter Elizabeth Richmond and Peter Brougham, was born. It is said she took a close interest in Henry Richmond Brougham as he grew up. When she died in 1739 she left High Head to him.

Henry Richmond Brougham had been left High Head Castle with the proviso that he was to inherit it on reaching his majority at 21 or marrying, whichever was the sooner. Under the terms of Isabella Miller's will, Commissioner Brougham held the castle 'in trust' from 1739-40, for his nephew, Henry Richmond Brougham, until he reached his majority. Isabella left Catterlen Hall to another of her tribe of daughters, Susanna Richmond. She was also left one moiety (share) of the rents and profits of High Head's buildings, land and mill to enjoy until Henry Richmond Brougham reached his majority. According to Hudleston in *The Brougham Family* (1960), Isabella Miller had poor relations with the Gledhill family into which her eldest daughter, Isabel had married. Probably as a result, Isabel Gledhill's son Joseph was passed over.

Mrs. Isabella Miller's will left Henry quite prosperous, but within two years of his reaching 21 and inheriting High Head in 1740 his finances were transformed. In November 1741, Commissioner Brougham died and on 3 December was buried at St Andrew's church, Holborn, Middlesex. He left most of his property to Henry Richmond Brougham. Henry proved his uncle's will. Though New Hall went to the Commissioner's sister Mary Brougham (d. 1754), his nephew received the rest, including

Brougham Hall and Scales Hall. Henry Richmond Brougham now had the enviable problem of where to live.

Henry Richmond Brougham's choice of High Head as a base rather than Scales or Brougham is puzzling. Perched on a cliff 100 ft. above the River Ive, which surrounded it on three sides, it had spent much of its life as a fortified pele. It had not been modernised at all after the threat of Border warfare vanished in the early 17th century. First mentioned in legal documents in 1272, High Head had been granted along with 67 surrounding acres to John de Harcla for a yearly rent of 66s. 8d. by Edward II in 1315. A 1317 Exchequer of Pleas roll mentions John de Harcla holding by grant 'a close called le Heghered ... in which close John had newly built a peel called Heghered peel ... within six acres of Inglewood forest around Laddestre ...'. In 1342 William Lengleys, yeoman and chief forester of Inglewood (granted High Head in 1328) was permitted to fortify it. The result was a square curtain-walled castle with a two-storey gatehouse (perhaps John de Harcla's pele).

Up to the mid-16th century High Head was little altered. After William Lengleys died, in 1344, his son Sir William Lengleys (then 30) inherited it. When he died, in 1369, it passed to his sister Juliana's son William Restwold (d. 1375). The Restwolds moved to the south in 1425. Eventually, in 1552, Edward Restwold sold High Head to John Richmond (d. 1575), a London merchant described in legal documents as 'Iremonger' and 'Armyrour'. According to Hugh Owen's *The Lowther Family*, he was later given the job of collecting the rents on the Dacre family's lands in Cumberland and Westmorland, then administered by Thomas Howard, 4th Duke of Norfolk (1538-72). John Richmond did most of the work, though his brother in-law Richard Lowther (1532-1608) was made receiver of the Dacre rents.

In 1551 John Richmond had married Margaret (1534-68), daughter of Hugh Lowther of Lowther (d. 1555). On the castle's west side, using the medieval south and west walls, they built a gabled Tudor wing in the third quarter of the 16th century. This had mullioned windows with flat arched label moulds (which remain) and the Richmond coat of arms on the courtyard wall. Overlooking the inner courtyard and projecting from its roof was a dormer window with pointed finials. John and Margaret Richmond had five sons and seven daughters, Margaret dying at High Head in December 1568. But later Richmonds seem to have done no further building. They may have preferred living at Catterlen Hall, acquired in 1644 when Mabel Vaux (daughter and heiress of John Vaux of Catterlen) brought it as a dowry on marrying Christopher Richmond (b. 1623). Sometimes tenanted, High Head did not bring in much. Edward Sandford's *A Cursory Relation of all the Antiquities and Familyes in Cumberland* (1676) put its worth at '£300 per an'.

On Isabella Miller's death, in 1739, High Head looked an uninspiring, even depressing, base for a young country squire. It was remotely sited, barbaric-looking and semi-derelict. Shown in Samuel and Nathaniel Buck's print of March 1739, its site had more potential than its other features. Though the 14th-century walls and Tudor wing were intact, trees grew in the courtyard and over the tops of the curtain wall. A medieval residential block on the east side seems to have been a shell. Though the Tudor wing was roofed, the medieval gatehouse may not have been. It still had a moat to the north. The only outbuilding seems to have been a dovecot in the grounds. The approach to the castle's gatehouse was windswept, the land on its left and right falling desolately east and west down to the Ive.

Henry Richmond Brougham was an enigmatic figure. He was an educated man who matriculated (like so many from Cumberland) at Queen's College, Oxford on 18 November 1737 aged eighteen. He entered Gray's Inn eight days later, on 26 November, but seems not to have become a lawyer. He was admitted to the Tanners' Guild of Carlisle in 1740.

11. Samuel and Nathaniel Buck's view of High Head Castle (1739).

It is said that he went on the Grand Tour, which seems likely. In 1742 he served the first of two terms as Sheriff of Cumberland. But his greatest achievement was to build a spectacularly-sited Classical mansion at High Head. Even ruined, it is one of the great architectural sights of Cumbria.

Accounts of Henry Richmond Brougham's building of the new mansion are strewn with legends which are either wrong or unprovable. There is unfortunately only scanty documentation of the work. Henry seems to have thought the medieval castle's condition was disgraceful. Perhaps work started on its demolition soon after he inherited it in 1740. This might account for the story that Commissioner Brougham assisted in some way. Henry Richmond Brougham decided to build a new house, and this probably took place in 1744-49. Henry razed most of the Castle to the bedrock, leaving a small medieval turret and the Tudor wing. He filled in the moat in front of the castle to make a garden. He used the stone from the old castle for internal walls, to create a flat base and extend the site towards the river on the south side, forming both a plateau for the house and a parterre on which people could walk.[5] Surplus stone from the demolition was used in a substantial wall along the north bank of the Ive, and in the high wall surrounding the formal terraced garden.

12. Henry Richmond Brougham (1719-49) by Allan Ramsay.

High Head's architect is unknown and no really credible candidate for it has been put forward, except James Gibbs. Some of his designs resemble High Head. Gibbs' only connection with the Cumberland and Westmorland area, however, seems to be that in c.1717-18 he produced drawings for a remodelling of Lowther Castle for the 3rd Viscount Lowther.[6] What adds to the mystery of High Head is that there was little building of Classical mansions in Cumberland and Westmorland until the last quarter of the 18th century. There had been exceptions like Armathwaite Castle, a pele converted into a Vanbrugh-style country house probably in the 1720s and Dallam Tower at Milnthorpe (1720-22). But the only Classical mansion exactly contemporary with High Head seems to be the 1746 range at Warcop Hall. Its interiors were identical to High Head's and seem to have been done by the same craftsmen, sheltering from the '45 Rebellion. All High Head's interiors were drawn by Antony Sharp, RCA, in October 1953.

In 1744, work started on a Gibbs-style classical mansion on which Henry Richmond Brougham was to spend £10,000. Using red Annan sandstone similar to the pink Lazonby sandstone distinctive to the Penrith area, from which the original castle had been built, he constructed a fine 11-bay façade of three floors facing north. Three rusticated bays projecting from the rest in the centre of the front drew the eye cleverly. The centre of the front was further emphasised by a set of double entrance stairs (a rare feature) with fine ironwork leading up to the front door. Further subtlety was achieved by the use of lighter yellow ashlar for details in and above these three centre bays. One was a 'Gibbs surround' with a grotesque headstone, used for the front door. The other, topping the three central bays, was a yellow ashlar frieze of the Brougham armorial bearings – a triton and a mermaid supporting three fish and an inverted chevron. Crowned by a balustrade of red sandstone, the whole front has a theatrical quality.

On the new block's east side, Henry built a five-bay façade. Here, like the entrance front, the central bay had a first-floor Venetian window. This had a pediment above it which contained, in ashlar, the Richmond arms. A set of double stairs lined with iron railings led to a door on the ground floor. Intermittent long and short quoins marked the corner of the east elevation with the south one and the front and east side. Directly facing the River Ive, the south front was nine bays long and enlivened by one splendid feature: the large first-floor Venetian window whose keystone was embellished, like the front door's, with a grotesque face. The Venetian window and rusticated door and window surrounds beneath it projected slightly from the rest of the façade. As with the east side, double stairs led up to a door on the ground floor.

Records of the progress at High Head between 1744 and 1748 are sketchy. In 1745 things did not go according to plan. Work went well enough for Henry Richmond Brougham to sign his name, rather self-consciously, on one of the castle's new windows. So perhaps, with these in place, the main block's roof and façade were nearly complete. Then came an unforeseen problem: the '45 Rebellion. On 31 October the Young Pretender's army left Edinburgh. On 8 November the Prince was at Brampton. On 17 November, his army triumphantly entered Carlisle. Henry Richmond Brougham's building project was now almost in its path. The prince entered Penrith on the night of 21 November, and most of the surrounding country houses, except for Lowther Hall, sent food to the rebel army. Henry's response was to give the craftsmen involved at High Head an enforced break. They seem to have gone 25 miles east, to Warcop Hall.

In 1747 High Head's stable block was built. An entirely classical building of Lazonby sandstone, it has an arched entrance surmounted by a pretty white-domed cupola and with alternate large and small quoins at its corners. It is unclear exactly when Henry constructed three other features: the entrance gates, the garden behind them and the castle, and the large, walled, terraced garden on the castle's north-east side. It is reasonable to assume they are contemporary with the rebuilding of the castle. The entrance gates have coupled Ionic pilasters, rampant sphinxes and pilastered niches set into rusticated gate-piers. They were built in front of the house bordered by an unpretentious low wall, and added to the theatrical effect of the front façade's pediment. A garden was made behind them. To the north-east of the castle, Henry constructed another, this one terraced on three levels and entered by a doorway with a fine 'Gibbs surround'. Creating this garden of almost two acres must have needed a great deal of earth-moving. The finished product, stretching down to a small watergate on the River Ive gives stunning views of the castle's front.

13. High Head Castle: the front facing the drive in Edwardian times.

Henry Richmond Brougham did not complete High Head. Externally, he left two main things part-done. Firstly, he left an exposed Tudor gable to the west of the main Palladian block, surmounting an awkward-looking square arch of Doric pillars, at right angles to the main façade. Secondly, he never finished the stately balustrade on the south side of the mansion. He left some old buildings standing, which may have been hard to integrate with the new Classical house, perhaps intending to replace them with a new wing. On the south side, a one-bay section of the Tudor wing and a medieval turret was left huddled up awkwardly against accomplished new work.

It is unclear how far Henry's plans came to completion internally. The rooms he created were little documented at the time and panelling was removed from them to Brougham Hall in 1858. An inventory of 8 May 1753, taken of the goods of Henry's successor in the house, his executor, John Gale of Whitehaven, lists six rooms, a 'Drawing Room, Oke Room, Best Drawing Room, Chints Room, Dressing Roome, Yellow Roome ...'.[7]

In 1921 architectural historian Christopher Hussey noted that seven rooms remained from Henry Richmond Brougham's time. These included a sumptuous panelled drawing room, a library, and two first-floor apartments which had been made into a bedroom

14. Sketches by Anthony Sharp, R.C.A. of High Head's splendid drawing room and its ceiling, completed in December 1953.

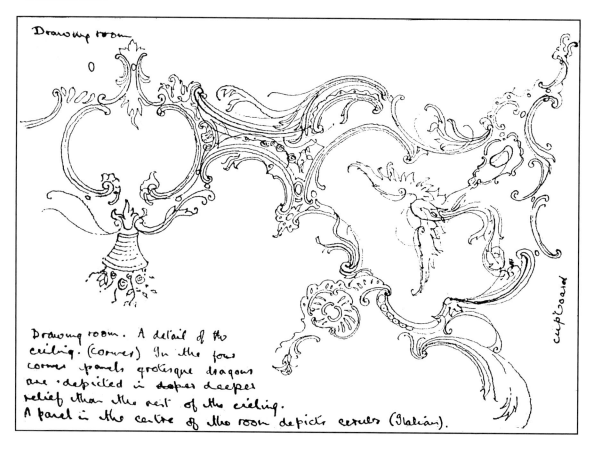

Drawing room

O

Drawing room. A detail of the ceiling. (corner) In the four corner panels grotesque dragons are depicted in ~~dopes~~ deeper relief than the rest of the ceiling.
A panel in the centre of the room depicts cerrers (Italian).

cupboard

with a spectacular door-case. Other parts of Henry's work were a majestic barrel-vaulted corridor lined with Doric columns and floored with black and white marble. The entrance hall, its fine staircase and the old dining room were also from Henry's time. This last room had some unusual panelling displaying the crests of Henry's forbears and relations: Brougham, Richmond, Richmond allied with Clerbaux-Chaytor, Hasell, Dacre, Richmond allied with Vaux of Catterlen, Richmond of Corby, Delamore, and Brougham allied with Richmond.

Henry Richmond Brougham's triumph was considerable but short-lived. In January 1749 he was again made Sheriff of Cumberland. A well satisfied man, he sat for Allan Ramsay, one of the leading portrait painters of the time. In the portrait he appears a commanding figure, albeit running slightly to fat. But sadly, on 23 April he died prematurely and unmarried, aged twenty-nine. Commissioner Brougham and Isabella Miller's plans to combine most of the Richmond and Brougham properties in one large holding had failed. The break-up of Henry Richmond Brougham's estates was now inevitable. Henry disliked his paternal Brougham relatives (a feeling they reciprocated) and omitted them from his will. This was proved at York, on 25 May 1749. In it, Henry left his property at High Head to descendants of Isabella Miller's daughters, Margaret and Isabel Richmond. He made his cousin, John Gale of Whitehaven, the son of Margaret Richmond (1689-1759) and William Gale (1693-1773), his executor. He also gave Gale half the castle, with dire consequences. The other half he left to another relation, Robert Baynes of Cockermouth (1717-89), Baynes, a lawyer, had married Elizabeth, daughter of Colonel Samuel Gledhill by his wife Isabel Richmond, daughter of Isabella Miller. Predictably, the Gale (later Gale-Braddylls of Conniside Priory) and the Baynes families began to quarrel, in the courts, over High Head's ownership.

15. The entrance hall at High Head: a postcard of 1910.

Henry Richmond Brougham had never lived at Brougham Hall in his tenure of the Brougham estates. Perhaps he associated it with his paternal Brougham relatives. But, in spite of this, the Hall did play a minor role in the '45 Rebellion. On 18 December 1745 the Battle of Clifton Moor, the last battle fought on English soil, took place in the meadows beneath the Hall. The Hall seems to have been used, in a minor way, by Cumberland's irregular cavalry.

As the Jacobite army retreated north, pursued by the Duke of Cumberland's army, its rearguard, baggage and artillery, under Lord George Murray, fell somewhat behind the main army, hampered by poor weather and inadequate roads. So while the Young Pretender and the main army entered Penrith on the evening of 17 December, Murray's section (led by the Macdonalds of Glengarry) spent the night six miles behind them, at Shap. There they joined up with a regiment of 200 men under Colonel Roy Stewart. Murray was marching to join the Prince's army at Penrith at dawn the following day when he found 'several parties' of enemy cavalry on the heights between him and Clifton village, three miles south of Penrith. This local volunteer cavalry galloped off when the Macdonalds of Glengarry charged them. Some, however, were taken prisoner including, fortuitously, the Duke of Cumberland's footman. He informed his captors that Cumberland was advancing with 4,000 horse.

The Young Pretender was told of Cumberland's advance and ordered Murray to retreat on Penrith. Macpherson of Cluny and his clan along with the Appin regiment, under Stewart of Ardshiel, went to Cliftonbridge to reinforce Murray's men. Cumberland's cavalry was now drawn up on Clifton Moor in the Highlanders' rear. The Highlanders then retreated through Lord Lonsdale's enclosures of fir trees. Murray now prepared for battle. He placed the Glengarry regiment on the high road within the fields, the Appin Stewarts in Lord Lonsdale's enclosures on their left. To the Stewarts' left he drew up the Macphersons, and on the right, stationed Colonel Roy Stewart's men, covered by a wall. On what was apparently a dark, occasionally moonlit night about a thousand English dismounted dragoons advanced towards Lord Lonsdale's enclosures to attack the Highlanders' flank. Murray ordered the Macphersons and Stewarts, then behind a hedge, to advance and take a second hedge in front, protected by a conveniently deep ditch. It was lined on the opposite side by enemy dragoons. They fired on the advancing Macphersons, led by Murray himself. But the Scots burst through the hedge, severely wounding their commander, Colonel Honeywood and sending them into retreat across the moor. Simultaneously, another body of Cumberland's dragoons advanced along the high road. They were repulsed by the Glengarry regiment and John Roy Stewart's. Some 12 Macphersons advanced too enthusiastically and were killed or taken prisoner.[8]

Pleased with his success, Murray offered to take on Cumberland's cavalry with reinforcements. But the Prince decided against this and Murray retreated over Lowther bridge into Penrith to join the main army. The skirmish had succeeded in slowing down Cumberland's advance, but next day the Prince's army had to retreat to Carlisle. On 20 December the Jacobite army crossed the River Esk into Scotland, meeting its nemesis at the Battle of Culloden on 16 April 1746.[9]

In the break-up of Henry Richmond Brougham's collection of properties, Brougham Hall and Scales Hall were entailed through Commissioner Brougham's will onto his other nephews, the sons of his brother Samuel Brougham (1681-1744). They went to Samuel's eldest son, John Brougham (*c*.1706-56), Henry Richmond Brougham's cousin. Henry Richmond Brougham's unexpected death started a decline in the Brougham family fortunes which were not to revive for more than 60 years.

1. This John, son of Thomas Brougham (1617-48), born *c.*1645, was High Constable of Kendal *c.*1680. Genealogist Peggy Stacey has recently discovered that he died at the home of his daughter, Agnes Mounsey of Patterdale, in 1730.
2. This he later sold to the Lowther family.
3. Carlisle P.R.O. Ballantine Dykes Papers D/BD/1 95.1
4. Carlisle P.R.O. ibid. D/BD/1 94.1
5. The bedrock beneath was a Permian sand dune, dating from 225 to 280 million years ago, when the whole Eden Valley was desert.
6. Mr. Terry Friedman in his book *James Gibbs* (Yale University Press, 1984) writes that there are a number of similarities between Gibbs' work and the centre-pieces in High Head's side and front. These are identical to plate numbers 43 and 57 of his *Book of Architecture* (1728). Friedman says that the castle's Doric hall screen is the same as that in Gibbs' Cambridge Senate House (of 1722-30).
7. Cumbria Record Office D/Cu.1/116
8. St. Cuthbert's church, Clifton's burial register records the burial of 10 dragoons 'six of Blands three of Cobhams and one of Mark Kerrs Regiment' on 19th December 1745. Seven Highlanders were killed and buried in Town End. Their remains seem to have been moved into Clifton churchyard at the time of the building of the railway (opened in 1862).
9. This account is taken from Sir Walter Scott, *Tales of A Grandfather, being stories from the History of Scotland*, Third Series, Vol. III (Cadell & Co., Edinburgh 1830), pp. 114-22.

Chapter Four

The 'Lost' Coffin 1749-1810

On 25 May 1749, Henry Richmond Brougham's will was proved at York. It left all his lands (except those that were entailed) to his executor, the merchant John Gale of Whitehaven, and £1,000 to Elizabeth Baynes, in addition to all debts Henry owed her husband, attorney Robert Baynes of Cockermouth. The will omitted Henry's paternal Brougham relatives, reinforcing their hatred for him, even in death. A letter written that day by Henry Richmond's cousin, solicitor John Brougham of Cockermouth (1706-82),[1] to John Brougham of Scales, now head of the family, was a typical reaction. Henry Richmond Brougham is described as

> ... his [Commissioner Brougham's] worthless adopted Heir, who as he lived without taking Notice of or shewing the least regard to any of us but Scandalous Treatment, so he Dyed, and shewed himself in his will and a scandalous exit he has made, for he has quite contrary to the intention of his Testator left all his personal estate and all his Reall that about 15,000 a [acres], and thereby very Shamefully and Largely Impoverished the Estate that was given him...[2]

John Brougham of Scales was one of the most obscure heads of the Broughams. Born *c.* 1706, the son of Samuel Brougham and Dorothy, daughter of the Rev. John Child, vicar of Penrith, John owned Brougham Hall for just seven years. He was allegedly a friend of the artist William Hogarth. Both his wife Elizabeth's maiden name and his own date of birth are unknown. In 1741 he was left £800 by Commissioner Brougham. In 1742 John is described as 'of Grays Inn' in London, but was neither a student there nor called to the Bar. The papers of his attorney and cousin, John Brougham of Cockermouth, yield a little about him and reveal a picture of family chaos.

John Brougham of Scales now faced two main problems. There was a sharp drop in income and prestige with the loss of the Richmond family lands and High Head Castle. Some of Henry Richmond Brougham's other lands had passed to his uncle, the Rev. Bernard Brougham, who was buried on 28 September 1750. Before his death he had sold them to John Brougham of Cockermouth. The remainder, Appletreethwaite in Inglewood Forest, Peestree in St Mary's, Carlisle, Hesket, land within the manor of Carlisle Castle, Scales Hall and Brougham Hall, estimated as worth £400 per annum, passed to John Brougham of Scales. Both estates were managed by William Whelpdale of Skirsgill, John Brougham of Cockermouth's brother-in-law. John of Scales also had to pay Henry Richmond Brougham's debts.

John Brougham of Scales' second problem was a legal battle against Gale and his solicitor, Robert Baynes of Cockermouth, developing even before the proving of Henry Richmond Brougham's will. Initially it was over the disputed possession of Beacon tenements and Denton's in the manor of Plumpton which Baynes claimed. By August 1750, Gale was also claiming Woodside tenement from the Broughams. In January 1749, however, John Brougham of Cockermouth had bought the Rev. Bernard Brougham's lands, Woodside included, for £2,100. The same month he had agreed to sell it to one Chris. Wyvill for £375, not realising that it might be affected by Henry Richmond Brougham's will.

John Brougham of Cockermouth was now the wealthiest member of the family. John Brougham of Scales, in contrast, was pretty impoverished. In an indiscreet letter of 29 October 1751 to his brother, the Rev. Thomas Brougham, John of Cockermouth described a visit to 'cous. Brougham' at Scales to get £100 owed to Thomas. 'Cous.' stumped up only £60, which his attorney promised to supplement out of his own Martinmas rents. Furthermore, creditors now harassed 'our Chief': 'I have been forced to preserve the Renown of the family you have the Honour & Happiness of being a Branch, by advancing above 100lb. for chief since I came down to prevent his being Arrested by a Jeweller & a Simon Draper ...'.

The Broughams' legal problems continued. On 2 December 1751 Baynes claimed a close within the manor of Catterlen through Henry Richmond Brougham's will, and wrote to Henry Brougham, 'Chief's' brother:

> My wife claims this Estate as Eldest Daur. of Mrs. Gledhill, who was the Eldest Sister of Henry Richmond Brougham's Mother. As it appears to me very clearly that my wife is entitled to this estate, I take the liberty to acquaint you with my Claim and hope if it appears to you in the same light – that you will be so ingenuous as to give it up without the Trouble of an eject-ment form ...[3]

Things moved slowly and attempts to reach an amicable settlement of this dispute failed, like an aborted meeting at Catterlen between Baynes and John Brougham of Cockermouth in May 1755. Robert and Elizabeth Baynes then obtained an ejectment order on the tenement, which was 20 acres of meadow and 20 of pasture and tenements in Newton parish, and brought a suit against John Brougham of Scales for £100. He had to surrender the tenement when it transpired that it had never legally belonged to the Rev. Bernard Brougham!

John Brougham of Scales lived at Scales Hall. It is not clear who lived at Brougham Hall in this period. John of Scales made little impact on either the family properties or the estates, perhaps partly because of ill health. On 24 March 1753, writing to the Rev. Thomas Brougham, John of Cockermouth referred to 'Chief' as 'a very Tender Twig', advising Thomas to get the annuity John owed him before the latter died. In 1756 John did die. He left two daughters Ann (c.1745-1810) and Dorothy (c.1746-1829) who died unmarried. His widow, Elizabeth (d. 1799), was granted letters of administration over his estate. According to his post mortem inventory, dated 5 May 1756, John Brougham left £400 3s. 10d., apparel valued at £200 and household furniture valued at £146 1s. 10d. His brother, Henry Brougham, now succeeded to Brougham Hall and the Brougham estates.

Henry Brougham the Elder (1719-82) is a far better documented figure than John. Baptised on 19 December at St Andrew's church, Holborn, he was working at the Six Clerks' Office in 1742. He earned his living as a solicitor. In 1741 he had been left £1,200 by Commissioner Brougham and had married Mary, daughter of the Rev. William Free-man, D.D. at St Benet's church, Paul's Wharf, London. In the Rev. Bernard Brougham's will of 2 February 1749,[4] he is referred to as 'of Took's Court, in the parish of St Andrew, Holborn' and is made Bernard's attorney, being assigned a bond of John Brougham of Cockermouth for the sum of £4,200. In a codicil of 12 July 1750, Bernard left him £600. In a letter of 16 April 1750 to the Rev. Thomas Brougham, John Brougham of Cocker-mouth called him 'that sly and insinuating youth', alleging that he was trying to ingrati-ate himself with the stricken Bernard. Henry eventually received an additional legacy of £170 from Bernard! In 1755 he enquired, fruitlessly, whether his cousin, John of Cocker-mouth, wanted to sell the estates he had bought from Bernard for £2,500.

Henry Brougham actually lived at Brougham Hall and was living there in 1758, on his election to the Tanners' Guild of Carlisle. The Hall seems to have become something of a family base again. Henry's third child, Ann, married at Brougham in August 1772. Scales was leased to one Jonah Peers in 1766 for seven years. Perhaps on becoming agent for the Duke of Norfolk's estates in Cumberland Henry wanted a larger establishment. However, accounts of Henry's employer, Charles, 10th Duke of Norfolk, do not shed much light on Henry Brougham's activities. The duke spent much of his time at Greystoke Castle, three miles from Penrith. His main achievement, according to George Edward Cockayne's *Complete Peerage*, was to write *Anecdotes of the Howard Family*. Born in 1720, the son of Henry Charles Howard of Greystoke and Mary, daughter and co-heir of John Aylward, a London merchant, he was made an F.S.A. and F.R.S. in 1768. He succeeded to the title in 1777, dying in 1786.

It is unclear how Henry Brougham's work for the 10th Duke of Norfolk benefited him. He seems not to have been poor, sending his second son John (baptised in July 1748) to Eton and later to King's College, Cambridge, in the early 1760s.[5] In 1766, when still working for the Six Clerks' Office, he entered into a lease and release agreement on Scales Hall. Henry, now 'of Castle Yard, Holborn', conveyed Scales Hall and 24 acres to Henry Pratt of London Street. These 24 acres were made up of Simpson's, Vaux's and Parker's farms in Skelton, and then occupied by John Pears and Thomas Simpson, were subject to a redemption payment of £300.

It must have pleased Henry Brougham to see his daughters marry well. Mary (1744-1812) married Richard Meux on 31 July 1767. The Meux family, from the Isle of Wight had acquired a baronetcy in 1641, bestowed on John Meux of Kingston, M.P. for Longtown, Isle of Wight in 1640. In 1705 the title had become extinct but Bartholomew, the 1st Baronet's brother, had descendants, including Richard. In 1831 Richard and Mary Meux's second son, Henry Meux of Theobalds Park, Hertfordshire, was made a baronet, a later baronet becoming Lord Mayor of London.[6] Another of Henry Brougham's daughters, Ann, married Thomas Aylmer of the Middle Temple, by special licence at Brougham on 31 August 1772.[7]

Despite having a London house, Henry Brougham the Elder may well have spent most of his last years in Cumberland and Westmorland. Though a treble voucher (a cumbersome stystem of transferring property from one party to another via a third party) of 1764 transferred Brougham Hall to his son Henry Brougham the Younger, it probably remained the family seat. In 1775, though, there arose the question of the manor of Brougham's ownership, and commissioners were asked to decide it. They found that the manor belonged to the Earl of Thanet and that the tenants, including Henry Brougham, were freeholders. Other tenants of parts of the manor were Sir Richard Tufton, the Earl of Lonsdale, John Jameson and the Mother and Sisters of St Anne's Hospital.

Henry Brougham the Elder's financial affairs were in some difficulty before his death in 1782. On 17 and 18 May 1779, he signed a release with Henry Pratt, Sir John Brewer Davis of Park Lane, St George's Hanover Square, and a merchant, Thomas Langley of Lothbury. As £3,000 remained owing to Pratt, of which the principal was £2,300, Henry conveyed all property he held excluding two estates, Murrell Hill and Musgrave Hall, to Davis and Langley. In 1782 the situation was little better. On 29 and 30 April, Henry Brougham signed another release, involving Davis, Langley, Pratt, Edward Stanley of Workington, James Craike of Hunby and the wealthy Cumberland landowner and industrialist John Christian. The linchpin of the agreement, Christian, agreed to pay off and discharge £2,870 9s. 4d. then due to Pratt. Another £2,588 9s. 8d. was to be paid to Henry Curwen and held in trust for Christian, along with a sum equivalent to that which Christian had paid Pratt. Henry Brougham now owed Christian £5,458 19s. 5d. He agreed to repay this and other sums paid by Christian to William Chapman and John Robinson, his attorney, at 5 per cent interest per annum.

Henry Brougham the Elder seems to have spent at least part of his last years at Brougham Hall, and took an active part in its management. In 1843, during the Broughams' bizarre law case against Thomas Bird, the testimony of 67-year-old William Elliott, a carpenter from Clifton, mentioned Henry manufacturing bricks at Wetheriggs Farm around 1778-9. After manufacture some were transported by his coachman and used on the farm buildings. Fittingly, Henry died at Brougham Hall on 21 December 1782. In his will of 20 May 1780 he asked that, if he died in Westmorland,

> ... to be buried at Brougham Church, which I think the properest burial place for a family that had its original in this parish who afterwards seated at Scales until part of its ancient possessions was restored and brought back again into the family by my late honoured uncle, John Brougham.

Henry could not script his exit to the last detail. On 26 December his funeral took place. Henry, 1st Lord Brougham described it:

> Neither my father, nor his brother John, were then in Westmorland, and Charles, Duke of Norfolk, who was an intimate friend of the family attended as chief mourner. At the funeral feast which preceded the funeral, His Grace addressed the guests: 'Friends and neighbours, before I give you the toast of the day, the memory of the deceased, I ask you to drink to the health of the family physician, Dr. Harrison, the founder of the feast'.
> There were more toasts, and the funeral procession set out for Ninekirks, a distance of three miles. At the church, the hearse and procession was met by the vicar – but the coffin had disappeared! On searching back it was found in the river at a place where, driven by a drunken coachman, the hearse had lurched against a rock. The outer oak coffin had broken to pieces, the lead had remained intact, too heavy to be carried away by the stream. The shock and scandal produced by all this had a sobering effect on everybody, and put an end to such disgraceful orgies in the county.[8]

In his will, proved on 19 April 1783, Henry Brougham the Elder left two leasehold estates, at New Cross, Surrey and in Kent (held of Christ's Hospital and the Company of Haberdashers respectively) to his wife, Mary. His daughter Mary Meux received a third leasehold estate, held of a Mr. Parker, at Hickmans Folly. His son, the Rev. John Brougham, received another estate at Lewisham, while Appletreethwaite in Inglewood Forest went to Timothy Fetherstonhaugh of Kirkoswald. Henry's eldest son, Henry (b. 1742) received a ninth part of the manor of Skelton. His daughter Rebecca (1753-1823), later Mrs. Richard Lowndes, received his 'Rucker' harpsichord and music.[9]

Henry Brougham the Elder's death was a considerable blow to his family. He had gone some way to reversing the impoverishment following Sheriff Brougham's death in 1749, without restoring the prosperity of Commissioner and Collector Peter Brougham's time. Unfortunately he left Scales Hall heavily mortgaged, and with an heir best described as 'honest and affectionate but dilatory, shambling and negative'.[10]

Born on 18 June 1742, and admitted to Grays Inn on 26 January 1765, Henry Brougham the Younger did not practise law. His father tried to groom him to take over the estate. In 1764 he had transferred Brougham Hall to his son and, in May 1768, filed a bill in Chancery with his son against Dorothy Brougham, tenant of Appletreethwaite,[11] and Elizabeth Richardson and her husband, who were tenants of Walker's and Wybergh's at Yanwath. But if Henry senior planned to hand over responsibility for the estates to his son he was disappointed.

Peter Brougham Wyly says there is no Whelpdale evidence to support the story that Henry the Younger was later betrothed to Mary Whelpdale, a distant cousin, who died on

16. Henry Brougham the Younger (1742-1810) in front of Brougham Hall and Lowther Bridge, *c.*1790, by an anonymous arti

the eve of their wedding. Around 1777, however, Henry abruptly departed from London to Cowgate, Edinburgh, where he settled in lodgings kept by Mrs. Mary Syme. Mrs. Syme was no ordinary landlady. Widow of the Rev. James Syme, minister of Alloa, Perthshire, she was the sister of the famous historian, the Rev. Dr. William Robertson, D.D. (1721-93). Author of *Charles V* and other widely-read books, he was Principal of Edinburgh University and Royal Historiographer of Scotland. He was also descended from the Robertsons of Gladney and, through them, the Robertsons of Strowan, Ayrshire. Mrs. Syme's unmarried daughter, Eleonora, then fell for young Henry Brougham. By their wedding, on 22 May 1778, Eleonora was some months pregnant with their first child.

Contemporaries of Henry, 1st Lord Brougham, describe Mrs. Eleonora Brougham as highly intelligent, practical and physically attractive (even in old age). Le Marchant, after a visit to Brougham Hall in 1833, wrote in his diary of her 'chaste, slightly severe air that plays over features that are chiselled with a precision and elegance which is seldom seen but in an ancient statue'. How could this remarkable woman have ended up marrying Henry Brougham the Younger, an eccentric and impoverished dilettante? Perhaps disappointment in him (if she felt it) was outweighed by devotion to their children. The first of these, Henry Peter, was born in Edinburgh on 19 September 1778 and baptised by his great-uncle, the Rev. Dr. William Robertson in St Giles' cathedral there. Other children followed: James (b. 1780), Peter (b. 1781), John Waugh (b. 1785), Mary (b. 1787) and William (b. 1795). Only James and William made much impact on life at Brougham Hall. Mary (who died unmarried in May 1856) was apparently a harridan, obsessed with cleanliness and dreaded by the Spalding and Brougham children who grew up there.

17. Mrs. Eleonora Brougham (née Syme) (d. 1839), attributed to Raeburn.

Henry and Eleonora Brougham soon moved with Mrs. Syme to a house in Edinburgh's prosperous St Andrew's Square. When Henry Peter was four his grandfather died, leaving his parents having to pay the mortgage on Scales Hall. As their income was only a few hundred pounds a year, and with three boys to look after, this proved beyond them. Henry Brougham tried to sell Scales Hall in 1785. Charles, 11th Duke of Norfolk, visited it on 26 September that year, leaving an interesting picture of its great neglect in his diary.

> ... called at Scales Hall, much out of repair, gives an idea of the stile of liv[ing] of Cumberland gentleman of small fortune in last century, a hall with carved oak ceil[ing], a large arched chimney kitchen and back kitchen a court surrounded w[ith] walls and buildings ... estate improveable, on sale next day only £2000 bid, let for £100, measures about 200 acres ... of great tythe.

On 25 and 26 January 1786, Henry Brougham signed an indenture with Edward Stanley of Workington, James Craike of Hunby and Peter Lamplugh of Dovenby Hall. Lamplugh (b. 1735), the eldest son of John Brougham of Cockermouth, had inherited the property of his father, his uncle, the Rev. Thomas Brougham, and the Rev. Bernard Brougham. He had changed his name from Brougham to Lamplugh by sign manual in 1783. He now wanted to buy Scales Hall. A release was drawn up between John Christian of Workington, Stanley, Craike, Henry Brougham and Mary Brougham, his mother. Scales Hall and 207 acres changed hands for £5,500 with Greenlands, Kiln Riggs and Longlands being granted and released to Peter Lamplugh and his heirs.

This did not end Henry Brougham the Younger's financial problems. On 3 and 4 April 1787, he granted and released Greenlands and Kilnriggs and some 11½ acres near Scales Hall to Robert Collins of Carlisle for £1,000. Collins later granted him a release so he could sell the land to Peter Lamplugh. On 5 and 6 April, a lease and release of the land in Greenlands and Kilnriggs was drawn up between Henry and his wife Eleonora for the sum of £230. On 1 October 1788, Henry, clearly impoverished, was granted a bond by Lamplugh of 'the penal sum of £400'.

Despite these financial problems, Henry and Eleonora Brougham moved back to Brougham Hall in 1790. Henry cut an eccentric, even bizarre, figure there, wearing his hair powdered and tied, dressed in a cut-away coat and white waistcoat, and wandering about the estate carrying a tall, gold-headed cane. Though he was a good and generous father, the Hall's housekeeping was in Eleonora's capable hands. Lord Campbell, in his *Lives of the Lord Chancellors* (1845-7) vol.8, quoted lines that Lord Murray wrote of her: 'She was kind, considerate, calm and intelligent; and ready without a shadow of pretension to help every person who stood in need of her unobtrusive aid'. Devoted to her eldest son, she had no favourites amongst her children.

Even by the time of the move from Edinburgh to Brougham Hall it was obvious that Henry Peter was a most gifted child. Though his ability would, given his steely determination, have emerged sooner or later, Edinburgh was a good place to grow up. Men of distinction adorned its public life, like Dugald Stewart the philosopher and the Adam brothers in architecture. Much of the city, like St Andrew's Square, was newly-built classical, or being rebuilt in that style. Its streets were surprisingly free from crime. Many of Henry's childhood contemporaries were to be distinguished men, like Francis Horner, later a Whig M.P. Strangely, for someone who lived until he was 90, Henry was a fragile child. When he was five or six he suffered from 'putrid fever' (possibly typhus), completely losing his memory. He forgot how to read, despite having just learnt from his father.

Henry was resilient, however. He recovered, was sent to infants' school and, in 1785, to Edinburgh High School. There punishments were severe and daily beatings common.

18. Peter Brougham Lamplugh (1735-91) in the style of Allan Ramsay.

PETER BROUGHAM LAMPLUGH *of* DOVENBY HALL
OBᵗ 1791. Æᵗ 56.

MARY, DAUGᵗʳ *of* Jʰⁿ BROUGHAM, WIFE to FRETCHEVILLE
OBᵗ 1785. DYKES *of* WARTHOLE

19. Mary Dykes (née Brougham) (d. 1785), sister of Peter Brougham Lamplugh and wife of Frecheville Dykes.

One story about Henry around this time illustrates two of his characteristics: his powerful memory and proud determination. He was punished when 11 by a master, Mr. Fraser, for an error in a Latin exercise. He turned up next day to the lesson weighed down with texts and authorities proving that he had been right and so forced the master to admit defeat. Younger members of the school referred to him after this as 'the boy who beat the master'.

Despite poor health in 1790, young Henry Brougham left Edinburgh High School as head of school, after spending a year in the rector Dr. Adam's classics class. He spent 1791 at Brougham Hall with his brother James under the care of a tutor, Mr. Mitchell. In their spare time they read, went riding, toured the Lakes, walked or called on neighbours. This may account for Henry's lifelong closeness to James. It probably marks the start of his love of Westmorland. He later returned to Brougham Hall at regular intervals. It is unclear how long the Broughams spent at the Hall in the 1790s. Henry Brougham senior does not seem to have liked the house and, in 1794, one Edward Scott is listed as its tenant.

In 1792 Henry Brougham entered Edinburgh University, aged 14, to read Humanity and Philosophy. The course included political economy, astronomy, ancient languages, rhetoric, logic, moral philosophy, mathematics and natural philosophy. Henry was fascinated by the art of public speaking, establishing a debating club with strict rules. He studied the oratory of leading divines and public figures. After three years he did a further course in law in 1795. Law was a natural career for someone like Brougham. In it the moderately able could earn a decent living and the outstanding could acquire impressive wealth and reputation.

Politics was the most common interest of Henry and his friends, who included future M.P.s and cabinet ministers: Francis Jeffrey, Sydney Smith, John William Ward, Charles Grant, Henry Cockburn, Lord Henry Petty, John Murray, John Allen, James Loch and Lord Webb Seymour. They endlessly discussed politics, philosophy and science, spent long evenings in oyster kitchens or each others' rooms, and drank heavily. Their talk was brilliant and often very funny. Pranks included tying together door-knockers of rows of terraced houses and sounding them in the small hours. Once they carried a coffin to the Edinburgh races. To the consternation of onlookers, the 'cortège' came to a stop by the track and Henry Brougham got out.

Henry Brougham had a striking diversity of learning and interests. One was science. In 1796 he wrote a paper entitled *Experiments and Observations on the Inflection, Reflection, and Colours of Light*, which was published by the Royal Society. He wrote *Further Observations* on the same subject in 1797. These papers attracted the adverse attention of a Swiss authority, Professor Prevost of Geneva, who questioned the thoroughness of the experiments. Henry also held a long, friendly correspondence on chemical matters from Brougham with a cousin on his mother's side, the Rev. Dr. Alexander Forsyth, Minister of Belhelvie, Aberdeenshire, and later proprietor of Forsyth and Co., Patent Gunmakers. In 1798, Brougham published another paper, *Porisms*, and kept up his studies with the scientist Black. He also founded an Academy of Physics and a Chemical Society!

Henry's lifelong scientific interests led him to become an F.R.S. in March 1803. But he was no Faraday. Politics gradually occupied more of his attention, and in 1798 he founded the Speculative Society in Edinburgh. Its rules were that one member would read a paper, and then the floor would be thrown open for discussion. It provided useful practice for the future in that debaters could make mistakes and not pay heavily for them. They could test themselves in a competitive atmosphere, learn to project themselves and argue their case before their cleverest contemporaries. In 1799 Henry went on a cruise to St Kilda, where he was wrecked hair-raisingly on the island's west side and had

20. Henry Brougham (1778-1868) in his twenties, oil miniature by an anonymous artist.

21. Henry Brougham (1778-1868) in his thirties, a pastel sketch.

to climb the cliffs, then travelled to Denmark and Scandinavia. One of his companions was Charles Stuart, later Lord Stuart de Rothesay and an ambassador in Madrid and Paris. In June 1800, he and Horner qualified as advocates in Edinburgh.

It is interesting to read of the reactions the young Henry Brougham provoked. Stuart thought him the cleverest man he had ever known, but the least steady.[12] Horner writing to John Hewlett on 17 July 1798 described him as 'an uncommon genius of a composite order ... he unites the greatest ardour for general information in every branch of knowledge and, what is more remarkable, activity in the business and interests in the pleasures of the world with all the powers of a mathematical intellect'.[13] What added to his unsteadiness was a family disaster in July 1800. Henry was devoted to his brother, Peter, who had joined the East India Company as a cadet for the 1799-1800 season. Aged only 18 he was killed in a duel with a Mr. Campbell of Shawfield, mate of the *Queen* at San Salvador on 7 July. Grief and anger at Peter's death sent Henry into a deep depression. He recovered after a few weeks but its effects were long-lasting. At regular intervals under strong pressure he would become mentally depressed, his behaviour alternately ungoverned and lethargic. Another legacy was a changeability which made him hard to live with, and a hyperactivity making work possible long into the night. Given these 'feet of clay' his later achievements are astonishing.

After a farcical first case as a junior counsel, when a man he was defending from a sedition charge openly admitted his guilt, Henry gained as much experience as possible, defending people who were virtually penniless. He was attracted by cases of people who were victims of the Government's censorship laws. He relied on an allowance from his father and his earnings were slight. But he was determined. Henry used ingenuous, albeit sometimes unconvincing defences and was not renowned for professional courtesy. He made life very difficult for one eccentric, plodding judge, Lord Eskgrove (?1724-1804). As Sir David Rae, Eskgrove had been a leading lawyer in the Scottish Court of Exchequer, being ennobled in 1782. After trying a series of men accused of either treason or sedition he had been made Lord Justice Clerk in June 1799. This made him a natural target for Brougham. In 1800 Eskgrove remarked 'I declare that man Broom or Broug-ham is the torment of my life'.

Henry's practice as an advocate gave him a certain notoriety but he made a name for himself through journalism. Originally a chance idea of John Murray, Sydney Smith, Francis Horner and Lord Webb Seymour, the *Edinburgh Review* of which Henry was a founding member appeared in October 1802. It attempted to cover all topics of learning and the arts from poetry to science. Henry immediately became one of its mainstays, contributing 80 articles to its first 20 issues. He had wide general knowledge, read extensively, and could work up a subject against a printer's deadline. But his reviews could be savage and unfair. One review of Byron's poems, *Hours of Idleness*, in 1808 drew the latter's permanent enmity. As late as March 1823, Byron intended to challenge Brougham to a duel if he ever returned to England.

With his number of cases as an advocate increasing somewhat, Brougham set out to write a book on the colonial empires. In it he argued that, contrary to what many commentators maintained, colonies were an asset and that the practice of slavery should be abolished and was repugnant in a Christian society. The book, *An Enquiry into the Colonial Policy of the European Powers*, was a compendium of information and statistics. Though somewhat ungainly, it drew Brougham to the attention of the Tory M.P. and anti-slavery campaigner William Wilberforce.

A lonely Henry Brougham was working long hours from seven in the morning until two the next day. He decided to try his luck in England (like his brother James, and Horner and Loch), and enter the English bar. His father's lack of enthusiasm led to a row between them. On 25 October 1803, Henry (in Edinburgh) wrote scathingly to Loch of his father's attitude:

> Mr. B. is the damndest lazy man to deal with in the way of business that you can possibly imagine, and generally goes upon the wise maxim that everything may as well be done tomorrow as today. The very reverse is always my principle so that things are often at a dead stop between us.

Eventually he won the argument, entering Grays Inn as a bencher in November 1803. On 27 December 1803 a friend, Andrew Clephane, wrote to Loch: 'Henry Brougham has at last determined on the English Bar, and sets out in a week or two for the South. It is my private opinion that he will never practise at any Bar whatever'.[14]

The young Henry Brougham left no 10 minutes of the day unfilled. This did not always guarantee success, though. In 1804 he endured the fiasco of the Edinburgh volunteers. Four hundred men chaired by him and supported by the City authorities offered the Government their services in the Napoleonic Wars, only to be ignored. Henry's anti-slavery pamphlet that year, *A Concise Statement of the Question regarding the Abolition of the Slave Trade* was more successful, however. It caught the public imagination, attracting the attention of M.P.s coming just before Wilberforce's Abolition Bill was read. Later, Henry, travelling with an American passport, made his way to Holland to support the anti-slavery cause. Then he recklessly travelled through Austria and down into Italy. He narrowly escaped arrest as an Englishman while on a boat travelling down the Rhine near Cologne, when his servant got into a brawl with some French soldiers. On another occasion Henry hid in the lavatory of a small ship while French soldiers searched it lack-adaisically for foreigners.

Escaping unscathed, Brougham returned to Edinburgh. In 1805 he decided to leave for London. He must have missed Edinburgh friends and the city's social life, such as the Friday Club (established in 1803). This met off Shakespeare Square at Boyle's Tavern, and later at Princes Street. Henry himself prepared the club's staple drink, rum punch ('a very pleasant but somewhat dangerous beverage') for the members who included Dugald Stewart (Brougham's former tutor), Professor John Playfair, Sydney Smith, Sir Walter Scott, Henry Mackenzie, Henry Cockburn (author of *The Man of Feeling*), Francis Home and the Earl of Selkirk.[15] In 1802, Henry had been thinking of London with dread and '... no small horror to five years' dull, unvaried drudgery, which must be undergone to obtain the privilege of drudging still harder among a set of disagreeable persons of brutal manners and confined talents ...'.[16] Once there, however, he defied grim predictions and flourished. In 1806 a friend, Wishaw, offered to be his banker. He led, despite his small allowance, an active social life, steering clear of the gaming tables and joining two clubs. These were the King of Clubs and Brooks'.

Brougham Hall stewed under his father's control. The Brougham family had spent such long periods elsewhere that in 1802 the Hall was still being called Bird's Nest by locals. From 1802 to 1810 its chapel was being used as a barn by the tenant of the adjoining land. In 1808, when Henry senior had to pay window tax, rather than raise more income from the estate he reduced the Hall's windows to between 40 and 50. Meanwhile, Henry junior was trying to obtain a parliamentary seat. At first he tried locally in Cumberland and Westmorland. In 1806, William Wilberforce wrote on his behalf to William, Viscount Lowther of Whitehaven (made Earl of Lonsdale in 1807) who controlled seven parliamentary seats in the area. His letter and one from Henry himself in 1807 were fruitless, however. Instead, Henry had to be content with two minor ill-rewarded jobs. The first was that of secretary to a mission to Portugal, headed by Lords

St Vincent and Rosslyn in 1806. It was something of a flop but Brougham displayed considerable ability. Substantial sums he spent went unrepaid after his return in December that year. The second job, during the following year, was to help the Whigs back into office in the 1807 General Election.

Doing unpaid hack-work, Henry wrote trenchant pamphlets, organised publicity and displayed a flair for propaganda, working long hours in Holland House. Lord Holland, the Whig patrician whom he had met through Edinburgh contacts, assisted him. But the Whigs were heavily beaten and the 'Ministry of All the Talents' lost office. In both jobs, Brougham discovered some noblemen's unwillingness to perform hard labour. They would sometimes, like Earl Grey, retreat at elections to their estates. They seemed unwilling to risk controversy and wanted to run their political lives through a network of relations. It was no accident that they had rewarded the great Edmund Burke with only a minor cabinet post. Brougham was unashamedly ambitious, however, and cared little if he was thought an opportunist or freebooter.

The years 1808 to 1810 marked a turning-point in the Broughams' fortunes. In November 1808, Henry qualified as a barrister at Lincoln's Inn, and started to practise on the Northern circuit. The previous month there had been controversy over the *Edinburgh Review*'s 'Don Cevallos' article, when Jeffrey, helped by Brougham, drew a parallel between the popular uprising in Spain against Napoleonic rule and Britain ('a lesson to all governments – a warning to all oligarchies'). Authorship of the article was ascribed to Brougham but his career continued to advance. Knowing his politics, the Liverpool merchants approached him with a brief to argue for the repeal of the Orders in Council, imposed by the Government in retaliation for Napoleon's Berlin and Milan decrees. They aimed to make trade with Continental Europe impossible and they allowed the searching of neutral shipping. They depressed trade between Britain and the U.S. and, naturally, the port of Liverpool. Henry Brougham argued the Liverpool merchants' case so compellingly before both Houses of Parliament that he drew large crowds. Though he failed to alter the Government's mind, this was a public triumph.

Henry Brougham, now reasonably well off, found himself at ease in the city clubs in the week, and country houses at week-ends. A man whose sporting knowledge was confined to hare-coursing, he found himself at a disadvantage at one shoot in 1810, when he set fire to his powder horn and burnt off his own eyelashes. Brougham tried to explain this upon philosophical principles but his companions, the Duke of Argyll and Lord Ponsonby, just laughed.

How much Henry Brougham entertained at Brougham Hall is not clear. A strange incident, in autumn 1809, indicates that Mrs. Eleonora Brougham was firmly in control there and that her Scots Presbyterian values conflicted with his liberal cosmopolitan ones. On their way back from Scotland, Lord and Lady Holland stopped at the Hall. Henry wanted to entertain them but Mrs. Brougham would not let Lady Holland (the mother of an illegitimate child) across the threshold, believing that her presence would somehow corrupt her unmarried daughter Mary, then twenty-three. This ignored the Hollands' friendship with Henry, the circumstances of Mrs. Brougham's own marriage in 1778 and Mary's unattractiveness. It also led to something of a rift between Henry and Lady Holland, lasting until 1815.

It was through the patronage of the Duke of Bedford that Henry finally acquired a parliamentary seat. After persuasion from Grey and Holland the Duke supported the idea. As a result, Lord Robert Spencer, the sitting M.P., quit the duke's Cornish pocket-borough, Camelford and on 4 February 1810 Henry Brougham was officially returned as its M.P. On 13 February, his father died, and Henry inherited the Hall and Estate.

1. He was the son of two cousins, Daniel Brougham (1679-1717) and Commissioner Brougham's sister, Mary Brougham (d. 1754).
2. Carlisle Record Office Ballantine Dykes Papers D/BD/1/95/2.
3. This letter and the one above are in Carlisle P.R.O. D/BD/1 94.
4. The information in this paragraph is in Carlisle P.R.O., D/BD/1/95.2 .
5. This John Brougham (1748-1811) Rector of Ballyhaise and Bailleborough in the diocese of Waterford, Ireland, founded an Irish branch of Broughams. See Chart 4.
6. This Baronetcy also became extinct, in 1900. The family brewing company, which became Friary Meux, was acquired by Watneys.
7. This Thomas Aylmer, only son of the Rev. Robert Aylmer of Camberwell, Surrey, clerk, was admitted to the Middle Temple on 3 July 1754 and called to the bar on 6 June 1788. He was probably descended from the Norfolk branch of the Aylmers of Aylmer Hall, Tilney St Lawrence, Norfolk.They included John Aylmer, Bishop of London (1521-94).
8. From *The Life and Times of Henry, Lord Brougham, by himself* (1871) pp. 9-10.During William Brougham's excavation of the chancel of Ninekirks in October 1846, a battered lead coffin was discovered, which could confirm part of this story!
9. P.C.C. Cornwallis 164, abstracted in Hudleston's paper, *The Brougham Family* (1960), p. 168.
10. Frances Hawes, *Henry Brougham* (Jonathan Cape, 1957).
11. Surrendered in 1769.
12. Loch's aunt, Louisa Adam writing to James Loch (25 February 1800), *Brougham And His Early Friends, Letters To James Loch 1798-1809*, collected and arranged by R. H. M. Buddle Atkinson and G.A. Jackson, London (1908), 3 vols., vol. 1, p. 107.
13. Ed. L. Horner, *Memoirs and Correspondence of Francis Horner* (London, 1843), vol. 1, pp. 65-6.
14. This quotation and the one above are from *Brougham And His Early Friends:Letters to James Loch 1798-1809, op. cit.* vol.2 p. 83 & p. 111 respectively.
15. According to *The Making of Classical Edinburgh*, by A. J. Youngson (Edinburgh University Press, 1966).
16. Letter from Henry Brougham to James Loch, Edinburgh, 20 August 1802, *Brougham And His Early Friends*, op. cit. Vol. I, 344.

Chapter 5

Eminence and Fame 1810-1834

Brougham Hall (1810-29)

In 1810 Henry made James responsible for the Hall, Eleonora for the household. The Broughams got back St Wilfred's chapel, whose tenant had found its doors were the wrong size and its location was poor. In 1813, the turnpike was re-routed from outside the chapel to across the bridge near Brougham Castle (now the Brough road). In 1819 blocked Hall windows were opened and a 'composition' (fixed sum) agreed for tax. Repairs were done and the Hall soon impressed visitors like Hobhouse. The estate expanded: in November 1831, Moorhouse's Farm and Scales Hall with 230 acres and 3 perches were bought from the Ballantine Dykeses for £12,500. James' bond and mortgage debts (exceeding £1,000 a year by autumn 1818) may have paid for some changes.[1] This borrowing, however, as will be described later, was to endanger the estate.

Henry's careers in law, science, journalism and politics, his dreadful handwriting, often undated letters and the vast array of material (over 110,000 items in the library of University College, London, alone) make formidable obstacles to the writing of a large, comprehensive biography of him. This will outline his career until 1835 and its effect on the Hall.

22. Brougham Hall, drawn by L. Benson, from Hutchinson's *History of Cumberland* (1794).

The Game of The Country

> Party is much the strongest passion of an Englishman's mind. Friendship, love & even avarice give way before it.

John Wilson Croker to John Murray, 21 January 1831 (University of Michigan, Ann Arbor, Croker MSS., Letter Book Vol. 25 ff 167-8).

Henry made his first important Commons speech, against slavery, on 15 June 1810. His oratory soon made him a leading Whig M.P. and he gained national fame in 1812 when Liverpool's merchants, injured by the Government's Orders in Council (a response to Napoleon's embargo on European trade with Britain providing for the searching of neutral shipping to Europe), engaged him as counsel. Arguing with great eloquence and a mass of statistics in the House of Lords, he got the Orders repealed on 16 June. A setback had come, however in May: Charles Duke of Norfolk told him to vacate Camelford. In June the Liverpool Whigs made him their parliamentary candidate with Thomas Creevey, the wit and diarist. Backed by the Earl of Sefton and the Roscoes, they almost defeated the Tories George Canning and Generals Tarleton and Gascoigne. After two weeks, however, they had to pull out on 19 October.

Now working on the Northern circuit, Henry resented political exile. 'I can't help thinking it a little strange that my being left out of parliament is, to all appearances now a settled matter', he told Creevey in 1814.[2] Time at Brougham in September 1813 and September 1814 (doing mathematical 'divertisements') perhaps consoled him. He returned there with depression in March 1815, studying bee-hives. William was also at the Hall, every long and short vacation from 1811-27.

Henry, offered the Winchelsea seat by the Earl of Darlington on 9 July 1815, returned to London in October. He caused the stunning defeat by 37 votes of Vansittart's Income Tax Bill on 19 March 1816.[3] The unpopular tax's abolition had been promised at the end of the Napoleonic Wars. Dominating the parliamentary select committee on popular education in London, Southwark and Westminster, he found grave abuses in private educational charity administration. This led to an Act setting up a commission of investigation, which later became the Charity Commission.

Brougham was a more commanding figure than Ponsonby, their official leader in the House, but the Whigs did not want to follow the newcomer. He was unpopular, indiscreet and devious. Creevey wrote: 'He has always some game or underplot out of sight – some mysterious correspondence – some extraordinary correspondence with persons quite opposite to himself'.[4]

Henry's ambition was to sit for Westmorland, and this meant challenging the Lowthers' parliamentary dominance. The ruthless Sir James Lowther had since 1774 held seven seats in Cumberland and Westmorland: one each for Appleby and Carlisle, one for Cumberland, both for Westmorland and both seats for Cockermouth. (Later, in 1780, he acquired Haslemere, a Surrey pocket borough with two members, thus completing the famous 'nine pins'.) Two Whig magnates had a small share. The Earl of Thanet had one of the Appleby seats, the Duke of Portland one at Carlisle and one for Cumberland.[5] The Tory Lowthers, led by William (made Earl of Lonsdale in 1807), were determined to keep Westmorland. In 1816 Henry told Creevey he had '... all the parsons, justices, attorneys, and nearly all the resident gentry (few enough, thank God! and vile enough) leagued agt. me, besides the whole force of the Government. The spirit of the freeholders, to be sure is wonderful, and in the end we must beat the villains'. He thought Lonsdale was 'now bleeding at every pore' financially.[6] But only in December

1817 did Wordsworth (made Distributor of Stamps for Westmorland in 1813, through Lowther patronage) hear a rumour in London that Henry was to contest the county.

Lowthers had been lord lieutenants of Cumberland and Westmorland since 1759. Sir Robert Smirke put Lord Lonsdale's income at £80-100,000 a year. Many of Westmorland's electors (composed of 2,500 40s. freeholders) voted for him by instinct, his ex-tenants being enfranchised to do so. He now named politically experienced sons as candidates for Westmorland: William, Viscount Lowther, M.P. for Westmorland since 1813 and a treasury commissioner, and Lt. Col. Henry Cecil Lowther, M.P. for Westmorland since 1812. A dramatic, bruising battle started. In early January 1818 Viscount Lowther hurried back from Paris to Westmorland. Though supported by many parsons, attornies and justices, *Kendal Chronicle* attacks troubled him. On 15 February he asked Croker to recommend a writer to respond to these attacks, complaining of a disorganised, inexperienced campaign.[7]

The Viscount's opponents were Quakers and non-conformists, Whig landowners like Lord Thanet, yeomen not under Lowther domination, and men in dispute with the commissioners, who had either broken Game Laws or opposed enclosures. But the Lowtherites subscribed £1,500 to set up their own paper, *The Westmorland Gazette*. They printed Wilberforce's letter of 1806 asking the then Viscount Lowther to give Henry a seat. They made new voters, buying land, dividing it into lots which supporters then purchased in order to be enfranchised. They said, justly, that Henry was not wholly supported by his party. Before polling Henry spoke for Lord Morpeth in Cockermouth, deprecating an election to save a 10-day poll. The Cumberland Whigs then refused to help in Westmorland.

Undaunted, Brougham spoke in every large village and town. Lambton wrote: 'He was at once counsel, agent, canvasser and orator and changing his character every hour; and always cheerful and active. Really his energy of mind is beyond anything I could even have conceived'.[8]

The Whigs promised £10,000 for Henry's campaign but Liverpool merchant John Wakefield probably provided funds instead.[9] Henry attracted the country gentlemen, middle-class professionals and farmers who were frustrated at Lowther despotism. William Crackenthorpe of Newbiggin Hall and Thomas Clarkson supported him, for example. Brougham promised to end Lowther domination, forming the 'Friends of the Independence of Westmorland'. He said the Lowthers (dominating local government, church and law) grew rich at the expense of the 'Blues'. This was a dangerous claim for a landowner to make. In March he claimed in a speech in Kendal that the Land Tax Assessment Bill would ensure his election. Viscount Lowther told Croker on 28 March that the Bill (enfranchising all with half an acre from a common) would increase Westmorland's electorate by a third, so they must oppose it.[10]

Venality and intimidation marked the campaign, but it had comedy. In Kendal, Henry attacked Wordsworth (a Lowther canvasser) saying his opponents used '... the most active of secret agents, a man with a sinecure in the country, with nothing else or very little to live upon', who worked hard at this although '... it was much harder to read his writings'.[11] Both sides, spurred on by *The Times* and *The Morning Chronicle*'s coverage, were confident. On 10 June Viscount Lowther told Croker that he faced 'a most turbulent mob', an unsympathetic sheriff and an assessor chosen by Brougham, but they would 'poll at least two to one'.[12] On 17 June he told Croker the campaign was '... quite a national question & an attempt to place the lower orders against those who possess property'. He added: '... our number of promises are two to one – & I think if he is backed by money we should beat him as 7 to 4 provided there is fair play'. His campaign, he said, was now well organised by experienced men.[13]

Henry told Lambton on 21 June that troops shadowed his meetings. After ordering legal action over a Lowtherite naval captain's letter offering his uncle £150 for four votes, he felt himself near a duel with Col. Lowther and begged Lambton's help. Henry had organised his forces in groups with leaders to march with music and colours. The lame were in carts, those with horses riding. Accommodation was in houses and barns. Polling booths were arranged in convenient places. The Lowthers were getting together a mob of miners, mainly from Alston Moor, but he expected to defeat them if fighting began.[14]

The poll was at Appleby. The Blues left Kendal early on 29 June, arriving there that afternoon. Henry, nearly hoarse, addressed them. The Lowthers had the local militia in and around the town and 200 special armed constables with illegal weapons. Col. Bolton of Storrs Hall, a Liverpool slave-trader, imported four or five stage-coaches of sailors and carpenters (for 5s. a day) for them. Henry wanted to get as many Blues as possible to vote early, persuading the Lowthers that resistance was expensive and futile. On the first day, Tuesday 30 June, he led, but fell behind on the next. On Friday he quit, promising in a last speech to persevere until the county's political independence was secure, announcing the start of an association for this. The result was very close: Viscount Lowther, 1,211; Col. Lowther, 1,158; Brougham, 890 votes.

In his private life Henry needed a resilient, elegant and educated wife. Instead, attractive to women but fearing domesticity, he had short-lived affairs. One in 1816-17 with Mrs. George Lamb (daughter of the Duke of Devonshire and Lady Elizabeth Foster) was followed by courtship of a Miss Pigou of Edinburgh. He proposed two or three times to her but she married a Mr. Meynell in mid-1818. In December 1818, he began an affair with Mary Ann Spalding. Widowed daughter of Thomas Eden of Wimbledon and niece of Lords Auckland and Henley, she was thirty-three. In 1807 she had married ex-Wigtownshire M.P. John Spalding of the Holme, Kirkcudbright, and had two children, John Eden and Marianne Dora. His death in 1815 left her with £1,500 a year and a house in Hill Street, Mayfair. Sydney Smith called her 'a showy, long, well-dressed, red and white widow', whose beauty impressed him.

Some gossips said that a brother of Mary Ann forced Henry to marry her. He did so furtively at Coldstream on 1 April 1819. Already pregnant, she came to Brougham with her children on 13 July. On 19 November a child, Sarah Eleanor, was born. Mary Ann, with a good income and distinguished ancestry, at first impressed Henry's family and friends. A hypochondriac, ill in 1820, she lost her new child in summer 1821 and was unwell in 1822. Though a second child, Eleanor Louise was born in 1821, Henry's philandering neglect, her depression, lack of social confidence and incomprehension of his work ensured that the marriage was a disaster. Usually at Brougham keeping accounts, she lived in a troubled obscurity, marked by illnesses and rows with Henry (some created by the Edens' Tory allegiance). They got on so badly by 1837 that Creevey wrote that Mary Ann was 'not only ... visible but as active with her legs as with her tongue. Brougham's hatred of her, absolute hatred, is too visible'.[15]

Thousands of surviving letters between Henry and his brothers show he needed and dominated them. Devotedly, James helped finance his election campaigns. John Waugh, however, feared Henry's anger despite his kindness. William (who got his degree at Jesus College, Cambridge, in 1819) still relied on Henry financially. They now helped him with the affair of Queen Caroline.

Caroline had made a hateful marriage to George, Prince of Wales in November 1794. Despite a child, Charlotte, born in January 1796, they soon separated. In 1806 the Portland Government's 'Delicate Investigation' of her actions had cleared her of misconduct, but not of imprudence. Brash and coarse, she was initially advised by Tory ministers Lord Eldon and Spencer Percival, but in 1811 Henry became her legal adviser. In May 1812 he

23.   Queen Caroline, by James Lonsdale *c*.1820.

and the Whig M.P. Samuel Whitbread became personal advisers. Henry also became
Charlotte's adviser. The position of both mother and daughter became more fraught,
however. 1813 saw further friction between Caroline and the prince because he forced
Charlotte to live in seclusion. She refused to marry William, Prince of Orange, as he
wished. In August 1815 Caroline went to the Continent. Scandal accompanied her
because of her 'friendship' with an Italian courier, Bergami.

Weakened by the old king's madness and her daughter's death in childbirth in 1817, Caroline refused the Government's offer of £50,000 to stay abroad. Her relations with Bergami now gave the promiscuous Prince Regent ammunition against her. In 1818, wanting a divorce, he sent a commission to Milan to investigate her. Brougham now used Caroline as a weapon against both government and Prince. In 1819 he sent his brother James to Pesaro to see her. Examining her finances, James sent him two reports in March, saying she and Bergami were 'to all appearances man and wife', that she had no wish to return to England, and that she should tell the Prince this. Henry, using William and John Waugh as messengers between London and Pesaro, offered Lord Liverpool's government a deal: Caroline, in return for not using the title 'queen', would stay abroad with an allowance for life. The Prince rejected it. Henry dissuaded Caroline from coming to England in August 1819, and again in March 1820, after George III's death on 29 January. But she was set on returning. Lord Liverpool offered to increase her annuity to £50,000 (in return for her not coming to England or assuming the title of queen) in April. Oddly, Henry, now her attorney-general, only told her of this when he, William and Lord Hutchinson met her at St Omer in June. But she rejected the offer, and sailed for Dover.

The government had a mountain of evidence against Caroline, but the public mood was that the king had treated her (even if guilty) shamefully, and that his promiscuity was worse than hers. The ministry, unpopular after the Peterloo Massacre of August 1819 and the Six Acts, was now frustrated by Henry. On 7 June, Castlereagh moved that a Commons Select Committee on the Green Bag Papers (the evidence against Caroline) be set up, but a brilliant speech by Brougham forced its postponement. On 5 July the Bill of Pains and Penalties, removing the queen's title and annulling her marriage because of adultery with Bergami, was introduced in the Lords. On 6 July, Henry opposed it in a fluent and impromptu speech. On 17 August, however, proceedings began. The Government lawyers Gifford (Attorney-General), Copley (Solicitor-General), Parke, Sir Christopher Robinson and Adams were demonstrably inferior to Brougham, Wilde, Lushington, Williams, Tindal and Denman. The Crown's witnesses, often ex-servants of Caroline, like Majocchi, wilted when cross-examined.

On 9 September proceedings were adjourned for the defence to prepare their case, Henry now departing for Brougham Hall. On 3 October Henry began his opening defence. Recalled by those who were present as a masterpiece of forensic eloquence, the speech, lasting until 1.30 p.m. the next day, destroyed the Crown's case. Creevey wrote that the closing appeal to the Lords was '... an exhortation to them to save themselves – the Church – the Crown – the Country, by their decision in favour of the Queen ... was made with great passion, but without a particle of rant .'[16] On 10 November the Lords passed the Bill by only nine and it was withdrawn.

Henry, now inundated with briefs, was granted the Freedom of the City of London and addresses poured in from corporations. Caroline gave him her portrait, but she did not pay him. After her death the Exchequer paid both Brougham and Denman. Henry was not made a K.C. until 1827, because he had lampooned the king in the trial. The privy council rejected his arguments for Caroline's coronation, as she was a wasting asset, dissipating goodwill, and could give Whigs no patronage. Literally locked out of the Coronation in Westminster Abbey on 19 July 1821, she died on 7 August. On 18 August, as executor, Henry had her coffin embarked at Harwich for Brunswick.

Whigs now hoped for a coalition with moderate Tories like Canning. Some thought Henry would trade his support for office when, in August 1822, he met Canning at a Northern Circuit dinner at Storrs Hall, Colonel Bolton's house near Windermere. Grey offered him the Leadership of the Commons if he formed a government, but Henry preferred the Mastership of the Rolls, a permanent post with a Commons seat. Grey knew that, dangerous out of office, Brougham must be in any Whig government.

On 4 February 1820, Henry asked the Duke of Devonshire and Lord George Cavendish to support him in a new Westmorland poll.[17] Viscount Lowther was at first dismissive of his chances. On 18 March polling began. Henry was second on the fifth day (22 March) with 1,126 votes to the Viscount's 1,140 and Colonel Lowther's 1,053. The Viscount wrote that, with a friendly sheriff and naming his own assessor, Henry had made 'nearly one hundred voters at a single decision for enfranchisements' in two or three months. Lord Thanet's influence had also increased the Whig voters:

> We are in a scrape & it will be a Godsend to be extricated – we think we have still four hundred at least of good votes – Brougham has polled already as many as we conceived him able to produce – but as his men come from no one knows where – I am unable to guess what number men can come.[18]

Polling ended on 25 March. The Viscount polled 1,530 votes, Colonel Lowther 1,412 and Henry 1,349, failing by only sixty-four. He did not get a Westmorland seat when he tried again in 1826.

Life at Brougham Hall could be unpleasant. On 20 September 1824 Hobhouse and Whig M.P. Edward Ellice came there. Hobhouse liked the first day, especially the hare coursing: '... only sort of sport in which Henry Brougham delights. Even that he takes very cooly [sic] & it is rather a queer sight to see him running with his hands in his pockets when a hare is started'. But the next day was depressing. Henry, silent and sullen, had 'none of that gay good humour which makes him in general one of the most delightful companions in the world'. He hardly gave Mary Ann, 'much of an invalid', any attention, and neglected his guests. It was impossible to guess that they were with 'the most extraordinarily gifted man in England ... perhaps in Europe'.[19] On 21 September Hobhouse left.

Family rivalry also emerged unpleasantly. In July 1825 James and William, sharing a house in Lincoln's Inn Fields, had a row. William had reluctantly lent James money in a bond to Henry Meux. This was for a loan to John Waugh. James and William now became mutually suspicious. James feared that Henry would learn of his debts. Parsimonious and retiring, he unjustly accused William (now a barrister) of extravagance. William had a horse and servant, but in 1825-30 never spent more than £600 a year. Henry, however supported James' criticism. When in summer 1827, William and John Waugh went abroad, returning to England on 20 September, Henry wrote to Lambton at Naples, censuring William for thus 'overspending'.

The struggle for power was now central to Henry's life and that of his brothers. Having become a national political celebrity in 1820, he even entered Disraeli's novel *Vivian Grey* (1826). In it Partenopex Puff, a minor author and wit, says:

> Oh! he is a prodigious fellow! What do you think Booby says? He says that Foaming Fudge can do more than any man in Great Britain; that he had one day to plead in the King's Bench, spout at a tavern, speak in the House, and fight a duel; and that he found time for everything but the last. [20]

In 1823 Creevey wrote: 'His lunacy ... is to be in power. He cannot endure for a moment anything or any man he thinks can possibly obstruct his march'.[21] But Henry showed great dedication to good causes. In 1824-6 he was Lord Rector of Glasgow University. In summer 1824 he attacked slavery in the Commons. Two hundred and twenty slave emancipation societies were then founded within a year, and Parliament received more

24. Henry Brougham by James Lonsdale (1821).

than 800 petitions. On 1 July 1825, he was chief speaker at London University's launch, and a founder of its University College in 1827. In November 1826 he founded the Society for the Diffusion of Useful Knowledge with Matthew Hill, M.P. for Hull. In 1828 the S.D.U.K. committee he presided over (including eight Fellows of the Royal Society, Lord John Russell (vice-chairman), Denman and Rowland Hill, inventor of penny postage) published the 'Library of Entertaining Knowledge', increasing the reading materials available to the working-class. In 1827 Henry's influence helped James to become M.P. for Tregony in Cornwall. James, a liberal reformer, refused office in 1827 and 1831 to remain Henry's aide. He lived with him at 48 Berkeley Square for three years, even missing breakfast if Henry had early visitors.[22]

Lord Liverpool's apoplexy in February 1827 led to Canning becoming prime minister. Many Whigs who had endorsed his liberal foreign secretaryship supported him, as did Henry. Excluding the Ultra-Tories, three entered the cabinet: Tierney, Master of the Mint; the Marquis of Lansdowne, Home Secretary; and the Earl of Carlisle, Lord Privy Seal on 16 July. The Catholic Emancipation issue was left open, and the Whigs and Tories split. Henry was made a K.C. provided he did not visit court to kiss hands. The offer of the Chief Barony of the Exchequer with a £7,000 a year salary for life (turned down), increased his law practice greatly. On 8 August, however, Canning died. Viscount Goderich, the new prime minister, could not form a government. The Whigs went back into opposition. On 9 January, the Duke of Wellington became prime minister.

Henry's health was indifferent in this period. He was often unkempt. In 1828 he was ill again, William nursing him. On 7 February, however, he made one of his finest speeches, on law reform. Lasting for six hours (the longest ever Commons speech) it led to two parliamentary commissions, on the law of real property and Common Law Courts. On the whole field of jurisprudence, it prefigured most of the century's legal reforms. On 3 March Creevey wrote in his diary that it ' ... produced a perfect torrent of retainers, I mean retainers from attorneys. This quite turns his head, already on the swing before'.[23]

The Brougham-Lowther feud continued even though Henry's Westmorland ambitions ended in 1826. He was furious at a false rumour that Viscount Lowther would be in Canning's government. Lowther for his part told Croker on 11 August 1827 that 'Brougham is a formidable opponent, but he would plague you less in that capacity than as a friend'.[24] Henry had a kind of revenge when the 1832 Reform Act ended the borough status of Haslemere, Appleby and Cockermouth.

The Tories were divided between 'Canningites' like Huskisson and 'Ultras' like Eldon. Disagreements over disenfranchising East Retford, a corrupt borough (in May 1828) made the former leave the Cabinet. Vesey Fitzgerald, President of the Board of Trade, was badly beaten that month in Co. Clare by Catholic Association leader Daniel O'Connell. Wellington then had to bring in Catholic emancipation in April 1829 with Whig support, alienating the Ultras. He could not, however, get a deal with the Canningites, or the Whigs (whom he approached in October). They remained disunited, with Grey 'exiled' at Howick.

Henry's patron, the Marquis of Cleveland (once Earl of Darlington), joined the Tories in January 1830, placing Henry in a dilemma. Without a Whig patron, he might have followed suit. When the Whigs planned concerted opposition to Wellington, he was quiet. Rumours that he had an agreement with the Duke angered other Whigs. The Duke of Devonshire's Knaresborough seat fell vacant when Tierney died on 26 January. Offered it, Henry accepted, realising that Wellington would not give him office. On 26 June George IV died. On 30 June Henry attacked the Government and narrowly escaped a duel after calling the Government front bench 'mean, fawning parasites of the Duke'. He attacked it again, especially Peel, on 6 July.

On 22 July Parliament was dissolved. On 23 July, Henry and Lord Morpeth (the Earl of Carlisle's eldest son) were adopted as Yorkshire's Whig candidates in the General Election. James negotiated this for him and was promised a close seat. On 27 July Henry started canvassing commercial and industrial Yorkshire. His campaign was a great success. The gentry feared him, but merchants and businessmen (remembering his defeat of the Orders in Council) and non-conformists (attracted by his opposition to slavery) flocked to him. He proposed radical changes to the Corn Laws, ending the East India Company's trading privileges and speedily abolishing slavery in the Empire. He advocated reform – enfranchising all resident householders, the large unrepresented towns and cities to return M.P.s, and three-yearly Parliaments. On 6 August Henry was elected.

The Whigs won 30 seats nationally. The Canningites would not support the Duke, and the Tories were split over Reform. Wellington talked to Canningites like Melbourne and Palmerston in July and September. They insisted on coming in as a group with Lansdowne and Grey, and favoured Reform, but Wellington rejected this. On 11 October Viscount Lowther predicted that 'The combined operations & attack of Whigs & Ultras will be more than ministers can stand'.[25] On 26 October (Parliament's opening) another dialogue with the Canningites failed. On 2 November the King's Speech omitted Reform and the Duke ruled it out in the Lords. On 15 November the Government was defeated on the Civil List by 29, and Wellington resigned.

Grey, forming a Government, and Althorp, Whig Commons leader, soon had a problem. Henry, persuaded to drop his Reform motion for debate in the Commons on 16 November, rejected Grey's written offer of the Attorney-Generalship made the next day. It is said he tore it up and then stamped on it, as he wanted to be Master of the Rolls. On 18 November Sefton told Creevey:

> He is really in a state of insanity, complains to everybody that he is neglected and threatens to put an extinguisher on the new Govt. in a month. In the meantime he keeps swearing he will not take anything – that he ought to be offered the seals tho' he would kick them out of the window rather than desert his Yorkshire friends by taking a peerage. All this, however, will subside in the Rolls, where, being lodged for life and quite beyond controul [*sic*], I don't envy the Govt. with such a chap ready to pounce upon them unexpectedly.[26]

Henry wrote to the Duke of Devonshire on 18 November: '... no other place than Chancellor is any temptation to me'.[27] Next morning, an anxious Grey offered him the job in Downing Street. Henry declined, saying he would not leave the Commons and Yorkshire. Later that day Lords Sefton, Althorp and Duncannon and James Brougham met him in the Lords to repeat the offer. Denman's advice may have decided him. Told that his refusing the Great Seal meant the Government's end and 25 more years in opposition for the Whigs, he accepted.

Lord Chancellor (1830-34)

> ... Brougham ... I should wonder little to see one day a second Cromwell: he is the cunningest and strongest man now in England, as I construe him and with no better principle than a Napoleon has: a feeling of virtue, a worship and a self-devotion to Power.[28]

Thomas Carlyle writing to John A. Carlyle, 4 March 1831.

On 20 November 1830, Henry made his last appearance as a barrister. Two days later he sat on the Woolsack as Speaker of the Lords and received the Great Seal. Henry was made Baron Brougham and Vaux of Brougham, Westmorland, introduced by Marquis

Wellesley and the Earl of Durham and made a privy councillor on 23 November.[29] On the 25th he was sworn in as Lord Chancellor.

The King told Lord Holland he had 'settled' Henry and he would 'not be dangerous any more'. But, though Henry never had a grandee's automatic political power, he had great national popularity, particularly with the middle classes. It has been argued that Henry's acceptance of a peerage naturally made him far less powerful but this did not necessarily follow. Only four Government ministers in Grey's ministry now sat in the Commons. A brilliant orator, he had formidable intellect and political astuteness. The great workload Grey gave him suggests Henry's importance, as does the scene on his taking his seat on the Woolsack. Members of the Royal family, peers, foreign ambassadors and spectators packed the chamber and gallery. Le Marchant, his private secretary, wrote that 'there was no instance on record of a Chancellor being equally honoured'.

The previous Lord Chancellor, Eldon, built up large arrears in the Chancery Court. Henry, a competent judge, started to clear them, mastering Equity law and even sitting from 10 a.m. to 11 p.m. or midnight hearing cases. He introduced a Local Courts Bill on 2 December. On 3 February 1831 the Cabinet decided that Henry should reform the Chancery Court and axe legal sinecures in the Civil List Bill. On 9 February Creevey told Miss Ord: '... the Beau [Wellington] said yesterday: "I am glad that Brougham is Chancellor. He is the only man with courage and talent to reform that damned Court".'[30]

Henry was over-ruled when he wanted to end some life pensions but on 22 February, the Chancery Bill, part of Grey's programme of

25.   Henry Brougham as Queen Caroline's Attorney General, sketched by A. Wivell.

'Peace, Retrenchment and Reform' was introduced. Ending many sinecures, it made good procedural changes, retaining the Masters in Chancery. Henry supported Melbourne's toughness on civil disorder as rural unrest and poverty saw the burning of hay-ricks and the destruction of farm equipment.

On 1 March Henry introduced the Chancery Bill in the Lords. That day Lord John Russell introduced the Reform Bill in the Commons in a two-hour speech. The Bill had been devised by a Cabinet committee of Russell, the Earl of Durham, Sir James Graham and Viscount Duncannon. Henry, who favoured more leniency than they did, was excluded. His draft Bill deprived pocket boroughs of a member each (he thought them a good route into politics for clever middle-class men), enfranchising larger towns and all householders. He was unhappy with the Bill's Schedules A and B. Despite these reservations, however, Henry did his utmost to get the Reform Bill passed.

The Bill axed 60 boroughs with two M.P.s in Schedule A, depriving another 47 of one M.P. each in Schedule B. Schedule C enfranchised towns like Manchester, Birmingham, Leeds, Sheffield, Sunderland, Wolverhampton, Bradford and parts of London, making them boroughs with two M.P.s. Schedule D made towns like Ashton-under-Lyne, Cheltenham, Gateshead, Huddersfield, Salford, Whitehaven and Kendal parliamentary boroughs with one M.P. each. Extending the county franchise, it gave all £10 borough householders the vote. After its first reading to a startled House, Henry organised large meetings in its favour in London and the large cities.

The Bill's passage was fraught with difficulties. On 23 March the Commons divided on its second reading. Amid Whig jubilation it passed 302 to 301, but still had to get through its committee stage and the Lords. Two Government defeats (on 19 April by eight and by 21 on 21 April) made Grey decide on a general election. On the morning of the 22nd, with the Lords about to pass a resolution begging the king not to prorogue Parliament, Grey and Brougham forced the king to do so.

In the General Election, some 90 per cent of English popular constituencies and counties elected reformers. When Parliament reassembled in June, Grey had a working majority. On 21 September the Commons passed the Bill by 109. Henry presented it to the Lords the next day before hostile Tories, who believed, like Croker, that 'Reform means the destruction of the aristocracy – nothing else'.[31] After Grey's and Lyndhurst's speeches and Tory interruptions, Brougham's speech on 7 October was regarded as his finest since the opening one in Queen Caroline's trial. He attacked the Earl of Harrowby's argument that abolishing close boroughs excluded peers' eldest sons from politics, and also commented forcefully on the venality of rotten boroughs:

That a Peer, or a speculating attorney, or a jobbing Jew, or a gambler from the Stock Exchange, by vesting in his own person the old walls of Sarum, or a few pigsties at Bletching-ley, or a summer house at Gatton, and making fictitious, and collusive, and momentary transfers of them to an agent or two, for the purpose of enabling them to vote as if they had property, of which they all the while knew they have not the very shadow, is in itself a monstrous abuse, in the form of a gross and barefaced cheat, and becomes the most disgust-ing hypocrisy when it is seriously treated as a franchise by virtue of property. I will tell these Peers, attorneys, jobbers, loan contractors, and the Nabob's agents, if such there still be amongst us, that the time is come when these things can no longer be borne, and an end must at length be put to the abuse which suffers the most precious right of Government to be made the subject of common barter, to be conveyed by traffic, pass by assignment under a commission of bankruptcy, or the powers of an insolvent Act, or to be made over for a gaming debt.[32]

He denied that 'the real nobility' opposed Reform, saying 56 of those ennobled before George III's reign were for it and 21 against. He ended: 'By all you hold most dear, by all the ties that bind every one of us to our common order and our common country I solemnly adjure you, I warn you, I implore you, yea, on my bended knees I supplicate you, reject not this Bill'.[33] After speaking for six hours and drinking three large soda water tumblers of hot negus (port, hot water, spice and lemon) he fell on his knees before the Woolsack. The Lords divided at six the next morning and rejected the Bill by forty-one.

Parliament was prorogued on 20 October with the country in crisis, depressed by rural poverty. Althorp's budget had been ineffective, and the Reform Bill was stalled. After a break at Brougham, depressed and weak, Henry returned for the new session in mid-January. He and others advised Grey to create peers to pass the Bill. The king agreed to this on 15 January, while the Cabinet agreed on it, should the Lords reject the Bill or greatly weaken it in committee. In late March it passed its third reading in the Commons. On 14 April it passed the Lords by nine. On 7 May, however, Lord Lyndhurst got a motion passed in committee by 35, postponing its disenfranchising clauses until discussion of its enfranchising sections ended. The Government had lost the initiative. The next day Grey and Brougham saw the king at Windsor, and offered to resign. On the 9th he accepted their resignations. On 15 May, however, Wellington gave up trying to form a Tory government to pass Reform. Strikes and the recession worsened the deadlock, and inflamed an already potentially explosive situation. The king refused to make new peers to pass the Bill. Wellington and Lyndhurst attacked it on 17 May in the Lords. On the 18th Grey and Brougham persuaded the king to write a letter allowing them to make new peers if the Lords rejected it. The opposition almost absent, its third reading passed on 6 June by 106 to twenty-two. On 7 May Brougham, Holland, Lansdowne, Wellesley, Grey and Durham as commissioners gave the Royal Assent as the king refused to.

In the summer of 1832 Henry piloted the Scottish and Irish Reform Bills and more Chancery Reform through the Lords. Some Chancery Court sinecures and patent offices were axed. The Lord Chancellor's retirement pension rose to £5,000 a year, and the Scottish Court of Exchequer was ended. He brought in his Bankruptcy Bill, replacing 70 itinerant commissioners ('the Septuagint') with a Court of Review, presided over by a chief judge in bankruptcy. Three less senior judges passed sentence in disputed cases while six commissioners dealt with undisputed ones. The Chancery Court lost £17,000 a year of patronage. He also created the Judicial Committee of the Privy Council, to try cases from all over the British Empire. A committee of Law Lords and judges from the colonies and India, it greatly improved the previous system which had allowed any privy councillors to judge cases referred to the Privy Council.

In December 1832 Ireland was seeing an increase in crime, peasant impoverishment and a tithe war. Henry and Althorp pressed for the replacement of the Irish Secretary, Stanley, hated by the Irish, with Goderich or Melbourne. Grey disagreed. When Henry threatened resignation, Grey said that that would break the Government. Henry backed down.

On 29 January 1833 began the Reformed Commons' first sitting. The Government's majority was three hundred. Henry, however, had to steer much of the new legislation through the Lords: the Chancery Bill, the first Factory Act, the Slavery Abolition Bill, the Irish Church Temporalities Act (suppressing 10 Irish bishoprics). Lyndhurst savaged his Local Courts Bill, though, and it was rejected by the Lords in March. His swiftness in giving judgement and inattention to detail in court was criticised. He quarrelled with the Attorney-General Sir William Horne (who resigned) and with Sir Edward Sugden, a barrister expert in Chancery Law who had been Wellington's Solicitor-General.[34]

The Cabinet was divided. Durham resigned in March 1833, while Hobhouse was briefly Irish Secretary and then resigned. In a reshuffle Stanley became Colonial Secretary and Littleton Irish Secretary in April. With problems over the Irish Coercion Act, there were the 'resigning fits' of Grey, persuaded to stay that October by Henry and others.

There were now both political and personal crises for Henry. Arrears reappeared in Chancery by the end of summer 1833 because of his severe throat infection in December 1832. He was overworked, despite having the company of his daughter, Eleanor Louise. She is described by Creevey as 'a very sensible interesting little thing with her eyes and ears all about her'. She was ill, however, that year and Henry had more throat trouble. His autumn break at Brougham was interrupted by a cabinet meeting in London. Returning to the Hall for Christmas, he had a heavy blow: on 24 December James died. As M.P. for Winchelsea in 1831-2 and Kendal in 1833, James had been Henry's eyes, ears and 'brake'. He refused the job of Accountant-General in May 1831 to serve him, taking a sinecure as Registrar of Affidavits in the Court of Chancery in August 1832. He was also Clerk of Letters Patent. His loss revealed vast personal indebtedness of about £40,000.

Life for Henry was becoming dangerously unbalanced. His closest family confidant was William, his unofficial press secretary in 1831-3, but their relationship was difficult. In March 1831 William became a Master in Chancery, and M.P. for Southwark in May. He claimed that the election expenses and fitting out his nephew Henry Brougham with uniform for Indian service meant that he could raise money for James in 1832 only by borrowing from Le Marchant. In August 1833 James asked William for a larger sum. He thought he deserved it, having done and spent so much for the family. William lent it unwillingly, offended at James saying he had his Mastership not through fitness but as the family's 'trustee'. Henry then reproached William for being niggardly.

Henry disapproved of William marrying Emily Taylor, daughter of Sir Charles Taylor, Bt., an ex-Tory M.P., in August 1834. William felt that everything Henry did at Brougham or in London showed he wanted to avoid Emily and the Taylors. He suspected William gossiped about him to them. Writing to William at Easter 1835, Henry said: '... even if he shd. lose his Pension he prays God he may never be driven to apply to me for help – that I had once assisted James when he applied to me at his utmost need meaning in August 1833 & had repented it night & day ever since ...'.[35]

Henry started 1834 grief-stricken and, Le Marchant apart, with no close adviser. By late March he was deeply depressed. He attended Cabinet irregularly. He even introduced his own legislation as Government measures, including a Bill altering the House of Lords' functions when sitting as a court. His evidence before a committee on newspaper duties contradicted Government policy. On 30 April he complained to the Cabinet of overwork, sitting in court for seven hours a day, never being in bed before 2 a.m., and having to write some seventy legal judgements (each one needing one or two hours to read) since November. He was also flirting with a Mrs. Petre and writing a book on Natural Theology!

The Times, hitherto Henry's staunch supporter, attacked the Poor Law Bill he took through the Lords in April. The Government, too, was troubled. On 28 May Stanley, Sir James Graham, the Duke of Richmond, and the Earl of Ripon (once Viscount Goderich) resigned over the disposal of the Irish Church's spare revenues. The king had a nervous breakdown. Henry's one great triumph that session was the Bill setting up the Central Criminal Court, welcomed by all.

In 1833 the Government proposed an Irish Tithe Bill and Irish Coercion Bill. The Irish Secretary Littleton sought Daniel O'Connell's support for the first by offering to modify the second. On the advice of his father-in-law and Henry's close friend, the

Marquis Wellesley, Lord Lieutenant of Ireland, Littleton asked Henry's opinion, and Henry advised that the Coercion Bill's meeting clauses be omitted. Grey, ignorant of events, disagreed with Littleton's views in Cabinet on 29 June, as did Melbourne. Brougham and others who shared Littleton's view then withdrew their objections. On 1 July the bill, unchanged, entered the Commons. O'Connell then divulged his 'confidential' conversations with Littleton and a storm ensued. Grey and Althorp resigned on 9 July.

Grey's family and friends unfairly blamed Henry for the prime minister's resignation, even suggesting he had planned it. In fact he did his utmost to support Grey, but there was little co-ordination between ministers, and it had been naïve to trust O'Connell. Henry now helped Melbourne remake the Cabinet, telling the king that the cross-party coalition the latter wanted was unworkable. Henry persuaded ministers that they need not retire and that if Althorp returned Grey was inessential. A modified Coercion Bill would bring Althorp back, he argued. On 14 July Melbourne became prime minister.

On 19 July *The Times* attacked Henry for his statement that he had always opposed the controversial Irish Coercion Bill clauses. On 19 August, in a spiteful leader about the Bill's re-introduction without the vexed clauses, it said his mind was giving way (as its proprietor John Walter suspected). With Parliament prorogued on 15 August Henry went to Brougham. His subsequent actions show that, lacking the help of William or Le Marchant (with whom he had quarrelled), his judgement was flawed. He travelled into Scotland in better spirits, with his stepdaughter Marianne. He was welcomed in towns and at country houses with artillery salutes, processions, banquets and addresses. He was made a freeman of various burghs.

But Henry was undignified, and his speeches contradictory. As guest of the Dowager Duchess of Bedford at Rothiemurchus, he flirted with the ladies. They hid the Great Seal, which he had with him, in a drawing room tea chest in response! Blindfolded, he had to find it aided by a piano, which was played louder the nearer he got. At Inverness he defended the Government for having done too much rather than running the risk of doing too little. He said presumptuously that he would write to tell the king that he lived 'in the hearts of his loyal subjects inhabiting this ancient and important capital of the Highlands'. This drew ridicule. At Dundee he was more radical and controversial. At Edinburgh on 15 September, his speech at a great banquet for Grey brought him into conflict with Lord Durham, who thought himself largely responsible for the Reform Bill. Disaffected, Durham accused the Government of not doing enough. Henry in response accused Durham and other Radicals of advocating half-baked measures. In October, now back in London, he was unaware how much he had damaged himself. Misled by fluency and popularity he had mismanaged his 'stump tour'. He returned to Chancery appeals, unaware of the impression made on Melbourne and the king. Nemesis was swift and crushing.

On 10 November Lord Althorp's father, Earl Spencer, died. A new Leader of the Commons was needed. On 14 November, Melbourne saw the king at Brighton. The king told him that he had dismissed the Cabinet, a decision that he justified because of his opposition to the replacement of Althorp by Lord John Russell, his anger and amazement at Henry's actions, and opposition to the Ministry's Irish Church Reform measures. Melbourne immediately told Henry and Palmerston the news. The following morning *The Times* carried a 'scoop' about the Ministry's fall, alleging that Queen Adelaide was behind it. Henry was widely accused of being the source of the leak, but not by the queen, who later made Henry her executor. Croker (former Tory Secretary to the Admiralty) said the 'leaker' was Ellice, Earl Grey's parliamentary private secretary – an influential Whig. Few mentioned the unlikelihood of Henry's handing a story to a newspaper which had made him so utterly miserable.

Henry now wrote angrily to the king: 'You choose to ruin the country, I wash my hands of your proceedings, and hold you answerable for the consequences'. What Disraeli called his 'vagrant and grotesque apocalypse' ended in a foolish offer to Lord Chancellor Lyndhurst on 22 November to take the Chief Barony of the Exchequer (promised to Sir James Scarlett) unpaid. He could live on his £5,000 a year pension, claim only '£800 or £1,000' for chambers and court expenses, thus saving the Treasury £6,000 a year. His offer became public knowledge and damaged him, despite his hasty retraction.

Melbourne did not want Henry, a personal friend, to oppose the Whigs. However, William condemned his brother. He was ostracised at Brooks' Club and blamed for the fall of Melbourne's Ministry by Whigs and the Press. Henry complained of this to Melbourne. On 14 February Melbourne made it clear that he believed Henry's actions had been a principal cause of the Government's fall. In a letter to Henry, Melbourne wrote:

> You domineered too much, you interfered with other departments, you encroached upon the province of the Prime Minister, you worked, as I believe with the Press, in a manner unbecoming the dignity of your station, and you formed political views of your own, and pursued them by means which were unfair to your colleagues.

In April 1835 Peel's Government fell. Melbourne, now Prime Minister, rejected Grey and Russell's pleas to give Henry office. He put the Great Seal in commission. Legal congestion in Chancery and protracted pain resulted. Speaking 221 times for the Government in the 1835 session, and taking the Municipal Reform Bill very ably through the Lords, Henry hoped for the Great Seal. But, on 16 January 1836, Charles Pepys, Master of the Rolls, was made Lord Chancellor as Earl of Cottenham. Henry read of it in the newspapers. He felt devastated, bitter and betrayed, retiring to Brougham with a nervous breakdown, physically ill. He took long walks, said nothing and saw no one. In 1831 Macaulay had predicted that '... he will soon place himself in a false position before the public. His popularity will go down and he will find himself alone'.[36] Perhaps it was inevitable that his drive and brilliance were undone eventually by his poor judgement. Long afterwards, William wrote: 'There never was so little common sense or discretion & this has been his grand error throughout life – violent & totally without the power of controuling [sic] himself – & thus with many good qualities making himself disliked or dreaded – wch. is quite as bad'.[37] But Henry's failings were outweighed by great achievements. Despite the often spiteful criticism he received, his reforms substantially changed 19th-century Britain and have left deep traces in the law, politics and institutions of this country to this day.[38]

1. William Brougham, *Memorandum to Mrs. Eleanora Brougham*, October 1835.
2. *Creevey*, ed. Gore, op. cit., p. 114.
3. Nicholas Vansittart, 1st Baron Bexley (1766-1851), Chancellor of the Exchequer 1812-23.
4. Creevey to his wife, Gore, p. 104.
5. Appleby, Cockermouth and Carlisle, all boroughs, returned two M.P.s. The electors of the first two were burgages. Carlisle's were freemen. Cumberland and Westmorland each returned two M.P.s, elected by freeholders. Blue had been the Whig colour in the two counties since the Duke of Portland, whose colour it was, fought the Lowthers in 1768.
6. Gore, pp. 152-3.
7. Croker MSS. Clements Library, Ann Arbor, Michigan, Box 10, folder 2.
8. Lambton to Sir Robert Wilson, British Museum Additional MSS. 30108 fol. 18.
9. John Cropper put the amount of Wakefield money used in the 1818 and 1826 Westmorland Elections at c.£30,000 in his book *Notes and Memories* (Bateman and Hewitson, 1900).

10. Croker MSS. Box 10, folder 3.
11. Hunter Davies, *William Wordsworth* (Weidenfeld & Nicolson, 1980).
12. Croker MSS. Box 10, folder 2.
13. ibid. Box 10, folder 6.
14. Lambton MSS.
15. *Creevey*, ed. Gore, p. 376.
16. *Creevey*, ed. Gore pp. 192-3.
17. A. Aspinall, *Lord Brougham and The Whig Party*, p. 279.
18. Croker MSS. Vol. 11, folder 3.
19. British Library Additional MSS. 56549 ff 47-9.
20. Disraeli, *Vivian Grey*, Bradenham Edition (Peter Davies, London, 1926), pp. 63-4.
21. Creevey to Miss Ord, 11 March 1823, *Creevey*, ed. Gore, p. 242.
22. William Brougham, *Memorandum to Mrs. Eleanora Brougham*, October 1835.
23. *Creevey*, ed. Gore, p. 284.
24. Croker Papers, Box 16, folder 20.
25. Croker MSS, Box 19, folder 10.
26. *Creevey*, ed. Gore, p. 318.
27. Chatsworth MS. in Aspinall, op.cit. p. 187
28. *The Collected Letters of Thomas and Jane Welsh Carlyle*, ed. C. R. Sanders and K. J. Fielding, Vol. 5 (1976).
29. He retained Brougham in his title at Denman's urging, originally wanting to be 'Lord Vaux'.
30. *Creevey*, ed. Gore, p. 321.
31. Croker to the Marquis of Hertford, 8 February 1831, Croker MSS. Letter Book 25.
32. J. B. Atlay, *The Victorian Chancellors*, Vol. 1 (1906), p. 307
33. *ibid.* pp. 308-9.
34. In July 1832 Sugden raised James Brougham's Chancery sinecure in the Commons and Henry then attacked him in the Lords. Sugden (1781-1875) was later Lord Chancellor as Baron St Leonards in 1852.
35. William Brougham, *Memorandum to Mrs. Eleanora Brougham*, October 1835.
36. G. O. Trevelyan, *The Life and Letters of Lord Macaulay*, (O.U.P., 1978), p.174.
37. William Brougham's *Diary*, 7 August 1859.
38. The eclipse of Henry's political career enabled him to add greatly to his published output of works. These eventually numbered 133 titles. He also had time for a wide range of activities like growing olives at Cannes, spiritualism and his inventions. These included the famous Brougham carriage of 1838, first manufactured by the London firm of Robinson and Cook. Lázló Tarr, in his book The History of the Carriage (1969) wrote·that it was: "... the first coupé to which the new principles of coach-building were applied: not only was the carriage-body fixed on elliptical springs, but the perch was fully discarded and the body so suspended that the bottom part between the seat and the driver's box was sunk deep enough to permit easy entrance from the ground. It was a most ingenious innovation". The Brougham name is still used, by Cadillac, in motor car design.

Chapter 6

Building a 'Modern Antique' 1829-1847

... only where the taste of those who have the designs prepared for them is sufficiently imbued with Gothic to admire it in its simplest form can an architect dare to make things so true to 'old character'.

L. N. Cottingham writing to William Brougham, 5 August 1844.[1]

By the 1820s a new age of castle building had begun. Many landowners were no longer satisfied with the Strawberry Hill-style Gothic of the previous generation. They wanted a more scholarly, realistic 'medieval' appearance. Building an authentic-looking mock-gothic castle also helped newly wealthy families to establish themselves, and the adoption of dubious medieval pedigrees and armorial bearings gave a superficial impression of 'old money'. Charles Tennyson-D'Eyncourt, a Radical M.P. and Tennyson's uncle, is a good example of this. In 1835 he inherited a large amount of property in Grimsby, broad acres of Lincolnshire farmland and Bayons Manor, a small Regency house at Tealby, over-looking the Lincolnshire Wolds. An antiquarian and amateur architect, he claimed descent from the Earls of Scarsdale and the medieval D'Eyncourts through his grand-mother, heiress Mary Clayton. He and the local architect W. A. Nicholson began a massive rebuilding of Bayons in 1836-7. Professor Mark Girouard's *The Victorian Country House* describes how they continued in the 1840s, constructing a splendid complex of buildings, including a great hall, fine library, towers and ruined keep, even digging a moat. The effect was spectacular.

Professor Girouard says that most of the builders of the new castles were Tories. But castle-building also attracted Whig landowners who wanted to display dynastic strength and power, among them two of Henry Brougham's friends. George Lambton gothicised Lambton Castle, Co. Durham (*c.*1820-8) and William Edwardes, 2nd Baron Kensington (sometime M.P. for Haverfordwest) built St Bride's Castle, Pembrokeshire, in 1833. It was hardly surprising that in this architectural climate and with an unparalleled amount of money available, Brougham Hall seemed unsuitably plain and shabby to the Broughams. They may have had a sneaking admiration for Smirke's work of 1806-11 at Lowther Castle. Certainly Brougham was a good country house to Gothicise. It was built at different times, was old enough to look medieval and was very well sited. In 1829 an old tower at the Hall conveniently gave way, so James and William Brougham had to find a suitable architect to rebuild it.

It is clear what drew the Broughams to Lewis Nockalls Cottingham from Dr. Janet Myles' authoritative study, *L. N. Cottingham (1787-1847) architect: his place in the Gothic Revival* (1989).[2] He was a rising Gothic architect who had started restoring Rochester Cathedral in 1825, and had published accurate drawings of Westminster Hall and Henry VII's chapel in which he advocated a systematic study of Gothic to help in restoration work and new building in Gothic. In Southwark (where William Brougham became M.P. in 1831) he and another architect, James Savage, had led a successful campaign in 1832 to save the lady chapel of St Saviour's church from demolition, as buildings were cleared to make an approach for London Bridge. Cottingham also had a museum of medieval antiquities at 43 Waterloo Bridge Road, which was much visited by noblemen, architects and artists, and reported on in journals.

Country house architects were often engaged on personal recommendation. Some of Cottingham's clients knew, or were related to, friends of the Broughams. One was William Craven, 2nd Earl of Craven (1809-66), a Liberal peer and neighbour of William Brougham's in London – Brougham lived at 19 Berkeley Square, Lord Craven in nearby Charles Street. He employed Cottingham at Combe Abbey, his Warwickshire seat. Cottingham, originally from Suffolk, had made his name in London, being made Surveyor to the Cooks' Company in 1822. Afterwards the patronage of John Harrison, a Derbyshire landowner, had helped him greatly. Harrison, who had conveniently married the heiress of local squire Edmund Evans of Yeldersley House, Derbyshire, in 1813, commissioned Cottingham to design him a new country house in 1828. This was the massive Snelston Hall, near Ashbourne, Derbyshire, built in a striking Perpendicular Gothic.

Snelston (now vanished) must have made a considerable stir locally. Cottingham's ability aroused the interest of another Derbyshire landowner, Charles Stanhope, 4th Earl of Harrington. In 1830 he began employing Cottingham to rebuild his seat, Elvaston Castle (a castellated mansion of 1817), near Derby. The work Cottingham did there is significant, and he had a similar task of remoulding an earlier structure at Brougham. Cottingham's work at Elvaston, continuing until 1840, reflected his confidence and the client's romantic eccentricity. Lord Harrington (Lord Fitzbooby in Disraeli's novel *Coningsby*) was a retired colonel who, as Viscount Petersham, had been Lord of the Bedchamber to George IV until 1829. That year he had inherited 'less than £90,000' from his father, the 3rd Earl. His lifestyle made eccentricity an art-form. He dressed like Henri IV of France, sporting a similar pointed beard, never went out until 6 p.m., spoke with a lisp and was a great connoisseur of tea, snuff-boxes and the stage. Dressing his equipage in browns, he also designed the Petersham overcoat and Petersham snuff-mixture!

Cottingham had to assist Lord Harrington in making Elvaston a comfortable retreat for the pretty actress Maria Foote, whom he married in 1831. Maria's two illegitimate children from a previous relationship with Colonel Berkeley (who had promised but failed to marry her) and her past as an actress made her unacceptable in upper-class society. Cottingham enlarged and remodelled the house, constructing the Gothic 'Hall of the Fair Star', decorated with painted mottoes and symbols. He may also have assisted Lord Harrington, a keen gardener and tree-planter, in laying out gardens that included a topiaried enclosure, 'The Garden of Mon Plaisir', and a Moorish pavilion called 'The Alhambra Garden'.

Cottingham also worked from 1832 onwards at Adare Manor, Co. Limerick for Viscount Adare, probably on its 132-ft. long first-floor gallery. This added to his not inconsiderable country house experience, but he was never a very prolific country house architect. He clearly possessed the patience required to deal with occasionally difficult clients and had considerable technical skill in resolving structural problems. An instance of this was his well-known restoration of Armagh Cathedral from 1834. Through an ingenious application of science, Cottingham supported the tower during underpinning work, avoiding the expense of dismantling and rebuilding it. He was thus an excellent choice for William Brougham, who thought Cottingham a true medievalist, describing Pugin in contrast as working 'in the florid church style'![3]

Brougham Hall had changed little externally since the 1790s. It had a small medieval gatehouse, a 33 by 103 ft. 'ancient chamber' (perhaps an early medieval hall), a Tudor dwelling hall, pele tower and James Bird's small mansion of the 1680s. It was a somewhat rambling building, quaint and awkward rather than breathtaking. In 1829, Parsons and White's *Directory of Cumberland and Westmorland* described it as 'a plain but lofty and aged pile with an embrassured parapet and having been built at different periods'. There were two classical gazebos 75 yards south-west and south-east of the Hall's south wall and a curious folly in the grounds. This, the circular thatched Hermit's Cell, had matted seats, painted glass windows, and a recluse's hour-glass, cross, beads and skull. Its table was embellished with appropriate lines from Milton's *Il Penseroso*.

The Broughams must have been demanding and somewhat wayward clients. Without the resources of a man like Lord Harrington, they had equally ambitious ideas. So, to save money, they had the work done from Cottingham's blueprints by a local builder John Robinson (1837-40) and by another local contractor and architect, John Richardson. Richardson, who had designed Kendal's New Theatre and its Infants' School in 1829, acted as a kind of site building manager. The project, continuing until Cottingham's death in 1847, is not always easy to trace year by year. A comparison of the buildings in F. W. Hulme's print of the West Terrace of 1846 and in J. Stubbs' print of *c*.1830 shows why. The shape and skyline of the building changed almost out of recognition. Cottingham gradually restructured the Hall and made it a spectacular castle-mansion.

On the evidence submitted to the Commissioner of Taxes in 1844 by William Brougham, the part of the Hall which had fallen down in 1829 was rebuilt from its foundations with all but two windows remaining the same size. An old tower, once used as a woodhouse, was also rebuilt. A game larder was erected where a sycamore once grew. Its one entrance led on to the courtyard. The amateur architect George Shaw's diary entry for 26 September 1830 suggests that this was an initial phase of the project without much new building. He found the place

> ... built of rough, unsquared stones, without being dressed and battlemented. The modern windows the present proprietor is having pulled out, and replacing them with old-fashioned ones with mullions and round heads. The place is undergoing considerable repairs and when finished will present the appearance of a fine castellated mansion to the road [now the Kendal to Carlisle stretch of the A6].

This work had started in August 1830.

The building already had a slightly picturesque Border-fortress look. Shaw approved of the 'very romantic' entrance to the grounds at the head of an avenue leading down to Brougham Castle: '... a deep archway with a flanking turret, the whole covered with ivy. There is no window or outlet to be seen, except one place strongly grated with iron. The doors are folding, and made of oak, deeply pannelled, with a knocker of massive dimensions and huge size'. Impressed, he returned later that evening, standing 'beside the huge portal, examining its appearance ... admiring the fine effect produced by a light which·shone from the small grated window...'.

Henry Brougham's political career must have given work on the Hall an impetus after 1829, work beginning only four months before he became Lord Chancellor. Though his letters sometimes mention his annoyance at being exploited by more leisured, richer, aristocratic Whig colleagues, Henry may well have felt he needed a larger and more stylish residence, not just to entertain. He had to look after his two Spalding step-children, Marianne Dora and John Eden, and his own child, Eleanor Louise. His brother John Waugh, an Edinburgh wine-merchant, had died in September 1829 with debts of £20,000, leaving his nine children for Henry to look after. In addition James and William, frequently at Brougham, and Mrs. Eleonora Brougham, permanently there, would all have needed their own space.

Another reason for Brougham Hall's rebuilding was Henry's and his brothers' wish to reinforce their family's status in stone, as Henry and William both cared deeply about their family's pedigree, traditions and past. Henry was very proud to be a Westmorland man, claiming descent from the de Burgham family, the de Vaux family, the Nevilles, Earls of Westmorland, the Stricklands, the Lamplughs of Lamplugh and the Delamore family. But this was more impressive than real. The de Burgham name might well have become corrupted into Brougham. The Broughams of Brougham who became extinct in 1608 were probably indirectly descended from the de Burghams, but Henry's earliest traceable ancestor is Peter Brougham of Eamont Bridge (d. 1581). His great-grandson, Henry Brougham of Scales Hall (c.1638-98), mentioned in Sir William Dugdale's 'Visitation' of 1665 was the first of that branch of the family to hold any substantial amount of land.

The Broughams' claim to be descended from the de Vaux family, however, was false. William Brougham seems to have invented a 1553 marriage between Thomas Brougham and Jane Vaux of Catterlen. Research by genealogists Peter Brougham Wyly and C. Roy Hudleston has proved that neither existed. A 16th-century marriage between Catherine Strickland (born a Neville, and the widow of Sir Walter Strickland) and a Henry Brougham (alleged son of the disproved Brougham-Vaux marriage) on which the Broughams claimed descent from the Nevilles, has also been disproved. The Broughams' claim to be descended from the Stricklands (through Catherine Strickland) was spurious. So was their claim of descent from the Delamores (an Isabella Delamore had married a William Vaux in 1481).

The Broughams also claimed descent from the Lamplughs of Lamplugh. In their pedigree, presented in Burke's *Commoners*, Vol. 1 (1836) they said that Elizabeth, eldest daughter of Col. John Lamplugh of Lamplugh, Cumberland, had married Henry Brougham of Scales (c.1638-98) as his second wife, having a son, Samuel, from whom the 1st Lord Brougham was descended. In Burke's *Royal Families*, Vol. 2 (1851) Elizabeth Lamplugh was described as the daughter and ultimately heiress of Col. John Lamplugh, and to have married Henry in 1670, having seven children. The late C. Roy Hudleston, in a brilliant piece of genealogical research, proved that this Henry Brougham – Elizabeth Lamplugh marriage did not take place. The Brougham pedigrees in Nicholson and Burn, and Hutchinson, say that Henry had only one wife, Mary Slee, whom he married on 25 November 1660. One of their children, Anne, was born in 1683! There are two further conclusive pieces of evidence. Henry's 1697 will mentions Mary Slee as his wife. His friend and first cousin Sir Daniel Fleming's book of family history, in Lord Lonsdale's muniments, lists Henry and Mary's marriage and their 12 children – including Samuel. Lastly, it is recorded that Mary died, as Henry's widow, in 1718.

In 1831 Brougham Hall was beginning to undergo a radical rebuilding as Henry Brougham became increasingly absorbed in the Reform Bill in the House of Lords. When he returned from Parliament in December after the Bill's second reading, parts of the Hall were open to the winds and its freshly-plastered walls (probably in the Mansion House) were still damp. As a result Henry caught a chill and was suffering from diarrhoea and vomiting within a few days. 1832 saw work progress further with a new tower, probably in the kitchen area, built on the site of outhouses by the Mansion House. On 24 December 1833, the building project suffered a temporary blow with the death of James Brougham. That day, Creevey wrote in a letter to Miss Ord that '... no one ever discovered the slightest particle of talent in James of any kind'. But this was cruel and unfair. James seems to have been a capable collector of political intelligence as an M.P. and a shrewd adviser to Henry. He was also a competent administrator of Brougham Hall and its estate.

James left real problems, however, on his death. According to a letter from William to James Rigg Brougham of 26 June 1863, his substantial debts (of about £40,000) led to a crisis meeting of William, Henry and Vizard (Henry's solicitor) in 1834. It was decided that it was not worth selling land to try to meet the debts of James and John Waugh Brougham. They then drew up a complex set of mortgages to meet the debts. These were: on Brougham itself (one of £15,000 to William's marriage settlement trustees), on Howes (a Cumberland farm James had owned, for £5,000) and another of James' farms, Broadfield (for £5,000). There was also an obligation in John Waugh Brougham's name for £2,500. Lastly there were two assignments on the mortgages on Broadfield (for £3,000) and a bond debt (for £2,000) made out to William. This all made a total of £32,500 in mortgages. The job of paying these debts off and looking after the Hall and Estate now fell to William.

William is one of the most significant men in the history of Brougham Hall and the Broughams. A clever lawyer and capable businessman who was M.P. for Southwark from 1831-4, he acted as a kind of press agent for Henry when he was Lord Chancellor. William was also a Master in Chancery from 1831 until 1852. Most importantly for Brougham Hall he was a medieval architecture enthusiast who kept sketchbooks of possible designs and probably established links with Cottingham. Cottingham approvingly

26.   Anonymous watercolour of the ice-house and clock-tower area of Brougham Hall, 12 November 1844.

called his taste 'imbued with Gothic'. A really enthusiastic antiquarian, he was a compulsive builder. This sometimes led him to pass off the high-class fakery he had commissioned for the interiors of the Hall and chapel as genuinely medieval. He also invented bits of history. Besides devising the dubious Brougham pedigree, he may also have 'found' the legend of the Brougham skull. In October 1846 his workmen discovered the skeletons of the de Burghams at nearby Ninekirks church. William then seems to have kept the presumed skull, sword and prick-spur of Gilbert de Burgham at the Hall. The superstition ran that unless a skull was kept at the Hall its inhabitants would be disturbed by horrendous noises at night!

Cottingham both collected furniture for his museum and designed pieces for each commission. He designed most of Brougham's furniture for William, a keen collector. This may have been some compensation for being bombarded by him with long letters full of sketches and technical questions! Somewhat mean both to his brothers and in business, William most enjoyed running things for his brother at Brougham and improving the estate. His astute business sense led him to set up Wetheriggs Pottery at Clifton in an existing tile and brick works in 1841. He also made a financially significant marriage to Emily Frances Taylor in August 1834. The only daughter and eventual heiress of Sir Charles William Taylor Bt. of Hollycombe, Sussex, she brought an inheritance of 2,716 acres in Somerset and nine acres in Hampshire on the death of her brother, the 2nd Baronet. Worth £4,587 a year in 1883, this was to more than double the Brougham landholdings and yearly income from land.

A glimpse of what life was like at Brougham Hall while Henry Brougham was Lord Chancellor is provided by a letter from Charles Knight, publisher of the Society for the Diffusion of Useful Knowledge, to his wife. He tells her of staying at Brougham with Lord Brougham and Matthew Hill, M.P. They rose at seven, and after letters and papers breakfasted at a quarter to ten. At 11 a.m. they went to the library to discuss 'some point of national importance' for three or four hours. A drive to the Lakes (the Chancellor acting as guide) followed. They dined at six or seven, talked for two or three hours, took tea in the drawing room and went to bed at eleven.

Henry Brougham's relationship with Brougham Hall was one of affection and distance, particularly after he ceased to be Lord Chancellor in November 1834. Spending much of his time at Hill Street and from 1838 at 4 Grafton Street, London, he would come up to Brougham in the autumn between parliamentary sessions. He visited the small fishing village of Cannes in the South of France by accident, while avoiding a cholera epidemic as he tried to cross the Italian border at Nice in Autumn 1834. Later he returned and eventually built a house, Chateau Eleanore-Louise at Cannes for himself and his fragile daughter, Eleanor Louise ('Tullia'). From 1840 he spent several months there every year. Around that time he considered selling Brougham Hall, but the idea got no further. William would not have been very receptive to it. A glance at what had taken place at Brougham by 1840 reveals why.

It is difficult to date all Cottingham's work at Brougham. By 1834, however, he was well into his stride, producing a convincing pastiche of an ancient Baronial Border fortress-mansion which had been added to from medieval to Elizabethan times. Some parts were built with a deliberate and charming incongruity. An example is the inner stable court-yard shown in a sketch by Fairholt of around 1838. This had a large variety of different lines and assorted sizes of windows. On the turnpike road's side was a grotesque but remarkable seven-day clock constructed by Richardson. At the top of two intersecting walls, its base had an oversized gargoyle beneath it. This area was in use by 1838.

Change elsewhere was considerable. By 1835 the medieval 'ancient chamber' had been swept away. By 1840 Cottingham had heightened Bird's Tower, the partly 17th-century pele in the centre of the Mansion House. He may also have designed for its top a large tank holding 5,000 gallons of water. This supplied the house, estate and drove two organs including the early 17th-century one in St Wilfred's chapel. Cottingham had also added two storeys to medieval buildings on the right of a minor gate facing the road. He had built around Bird's Tower a striking oak roofed armour hall 42 ft. long and 20 ft. high and wide, a cloistered passage running along the entire face of the Mansion House, an octagon room, the new library, the dining room and the Norman bedroom. On the first floor he had built the Norman corridor, later decorated with a painting of the Bayeux Tapestry. This new building work extended the Mansion House into an 'E' shape.

Events in 1838 and 1839 transformed the Brougham family and life at Brougham. One of the most important changes was the disinheritance of Patrick, Henry's nephew and John Waugh Brougham's second son. John Waugh's eldest son was Henry (born on 7 February 1813) who had stood to inherit the Brougham property on Lord Brougham's death, but not his title. This could only have been passed to male children of Lord Brougham, who had none. Patrick, born in 1819, at first looked unlikely to inherit much from Lord Brougham. Rather reckless and ill-disciplined, he got into a series of discreditable escapades. The last straw came in August 1837 when he was working in Edinburgh. On 4 September Henry wrote to his brother William, describing what had happened:

27. Henry Brougham (1813-39), nephew of Henry, Lord Brougham.

> The lad had *in three months* got into debt above £70 – chiefly by buying and riding a horse and other follies of the same kind and he took the money out of a check [*sic*] of his employers and was of course found out the same day or next morning ...

In December 1837 Patrick may have been in prison. Lord Brougham was furious: 'I would not send the wretch a pound to rescue him from lying there all his life – not if I had a million', he wrote to William on Christmas Day. But he later relented and intervened to stop Patrick's case coming to court. Patrick set off for Australia from Leith in the ship *Countess of Durham* in April 1838, armed with letters of introduction from Lord Brougham to Sir John Franklin in Hobart, and Governor Gipps of New South Wales. Arriving in Sydney in September he eventually became a sheep farmer. In 1839 his brother John Brougham joined him in New South Wales with the news that Lord Brougham had sent £200 to help them establish themselves there. Well into 1840 they would have learnt of their brother Henry's death, in October 1839. By this time Patrick, who would have been next in line, stood no chance of inheriting. Patrick and John stayed in Australia, founding the Australian branch of the Broughams on Chart Seven.

In November 1839 the death of Tullia, then 17, from consumption, was a devastating blow to Lord Brougham, leaving him grief-stricken. A great unifying force in the family, particularly in the squabbles between William and Henry, was lost when the remarkable Mrs. Eleonora Brougham died in December.

Patrick's disinheritance reinforced William Brougham's position at Brougham and in the family. In a letter to his nephew, James Rigg Brougham, on 26 June 1863, he maintained that from 1840 onwards he had 'paid every thing that has been laid out at Brougham'. Under his management, Cottingham continued to embellish the Hall. In 1842 a stair-bridge was built over the turnpike between chapel and Hall. Wrought-iron gates, probably designed by Cottingham, were added to it at the chapel end. He had published the book, *The Ornamental Metal Worker's Director* in 1823 (reissued in 1824 as *The Smith and Founder's Director, containing a Series of Designs and Patterns for Ornamental Iron and Brass Work*) and was an influential expert in the field.

On the Hall side of the stair-bridge there were more developments. It was probably here that (according to William Brougham's 1844 submissions to the Commissioner of Taxes) an extremely old part of the Hall had given way in October 1842. Certainly another intense spate of building followed there in 1843-4, radically changing the look of the Mansion House.

In 1843 a new room was added at the west end of the Mansion House. The new library was also built on the ground floor there, eventually containing oak panelling, antique furniture and more than 12,000 volumes. In addition a small turret was added at the corner. According to the Case for the Opinion of the Commissioner of Taxes of 1844, this area was rebuilt on its old foundations with 16 rather than 18 windows, the new ones square-topped, replacing the original round-topped ones. It says that parts of the exterior walls in this area were rebuilt, some from the first storey up, others from the foundations. This indicates an extensive rebuilding.

During the rebuilding of the west end of the Mansion House, the earth above the road and woodland walk was banked up creating the west terrace, reinforced with heavy stone flags and buttressed walling. This raises interesting questions about what influenced Cottingham's west terrace design. Sir Robert Smirke and Cottingham were friends and corresponded. There is, however, no evidence of collaboration between them. In 1841 Cottingham had been rebuilding the tower of Milton Bryant church, Bedfordshire, for Sir Robert Inglis, a high churchman, F.S.A. and Tory M.P. for Oxford. Smirke had previously submitted designs which were not used. The designs Cottingham used on the Brougham Hall west terrace, however, bear a strong resemblance to Smirke's designs for the east terrace of Windsor Castle, now in the R.I.B.A. Library. Did Smirke show his friend the designs and indirectly inspire Brougham's west terrace?

The work in 1843 spread out over other areas like the north front and the stable yard. In late September that year, a Mr. George Pugmire surveyed the Hall's windows for the

28. Three sons of John Waugh Brougham and their wives, at the back, left to right: James Rigg, Patrick, John and Caroline; front, left to right: Isabella, Mary. Caroline and Mary Brougham were sisters, daughters of John Kennedy of Keswyck, Gunning, New South Wales, Australia. Isabella Eliza Brougham was the fifth daughter of John Cropper of Dingle Bank, Liverpool.

Commissioner of Taxes, and listed the rooms still incomplete. In the north front two larders, a bedroom, water-closet, two towers and a passage were unfinished, and in the stable yard a tower, stable boy's bedroom, larder and a passage had not yet been completed. These rooms had 14 windows between them. The work done in 1843 also included new gardens and hothouses on the way to Penrith, and an 1848 map of the Hall and estate shows a garden of about two acres on the chapel side of the turnpike. Between 1843 and 1844 (probably after Pugmire's survey) more work was done on another two areas. New stables were built on the south side of the house. A Norman bedroom supported by pillars and projecting from the Hall with a groined arch was fashioned by Richardson in 1844 to Cottingham's designs and advice.

In 1843 there came a bizarre challenge to Lord Brougham's ownership of the Hall. It resembled one of Henry Brougham's own pranks except, of course, that he was its target. Thomas Bird of Ashton-under-Lyne asserted that John Brougham of Scales' purchase in 1726 of Brougham Hall had been illegal, that he owned the Hall and estate and that Lord Brougham therefore owed him rent. Not content with this, Bird continued his argument in a bizarre, melodramatic, feudal way, threatening to steal a grey mare (in lieu of rent) from Wetheriggs and to break into Brougham Hall kitchen demanding rent! The Broughams' case against Bird came up at Appleby Assizes on 11 August. On 12 September Bird was soundly defeated!

In 1844 William pressed on with Brougham Hall. Parts of the house, according to the 1844 Case for the Commissioner of Taxes, were still uninhabited. On 25 January Richardson wrote to William telling him that he was putting up the clock tower, reinforced with iron bars ('the most Difficult work of anything we have done') and that they had finished the magnificent fireplace in the Armour Hall, whose pillar and cornice he was planning to erect once the room had been painted. The courtyard's walls were incomplete but its stone slabs were in place with the ice-house ready for use, he reported. On 11 February Richardson wrote that W. Scott intended to begin painting the Armour Hall 'tommorow'. He enclosed plans of the proposed 14 by 14 ft. Octagon Room. Though recent bad weather had stopped work outside, he had taken down the quoins of the library and cut a new foundation for it.

Meanwhile, William ended a typically long-drawn out negotiation with the Commissioner of Taxes. By having the cloister closed off in one area as requested by the tax authorities, William, typically, saved some money. In May 1844, Brougham Hall's window tax was set at £14 8s. 9d., as it had been in April 1835. In a more exciting vein, in July and August Cottingham had a vast door-knocker cast for William by Thomas Potter in London. Nearly two feet across, this was an exact replica of the 1140 Durham Cathedral sanctuary lion-headed door-knocker. Letters from Cottingham to William Brougham around this time show that the interior of the Mansion House was being decorated. On 31 July Cottingham wrote to William, from London, enclosing a bill for armour from a Mr. Falckes, telling him he had just sent furniture-maker Samuel Pratt a

29.   Hartwood Station, Deniliquin, New South Wales, Australia, built by Patrick Brougham in 1853-4.

sketch for valances to bed and dining hall curtains, and drawings for a screen beneath the staircase. In early August he was in London arranging for the shipment to Brougham of furniture he had designed – a sitting room table, frames for a dressing room table and a washstand. He was also having some firescreens made by Pratt, advising William on chairs and advocating red and grey stone paving for the armour hall.

After 1844 it seems that Cottingham continued to advise and assist William Brougham giving technical advice on furnishings, fittings and interior decoration where needed. His son, Nockalls Johnson Cottingham, increasingly took over the work. William Brougham seems to have been his own master for much of the time, continuing to collect. George Shaw's account of Brougham Hall, in 1848, mentions the old drawing room as having some arms of Edward VI over its chimney-piece, and a large array of tapestries and stamped leather around the house. It mentions the stained glass in the great dining room and a fine collection of armour in the armour hall. Though the bell for the eight-day tower clock (made by Vulliamy) was cast in 1846, by 1847 the great rebuilding seems to have slackened pace. Then Lord Brougham made an important legal move. The Brougham estate had been entailed by Lord Brougham's grandfather, Henry (1719-82), and each descendant who inherited it was a 'tenant in tail'. In March 1847

30. F. W. Hulme's lithotint of Brougham Hall's terrace (1846), from S. C. Hall's *Baronial Halls*, Vol. II (1848)

Lord Brougham took advantage of an 1833 Act enabling a tenant in tail to break an entail through a deed enrolled in Chancery. On 18 March 1847, William wrote in his diary:

> ... H. executed a deed conveying all his real estt. to Liman upon such trusts as H. might by any Deed direct or appoint & in default of appointt. & subject there to then to the care of H. for life without Impeachment of waste & after his decease to me in Fee – It was witnessed by Ld. Cottenham & Lord Lyndhurst – & is deposited at Bouverie & Co. for safe Custody.[4]

Henry had broken his grandfather's entail with a deed that enabled William and in his turn, Henry Charles, to succeed to the estate.

By 1847 Cottingham's work at Brougham Hall seems to have been externally complete. He had wrought a tremendous, eye-catching transformation. It was largely his work that gave even passing travellers a thrill of importance and drew the praise of distinguished visitors. On 13 October 1847 Cottingham died, after a long illness, and was buried in Croydon.[5] The Brougham family had lost one of its best servants.

1. Brougham Papers, University College, London.
2. Submitted as a Ph.D. thesis to Leicester Polytechnic.
3. Letter from William Brougham to the Earl of Carlisle, 25 November 1844, Castle Howard archive.
4. The 1st Lord Brougham's solicitors were Bouverie and Co. In 1865 they were called Ransom and Bouverie and Co. and, describing themselves as bankers, were at 1, Pall Mall East, S.W.
5. In 1854 his elder son, Nockalls Johnson Cottingham (b. 1823), also an architect who had continued his father's business, was lost, along with his father's drawings, when the steamer *Arctic*, en route to New York, sank with all hands.

Chapter 7

Helping the Patriarch and Completing the Hall 1847-1868

I think no one ever took old age less gracefully or showed more constantly the baneful effects of having been allowed his own way – neither self-control – nor any effort to submit to immutable necessity – this shows itself in every thing he does.

William Brougham on Henry, Lord Brougham (*Diary*, 5 May 1864)

By the time Lord Brougham signed the first entail of 18 March 1847, William ran the family's property and finances in Cumberland and Westmorland. He led a life of concentrated, bustling activity. From March 1831 until the end of 1852 William was a Master in Chancery in London, while at Brougham he shot grouse, helped to organise the local militia, saw to the accounts, researched papers for Henry, played real tennis and wrote long letters of advice to his children.

William's burdens were many. They included his insane sister-in-law, Mary Ann (whom he called 'the old brute'), and he also had to deal with his wife Emily's ill health and their children. By 1847 they had five children: Henry Charles, Alice, Emily Evelyn, Wilfred and Adela Mary ('Tib'). William also helped John Waugh Brougham's children (sending Patrick and John £520 in March 1853), and the Irish Broughams.

William's diary gives a fascinating insight into life at Brougham. It shows the contradiction between his family's public prestige and sometimes bleak private face. For example, by 1847 Lady Brougham was insane, after years of self-destructive, neurotic withdrawal and Henry's ill-treatment. Incurable, even menacing, her life was a miserable path of pain and mindless over-eating. William's

31. William, 2nd Lord Brougham (1795-1886), from Sir George Hayter's painting *The House of Commons, 1833*.

family dreaded her. His unstable sister Mary had been 'kept' in Reading since 1834, another family tragedy.

From 1834 the Hall was dominated by the difficult relationship between Henry and William. Henry, hard to live with, suspected that William's family wanted him dead. He treated Emily insensitively, even unbearably, and was suspicious of her family as Sir Charles Taylor, 1st Baronet had been a Tory M.P. His anger and periodic rudeness to visitors annoyed William. One day in October 1848, Hobhouse (a guest) said in conversation that the illness of Thomas Duncombe, Radical M.P. for Finsbury, was all pretence. Henry replied: 'None but an inane fool would assert such a thing'. Hobhouse, incensed, tried to leave the Hall at 2 a.m. Henry was eventually persuaded to write him an apology, which fortunately Hobhouse accepted, staying.

William could be heartless. On the death of Mr. Vignati, Wilfred's father-in-law, his diary for 4 April 1864 reads: 'This is fortunate as it ends all trouble & risk arising out of the [marriage] settlement'. He could be vindictive, banning Henry's stepdaughter Lady Malet from Brougham in 1848, and calling her brother, John Eden Spalding, 'the swindler'. He felt Henry treated Emily 'as if she were the dirt beneath his feet'. Rows punctuated his relations with Henry, and both felt longstanding mutual hurt. William had left Brougham within days of Eleanor Louise's death in 1839, hurting a grief-stricken Henry who then arrived there. Henry's devotion to Henry Charles, Wilfred and Reginald (b. 1853) sometimes provoked William's resentment. This relationship of reproach and critical, hurt affection is typified by a row recorded in William's diary for 6 September 1851. The mislaying of manuscripts, which Henry had marked while researching a book, led to a bitter quarrel at the Hall. He said that William

> ... cared for nothing – paid no attention to anything – wd. be as like to throw them into the fire as valueless – I calmly said, nothing could be more unjust – as my whole life was spent in keeping things together & taking care of what belonged to him – as witness the pains that had been taken to preserve all the letters & MSS.

On 31 September William wrote that after Henry's recent behaviour '... it required all my resolution to avoid a total and absolute quarrel & leaving the place for ever'.

Despite the rows they respected each other. Lord Brougham gave William a virtually free hand to manage the family property, taking a close interest in his nephews and their education. In return he expected William's help with his own activities, imploring William's family to be with him at Brougham or Cannes. They tried to tolerate his periodic burning anger, rudeness and alarming depressions. This understanding between the brothers benefited Brougham. During his long stays William could administer the Hall, and he directed building work on the spot (with architects' advice) or by voluminous, painstaking correspondence. Henry had little interest in architecture but had to approve the work. In July 1852 he expressed his dislike of a new covered passage from Hall to chapel, and it was promptly demolished! William consulted him carefully about legal problems, for example a farcical dispute in August 1847. This erupted when the Hon. Rev. Thomas Edwardes, Rector of Brougham, refused to read the service in St Wilfred's chapel for the Broughams and their servants. He, like the Broughams, claimed jurisdiction over it. The dispute ended inconclusively in October.

Building Work at Brougham Hall 1847-52

William was happiest working on Brougham. He was advised by the local architect John Richardson, estate staff Joseph Richardson, George Slee, George Scott and John White, a Robert James in London and a friend George Shaw (1810-76), an amateur architect and mill-owner. Shaw, an eccentric and rather obsequious antiquarian who loved Gothic and Tudor architecture, would travel hundreds of miles to see it. With enterprising untrained talent and a small building company at St Chad's, his Saddleworth estate, he built churches in the north of England, and even mansions in Tudor and Gothic. Clients included local squires and aristocracy, such as the armour expert Sir Samuel Meyrick, Sir Stephen Glynne (Gladstone's son-in-law) and Lord Londesborough. His enthusiastic but often vague letters to William show that he was consulted only for interior fittings at Brougham.

The architect Richard Charles Hussey sketched the Hall's terrace front on 4 October 1847. It looked complete but work continued as he drew. That month William worked on the Norman room. Mr. Walton, the painter, created mask heads, kings, and a scroll for its interior, and laboured at the Bayeux Tapestry in the Norman corridor. In early November Walton was working on the great staircase area (built by John Richardson).

During the next year work evolved slowly. In early March 1848 a drain tunnel was being cut under the terrace gravel. Six- and eight-inch drainpipes had been manufactured for it at a foundry. In mid-May William came to Brougham, and work restarted. In August the painting of diaper design on the staircase walls was finished, as was the planning of the Norman room's cornice and ceiling. On 1 November William and George Scott settled the plan for the passage painting. William stayed at Brougham over Christmas. On 26 December arrived a thankless letter from Henry proposing to sell Brougham. William wrote in his diary: 'answered this, so as to put all such nonsense out of his head'.

William developed the Hall and its gardens as money allowed. By February 1849 the great staircase area's panelling (including napkin panelling from Scales Hall) had been

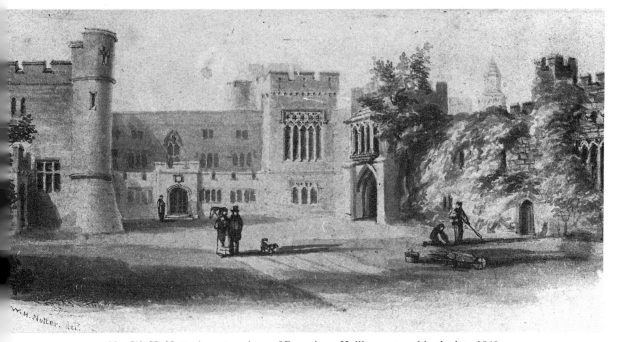

32. W. H. Nutter's watercolour of Brougham Hall's courtyard in the late 1840s.

inserted. Work took place on the staircase on the west side of the Mansion House. Coming to Brougham in early August, William had the Norman room finished by mid-September, then settled plans for its brass ornaments. In October he decided to build a peach house for £150, acquired four stags' heads from Leonard Edmunds and ordered 508 ft. of piping for the Norman passage. In early November William and Robert James decided to make the dining room ceiling (from old mouldings) and the deed room using old oak pieces for shelving. William also planned a terrace walk to Brougham Castle. On 3 December he returned to 19 Grosvenor Square. There he bargained with a Mr. Paull for cutting quarterfoils on the great staircase window and approached Youngs of Parliament Street for a deer fence for the park.

In January 1850 George Shaw suggested altering the line of the road from Lowther Springs to the end of Oak Bank. This may have led to the rebuilding of the park walls under Joseph Richardson's supervision. Costing 18s. 6d. per rood, 732 yards of stone were built around the park and Hall kitchen by mid-March. February saw work on the peach house. Pipes were installed up the kitchen roof and the library tower was worked on. On 2 March Robert James wrote to William about raising the Hall's height to allow new bedrooms. In early March the dining room ceiling was being made, with timber and joists about to be installed. On 8 April William arrived from London. Soon the dining room ceiling was completed and the colour chosen for the Octagon Room ceiling. The room resembled one William had studied at Brougham Castle. More house-painting followed. On 29 July George Shaw, impressed, wrote to William describing Brougham as '... really without doubt the best done up place in existence ...'.

A lull in building followed. On 10 January 1851, however, William settled the design of the library tower tables and old drawing room with Robert James. The new passage needed an oak ceiling and new brick lining, increasing costs. In 1852 a real tennis court was built in what is now the yard of Eamont Bridge's *Crown Inn*, shut up until spring 1853 and then much used. The west dressing room was finished on 23 November 1852.

Brougham Family History (1848-58)

The years 1848-52 were trying. By 1840 it was obvious that the Whigs had shelved Henry, as his judgement was distrusted. In 1845 a plan for him to change places with Lord Chancellor Lyndhurst in Peel's Conservative government failed and his hopes of ministerial office ended. In early 1848 he applied for French citizenship to Crémieux, the French Minister of Justice, wanting to stand in the National Assembly for the Var district around Cannes. The English press, especially *The Times*, made fun of him unmercifully. William wrote sadly in his diary on Thursday 20 April:

> ... What a fatal want of the right sense of things this shews! The <u>pretence</u> that it was to secure that miserable property at Cannes is too transparent to deceive a child. Everybody will believe that it was that insane desire to be meddling, wh. has actuated him. It is strange how he contrives always to do the thing that is most to lower him in the eyes of all men!

Henry's scheme naturally died, a half-baked idea created by his emotional isolation and fear of being challenged. He recovered quickly from the publicity and in November corresponded with Metternich and Guizot from Cannes.

There were other misfortunes including the death of Emily's mother, Charlotte, Lady Taylor, on 1 June 1848. William had not liked her or her 'Billingsgate' speech and 'Thompson temper'. On 6 June she was buried in the Thompson family vault at Roehampton. Emily was extremely distressed and William was angry at Mary Ann's indifference.

33. James Rigg Brougham, Q.C. (1826-1919)
by Fred Yates.

34. Isabella Eliza Cropper Brougham
(d. 1921) by Fred Yates.

1848 was not all disaster, though. William helped his barrister nephew James Rigg Brougham, who was talented, hard-working and well-liked. In mid-June 1848, William asked Lord Chancellor Cottenham to give James, then the Lord Chancellor's Secretary in Bankruptcy, the Liverpool Registrarship in Bankruptcy. The condition of his appointment was that he contributed £300 a year from his £800 salary, ostensibly to pay off family debts. On 7 August James took up his new duties. He subsequently became a regular visitor to Brougham and a trusted family legal advisor.

The Broughams needed regular legal advice: Henry's scrapes alone would have required it. In June 1850 he was associating with one H. Martin, reputedly a rogue. An alarmed William was told by his London solicitor Vizard that Martin, the son of Lord Saye and Sele's footman, was a whorer and swindler. But William wrote, '... such is H.'s madness & infatuation that he is doing all he can to uphold the blackguard'. Much of 1851 (and perhaps the first half of 1852) were clouded. William examined an anxious Henry's 'excessive' bills on 18 January, suspecting that Martin's wife Betty was behind them. Examining Henry's accounts in June he found 'hush money' had been paid to Martin. Henry was being blackmailed. In another scandal, Lady Brougham attacked a policeman and spat in another's face in London on 15 June 1851. William wrote to Sir Richard Mayne, Chief Commissioner of the Metropolitan Police to try to prevent her insanity becoming the talk of London. Mayne ensured that a charge entered at the Vine Street office by the policeman she attacked never came to court.

At this time William made the family's last attempt at high office. A Master in Chancery, he stood to suffer in future reforms and now tried to become Vice-Chancellor. Sir Thomas Wilde, Lord Truro (1782-1855), a good family friend, had been Lord Chancellor since 15 July 1850. He had entrusted Henry with the Lords' appellate jurisdiction. On 19 June 1851, with Henry's support, William approached the prime minister, Lord John Russell, through the Earl of Minto (Lord Privy Seal and Russell's father-in-law) about the Vice-Chancellorship. But this fell foul of Lord Truro. Truro's reforms led to the office of Chief Clerk replacing that of Master in Chancery; the next Lord Chancellor, Sugden (appointed 4 March 1852) told William on 2 November 1852 that he would soon cease to be a Master. On 17 December William left 25 Southampton Buildings after nearly 22 years, 'without much regret', his legal career ended.

William needed more income. On 21 September 1851 he found he had made a £3,000 loss in a Bantry lead mine. New work on Brougham Hall virtually stopped from 1853-7, but it is unclear why. This did not lead to more domestic peace. On 3 July 1852 William arrived at Brougham. Emily, who had a miscarriage on 28 July, felt bitter and neglected. On 18 September William wrote:

> This morng. had a very disagreeable conversation with E. who declared distinctly her horror of this place – partly owing to the madness of the old woman, partly to H. & the feeling that she was always on a volcano – partly to the dullness of the life & being obliged to live always *in a garret*. She said that for 17 years she had been sacrificed – nothing was spent on her altho' money cd. always be found for anything else that I had my amusement and fancy indulged – that she had too much conscience to spend money upon herself – & so on – but over and over again repeating her hatred of this place, her anxiety to leave it & never to see it again – in all of which she shall certainly be indulged –

William now spent more time with her. She bore a son on 2 December 1853, christened Reginald Thomas Dudley Brougham on 20 January 1854. A crazy legal challenge in mid-May from some obscure Birds claiming ownership of the Hall followed. But a reasonably secure financial position had now been established, allowing William to buy King

Arthur's Round Table and Yanwath Castle in 1853, and High Head in April 1854. But William continued to be annoyed by Henry. During his stay at Brougham in August and September 1853, Henry spoke to no one, even refusing to answer when addressed, for 10 days. Henry thought they all wished him dead.

Family life at Brougham was not always acrimonious. There was great affection between William, Emily and their children with tearful partings before school terms. Henry enjoyed his nephews' company too. In late September 1854 he begged William to let Wilfred stay at Brougham until he departed on 2 October, then left with Henry Charles and Wilfred on the London train on 5 October. Emily, though, was unhappy. On 10 November she 'exploded' after dinner, saying she loathed the Hall, life in it and the local climate. William wrote: '... a repetition of this sort of thing wd. decide me on a separation'. Another quarrel arose when Alice proposed to the Rev. Thomas Edwardes on 29 July 1856. Next day William told her that marrying Edwardes was 'impossible'.

While William spent much of his time at Brougham, Henry's energy was undiminished. In mid-1857 Henry Charles (now a House of Lords clerk) worked as his secretary. In the evenings Henry attended the Law Amendment Society: he was still having new ideas. In 1857 he founded the prestigious National Association for the Promotion of Social Sciences, and became its President. Henry continued his educational interests, helping those who had supported the S.D.U.K. In late 1857, for instance, opening the Kendal Mechanics' Institute, he spoke about his educational and anti-slavery work. Its chairman, John Cropper, described him as:

> ... then an old man, and evidently gave no thought to appearance, or to manner. A striking almost grotesque presence. Careless dress, large ill-tied neckcloth and unsmoothed hat; but he came forward with the perfect authority and position of a king. He sprung into his subjects with the greatest confidence, whatever they might be, urging us to value books, to study them, and to understand their meaning.[1]

Brougham Hall 1856-60

In 1856, the Hall narrowly avoided disaster. A fire ate into a fresco of the Siege of Troy and the dining room ceiling but, according to the *Carlisle Journal*, did only £20 damage. The Broughams played host to Edward, Prince of Wales in May 1857 but mist marred his three-day visit. On 16 November 1857 William received the rest of the Brougham properties from Henry in an entail. Between 1858 and 1860 he made slight changes at Brougham. By mid-March 1858 he had established a new garden with two urns at the entrance and a glass wall for growing apricots. In summer 1858 a water-course was being built with Wetheriggs bricks. Whellan says that carved woodwork was removed from High Head to Brougham that year.[2] The most major development, though, was the Clifton-Appleby line which cut through the estate in 1862. Operated by the Eden Valley Railway Co., it conveniently brought West Cumberland coal to Wetheriggs.

Henry was still vigorous. He continued speaking in public. On 10 October 1859 (aged 81) he went to a meeting in Bradford. He had two remaining triumphs to savour. On 27 October he was elected Chancellor of Edinburgh University, beating the Duke of Buccleuch with a crushing 236 majority. He and William had agreed by now about the Brougham title. The original patent of 1830 was to Henry's 'heirs male', but he had none. So the brothers lobbied Palmerston and Prince Albert for a separate creation for William. On 23 December 1859 William wrote in his diary that he had 'partly settled on Delamore'. But Palmerston was reluctant to give him a peerage since as politician, lawyer and judge he had never been a national figure.

On 24 February 1860, at Cannes, William received from Henry 'the announcement that the Queen has offered him a new Patent with special limitation to me'. The next day

35. Henry, Lord Brougham in old age, photographed by Herbert Watkins.

he got a letter from Prince Albert, summarised in his diary: 'he puts it on the Precedents of Nelson and St Vincent – & that the Queen agrees to it in order to preserve the Brougham peerage acquired by H. and not to make a new one'. On 8 March Queen Victoria issued a patent for the special limitation of the Brougham peerage with special remainder to William. Henry, 'in consideration of eminent public services, especially in the diffusion of knowledge, the spread of education, and the abolition of the Slave-trade and Slavery', was made Baron Brougham and Vaux of Brougham, Westmorland, & of High Head Castle, Cumberland. Always economical, William then persuaded the Treasury to remit the peerage fee and stamps, despite opposition from the chancellor of the exchequer, Gladstone. The move displeased the sons of John Waugh considerably. The normally equable James Rigg Brougham wrote to William to complain about the covert manner in which the new peerage patent had been obtained on 17 August 1863. He called the move '... so entirely unprecedented as passing over so many legitimate heirs to the natural succession'. He wrote: 'As it now stands it makes us appear to the world as if we were illegitimate'. It is clear that his brothers in Australia shared this hurt and anger at being cut out of the succession.

There were less pleasant problems, too. After bearing six children, Emily was diagnosed on 25 September as suffering from a displaced womb. Wilfred was a worry, being chronically indebted. In 1858 and 1860 he had cost William more than £2,600.

From June to December 1859 he spent 'the greater part of £800, in 6 months'. On 11 July 1860 William had to send him £250 and settle the rest of his unpaid bills with his agent Leonard Edmunds in November. £985 15s. 6d. in debt that year, Wilfred was becoming a financial drain and disappointment. He was unsettled in the 10th Light Dragoons, as a Cornet, and wanted to leave.

Henry continued to be active. Installed on 18 May 1860 as Chancellor of Edinburgh University, he was trying that month to get Cannes a railroad. But he became tired more often and attended the House of Lords less. Henry still travelled to public engagements, though, and was a prominent mourner at the funeral of the great naval commander, Thomas Cochrane, 10th Earl of Dundonald at Westminster Abbey on 14 November. But he knew that he must think of the future. He now made a will on Saturday 8 December. William wrote in his diary:

> H. executed last night a will confirming the Deeds of 1847 & 1857 & leaving me his personalty & appointing an excr. – this was duly witnessed by Garment & Stanford – ... made my will for the purpose of providing for Wilfred, in case of accidents – the draft as prepared by Hough, can be done at large hereafter.

The Last Rebuilding (1861-64)
William now embellished the Hall for pleasure rather than prestige. Henry Charles wanted a billiard room, so William selected Richard Charles Hussey (1806-87) to design it. Mainly a church architect, he had worked on four country mansions. In 1835 Hussey had gone into partnership in Birmingham with the more talented Thomas Rickman (1776-1841), inventor of the terms Early English, Decorated and Perpendicular. Though Rickman died in 1841, Hussey was made a Fellow of the R.I.B.A. in March 1852 and Vice-President in 1859. His office in 1861 was at 16 King William Street, Strand. Hussey's meticulous blueprints were neatly costed and his commissions were measured personally by hand. He made designs from sketch books of old buildings, could handle trowel, chisel, adze or saw like a craftsman, and could correct carving in stone or wood, never overlooking an error.[3]

In February and March 1861 William worked at the billiard room plans. He and Hussey then began a long series of meetings, site inspections and letters. On 8 July Hussey worked at Brougham on new plans for the room. More letters followed from August onwards about fitting the billiard room and library into a coherent complex. On 19 October Hussey suggested making the billiard room the thoroughfare to the library and the drawing room beyond. The existing passage's outer wall would be rebuilt from the front door to the library, which would be heightened, allowing the billiard room ceiling to extend to it or be carried to the full height of the house. The scheme was adopted. After three more meetings and drawing two more plans, William drew a final one which Hussey approved in a letter of 18 November. Hussey expected 'a good deal of consideration will be needful to bring everything to fit properly'.

In 1861 Hussey only built a small ice-house at the Hall, costing £3. From April to October 1862 plans for rib-vaulting the billiard room, library recess and library and building the walk and border in the gardens beside them were devised. On 17 November demolition started on the postern and library bay area shown in Nutter's painting of the late 1840s. A new late 14th-century and 15th-century-style tower was planned.

On 1 December the postern gate's demolition was finished. William decided to rebuild it as before using its doorway and groining as a passage from billiard room to terrace. In early December the new building's foundations were laid and its drains cut. After William made more plans, the new bay windows were built up to sill level and the

36. The armour hall at Brougham: an example of the magnificent interiors Cottingham created.

foundations of the library recess begun. One window was built to full height. On 19 and 20 December Hussey and William had two more London meetings. At the second they sorted out the postern. On 24 December William settled plans for a skylight in the new room with Hussey and a Mr. Farrady.

To Emily's chagrin, William tried hard to economise. An expensive year meant stringency in later ones. In 1860, for instance, William spent a total of £6,113 10s. 1d.; £3,843 5s. in London or abroad and the rest on Brougham Hall (£2,269. 15s. 1d.). On 28 January 1861, he decided on 'much economy this year to make matters square again'. In 1862 he invested more than £5,000 in the Eden Valley and Monmouth Railways with more than five per cent return. Perhaps as a result, at the end of 1862 finances were in 'moderate balance' for 1863. Out of it he paid £1,800 for Beacon Hill Farm and new building at Brougham.

William's optimism in 1863 proved misplaced. Building costs outstripped estimates and the project progressed slowly. In early January the library tower neared completion. By 1 March the billiard room's south windows were in place. Inevitably other features

37.   The drawing room at Brougham Hall.

38.   The library at Brougham, rebuilt by Hussey.

had to be added, including the east plantation wall and a marble fountain, ordered in March from Basso in Paris for 300 francs (a price including its delivery to London). That month William searched for curtains for the library arch and saw Hussey about problems with the library bay ceiling. On 2 April he took the 'Sun Light', made by Farrady in London, to Brougham, with all the billiard room windows now in place. The gable above the library arch was demolished in April, and the library bay ceiling (previously supported with a trussed beam and two columns) was completed. The cornice in its recess and a curtain rod were installed, the library's woodwork planned, and the ceiling of the library recess started. The books were returned and a gas pendant was installed in the library recess. By 30 June its staircase top was on and it awaited a parapet. The room's interior was soon complete. On 3 July William wrote: 'The success of the Library is beyond my most sanguine expectations – & when the Recess is open, the room will be perfect'. The exterior was finished with its battlements by 23 July.

In August 1863 the library recess was prepared for gilding and finishing, the billiard room's woodwork was finished and two-thirds of the deed room was vaulted. Externally the postern and wall-cutting were completed, and scaffolding erected for roofing the tower. In September the billiard room roof was slated and library recess completed. Tapestries were now hung over the billiard room door. In early November, William was having the library groined and vaulted. On 22 December the vaulting bosses were finished, and the flooring joists for the room above (Lord Brougham's study) were laid. On 24 December this floor was completed. Beneath it a twelve by six feet billiard table was installed.

In late December 1863, William wrote a brief account of the work's estimates and costs in his diary. He estimated the billiard room tower would cost 'from [£]14 to 1,500' including the deed room furniture but excluding the billiard table. The library would cost 'not less than [£]600' and the east wall, river wall and jobbing around £100. William expected a total cost of £2,200-2,300. By 31 December 1863, however, £1,800 had been spent on the billiard room area. With two family marriages that year costing £500, the cost of High Head's repairs estimated at £900, and Brougham's costs, more saving was needed. He now felt that as all these items of spending would cost £3,500 he needed 'two years of perfect quiet to restore the balance of accounts'.

Much of William's income went into Brougham. Perhaps this left less money to invest from an income which had failed to grow dramatically. A financial strain is evident: William decided to borrow £2,500 from a bank on 19 September 1863. He had also paid £340 for 17 Bank of Australia shares and spent 'a few hundred' draining land at Bewley Castle at Bolton on the River Eden. But these sums, outweighed by costs at Brougham and High Head, left 'not above £800' saved.

In early March 1864, William Brougham consulted with George Slee about colouring the Billiard Room ceiling and walls, and thought about planting in the gardens. Hussey sent advice and enclosed sketches for the Deed Room in long letters. These read like a Victorian interior decoration manual. On 17 March he wrote:

> ... the style of architecture is of too late a date for a continuous diaper on the walls. The most common way, in Perpendicular times, of ornamenting wide spaces of walls was either spotting it over with flowers or single leaves (oak, thorn, maple &c.) as exhibited by the accompanying sketches at No. 1 ... I should suggest your adopting style No. 1 & working it out with your crest and a rose alternately: the rose may be single or double ...

The surviving ceiling ribs show his advice was taken. He also suggested introducing a heraldic shield for the window splays[1] at springing level, leaving the rest plain or with dispersed ornament. He proposed for the hollow space under the bottom of the vaulting a blue colour '... spangled over with gold stars alternately blazing & quiescent ...' of lead.

39. The rebuilt library and Hussey's billiard room at Brougham Hall.

On 19 March William selected the billiard room vault paint. On 23 March he began new, circular flower-beds in the gardens. On the 24th Hussey told him that '... the style of the new tower, the upper storey, having few characteristic details may pass muster as belonging to the time of Richd. II, but the lower storey cannot be carried much further than Heny. V, & is really in the style of Hen. VI & Edwd. IV'. He advised colouring the tower's interior in black and gold stripes 'copied from a sample of ancient colouring' in Hascombe parish church, near Guildford, and suggested the Palace of Westminster's painted chamber as another source of inspiration.

From the end of March to early April the craftsmen worked on the deed room ceiling. By 31 March the Hascombe black and gold pattern had been adopted, and was also used either side of the altar in St Wilfred's chapel. Hussey advised continuous colour testing before work proceeded on the new billiard room tower's decoration. The work was then finished smoothly. On 30 June William settled plans for a billiard room bookcase and places for the score-board and cues. In July he put a grate in the room and then all boxes, deeds and papers in the deed room. On 6 August the billiard room's carpet was laid. Despite John White's sad death later that month, on 25 August, William and Henry Charles planned great changes in the gardens. On 27 November William was planning brass work for the billiard room fireplace. This ended Hussey's rebuilding. Its external effect was magnificent and the library's interior had a fine, cloister-like atmosphere of learning. Little more was done, apart from setting up the library's brass fire front, resetting its fire-bricks (April 1865) and completing the new walk to the east of the terrace (September 1865).

Life at Brougham Hall (1861-June 1868)

In 1861 Lord Brougham's powers were obviously declining. On 4 June he had a fainting fit at Brougham. His memory failing, he had trouble writing his memoirs, started earlier that year. William, Alice and Evelyn helped, sifting papers in the Hall's deed room, while William studied piles of correspondence, but they were not equal to the task. Henry Reeve advised postponing publication 'at any price' on 2 November 1862. In November 1867, William arranged the publication of volume one of Henry's *Life and Times*. It was unreliable and inaccurately printed.

Henry could still be the luminary. On 10 March 1863 he made an excellent speech to 129 dinner guests at Cannes, including the King of Würtemburg, Stratford Canning and Edward Ellice. But sadly old contemporaries were dying, for example a political friend, the 3rd Marquis of Lansdowne, on 31 January 1863. William began to watch Henry carefully. He still had his good days, giving an address to a full meeting in Edinburgh on 7 October. He had farcical days like a dental appointment in Manchester on 1 August. Comically, he went to it under his manservant's name, Garment!

By now Alice and Wilfred were giving their parents anguish. Alice forced her father to agree to her marrying the Rev. Thomas Edwardes in 1861. He did so, providing Edwardes got a living sufficient to insure his life for £5,000. They were married on 30 November 1863 at Ninekirks. Wilfred was still extravagant and headstrong. On 12 June 1861 he bought a Lieutenancy in the 10th Light Dragoons from a Richard Lomax for £250, but was still in debt in 1863. On 21 March 1862 his parents said they disapproved of his connection with Francesca Vignati, a none-too-wealthy Irish-Italian girl he had met in Ipswich. In April he threatened to marry her, and in June William took his lawyer Leman's advice to yield. Amongst other conditions the couple received £500 per annum during their joint lives from Mr. and Mrs. Vignati and a similar sum from William. They were married on 4 June 1863. William liked Francesca and tried to help, restoring High Head for them although he felt the marriage was 'a wretched connection'.

1864 was depressing. Leonard Edmunds, a family friend, had lived at 4 Grafton Street, and had held the combined jobs of Clerk of the Patent Office and Recorder of the House of Lords since 1852. Now he was gradually exposed as an embezzler of public money. At Edmunds' urging (he was in dispute with a colleague, Woodcroft) two Q.C.s, Hindmarsh and Greenwood were appointed to investigate the workings of the Patent Office in March 1864. They found that Edmunds had withheld money from the Treasury since 1852. He had bought £500-worth of stamps with public funds in 1853 and in 1863 got £500 from public funds as 'repayment' for this and kept it. He had purchased stamps at wholesale prices, selling them at retail prices. He had removed public money for his own use without keeping accounts of it and withheld from the Treasury £399 7s. 4d., another sum of £5,190 over 12 years, and £2,682 more in fees. This made a total of £7,872 unpaid. A further survey in September discovered that even after repaying £2,682 he still owed £9,617. His immediate dismissal was recommended to Lord Chancellor Westbury. Unfortunately the problem he posed was extremely complex. Edmunds could now do both Westbury and the Broughams great damage.

For Henry and William, Edmunds was a singularly disastrous person to trust. Baptised on 15 March 1802 as the son of John and Mary Edmunds, he had been virtually adopted as part of the family in 1826, when his father died working for it during the Westmorland Election. His advance under Lord Brougham's patronage was as swift as it was undeserved. He became Pursebearer (with a £460 yearly salary) and Secretary of the Commisioners (about £500 per annum) in 1830, Clerk of the Patents (in August 1833, with £400 per annum), Clerk of the Gown (with a £1,000 a year salary in 1848) and Clerk to the House of Lords (£1,500 per annum) in 1848. In October 1852 he was made Clerk to the Commissioners of Patents (at £600 per annum). The Commissioners included the Master of the Rolls, Lord Chancellor and other Crown law officers. Edmunds' complete unscrupulousness now directly damaged Lord Chancellor Westbury, supposed to supervise him and the Broughams who had advanced him.

Westbury had already made some questionable appointments to the Leeds Court of Bankruptcy since he took the Woolsack in June 1861 (including that of his spendthrift son the Hon. Richard Bethell, arrested for debt at Ascot on 15 December 1864). He was under much pressure. He unwisely allowed Edmunds to resign from the Patent Office on 7 August provided that he repaid the Patents money to the Treasury. Eventually at his and William's urging Edmunds resigned from his House of Lords job. In October 1864, Westbury secured Edmunds a £800 yearly pension from the House of Lords. At a Lords Select Committee he presented Edmunds' petition himself.

At this point, however, two events made the 'Edmunds scandal' erupt. Lord Brougham discovered Edmunds' fraud on the Treasury and threw him out of 4 Grafton Street. Then Lord Stanley, hearing rumours, asked the Attorney-General about the case. Westbury then had to ask a Lords Select Committee to examine the affair. This, sitting in March 1865 confirmed the earlier investigation's findings and axed Edmunds' pension. It censured Westbury's actions over the Leeds Bankruptcy Court and Edmunds cases by a vote of six to five. On 7 July 1865 Westbury resigned when a vote of censure was passed against him in the Commons by 14 votes.

Living in lodgings without regular income, Edmunds still had power to injure, and knew many of the Broughams' family secrets. He used a 1833 family legal agreement (to which he was a party) as a 'lever' against them. During the Lords Select Committee sittings in March 1865, William had insisted that Henry had not benefited financially from Edmunds' corruption (which included the removal of £6,670 2s. 11d. of public money in 1834-57 into his Coutts Bank account). Though the Committee believed Henry's word on this, both the Broughams and Edmunds knew that that was not true. In fact Edmunds had been paying £300 in annual contributions from his salary since 1833 to William. These went to pay off a £5,000 mortgage on Howes farm dating from 1811 and entered into by the hapless James, its owner. Made out to a Margaret Robinson, the mortgage had Henry, James and Mrs. Eleonora Brougham as signatories. Edmunds' life had also been insured for £3,000 so that the mortgage would be paid off in the event of his death. Henry (James' heir) had long owned the farm. Edmunds now claimed that they owed him a £5,000 mortgage. Using all this to blackmail them and owed money by William (£1,200 borrowed from him in 1845), Edmunds took William to the Chancery Court. James Leman (the Broughams' former solicitor) now helped Edmunds in the proceedings.

On 26 January 1865 Lord Chancellor Cranworth gave his judgement on the case of Edmunds v. William Brougham. This was that Lord Brougham (though he had blamelessly forgotten about the 1811 mortgage) had to pay £5,000 with interest accumulated since 24 June 1864. He also decided that William owed Edmunds £1,200 and that the widow and children of John Waugh Brougham could have a case against William. Money paid by Edmunds had ostensibly been destined for them. On 6 November 1866 William paid them £5,000!

In 1867, Edmunds succeeded in getting the £5,000 from the Broughams. He threatened to get Sir Dennis Le Marchant summoned in legal proceedings. It was clear to James Rigg Brougham that Le Marchant, who had witnessed an agreement between James, Henry and Edmunds in 1833 (when Edmunds on getting the job of Clerk of the Patents had promised to pay £300 a year to James for John Waugh's family) would give damaging evidence in court. James Rigg Brougham and Frederick Vane proposed a compromise. William approved. So, on 27 March an agreement with Edmunds' solicitor, Horace Earle, was signed, whereby the £5,000 was paid over and the incriminating documents destroyed in the presence of James Rigg Brougham and Earle. It appears that the money was paid to Edmunds. The matter did not end there, however.

There were other family difficulties. Henry Charles' absences from the Hall seemed selfish and insensitive. But he spent little: on 14 April 1863, William wrote in his diary that he had cost him only £470 in four years. William gave him a £100 yearly allowance and he had 'above £150 from his place'.

The Westmorland Militia absorbed William. On 25 June 1862, speaking at a Carlisle dinner, he criticised 'the shabby country gentlemen of Cumberland' for their niggardly support of it. Lord Lonsdale then offered a cup worth £50 and 10 guineas a year to the winner of the regiment's rifle competition; Sir Richard Tufton added £25. On 3 November 1863 William was made a Lieutenant-Colonel. However, on 17 March 1864 his mistaken offer of a Militia company to Wilfred produced a rash of officers' resignations. Wilfred, now unwell, had had a fit by 15 June. He was transferred to the 17th Lancers on 12 December 1865.

By mid-1864 Henry, angry and impatient, was getting progressively more difficult to live with.On 5 May William wrote: 'what a wretched ending all this portends – not only for himself but for all of us, who cannot escape him'.

William was genuinely pleased at becoming grandfather to Alice's first child in September and to Wilfred's son, Wilfred Francis. He was born in November and christened at St Wilfred's chapel on Christmas Day 1864. But Evelyn had now fallen for a Mr. Christiani, whose chief fault in William's eyes was that he was foreign. His possessive disapproval made Evelyn and Christiani communicate in cypher, and the relationship continued during 1865. William, annoyed at Evelyn's 'studied and determined deceit', had looked forward to her company in old age. But the strangest crisis came after Mary Ann, Lady Brougham died at Brighton on 12 January 1865. On 15 January Vane told William that Henry was now committed to a Sylvia Doyle! He was flabbergasted: '... if he refuses to marry her, she will give much trouble in writing and dunning for money'. Two friends, Colonel North and the Marquis of Douro, were keen to help and William wrote that if they married '... my course is plain. I shall at once shut up Brougham & take a place somewhere in the South, waiting till we are all set right by H.'s death. Seeing, knowing, or in any way recognising such a marriage is wholly impossible'.

The affair melted away, though Lord Brougham's health worsened with a mild stroke on 14 March. He could not bear solitude, but unfortunately Henry Charles was too often absent to keep him company. Things were now depressingly grim: Emily's health had worsened and Wilfred was usually in debt. In February 1866 Francis Sandys Dugmore, son of a Q.C., proposed to Evelyn. William loathed him and refused to consent to the marriage, but the engagement was announced on 7 April, and the couple were married on 23 April 1867.

The Broughams' biggest problem was Lord Brougham's health. By July 1866 he was getting weaker every month, while his nephews and nieces gradually departed from Brougham. In November 1866 William resigned his commission, perhaps to look after Emily and Henry. But with the family dispersed there were fewer visitors to the Hall.

Reading William's detailed, morbid account of Henry's decline is very depressing. It is enough to say that on 24 November 1866 he was too feeble for Garment to get him up the Hall's stairs. His bed was moved to the dining room. Later Henry's memory failed completely and he developed odd quirks, for example neglecting his personal hygiene. By the end of May 1867 Henry was totally disorientated, by mid-June unable to sign his name. On 10 August at 6 p.m. he arrived at Brougham, only being persuaded that his journey was over when the coachman had driven for some time around the courtyard. Leaving Brougham with a physician, Dr. Taylor, on 5 November, Henry was at Cannes at the start of 1868, his sole pleasures being eating and carriage driving. On Wednesday 6 May, when the family were about to leave by train, he was very weak. A physician, Dr. Dickinson, was called, advising William and Emily to delay travelling. William describes the next day:

> ... Thursday 7th. H. seemed so much better this morng. (altho' after the hottest night we have had 59°) that I went to the station & ordered the invalid carriage – He looked better than usual, at luncheon – but Garment said his weakness had manifestly increased – & Whiteley calling (not sent for) saw him & ordered some bitters – & a stimulant – I went to Whiteley at 2 – & found Dickinson there – on hearing that he (Whiteley) found the pulse very frequent, feeble and fluttering I was convinced it would not last many days & at once went to the Station & countermanded the Salon – at 6. H. dined & ate with appetite & Whiteley being with him before and during dinner, said he had rallied – that there was healthy moisture in the skin – & that all he thought unfavourable, was that the breathing was not quite free – still, on the whole, there was decided improvement – He went to bed before 9 only complaining of the fatigue of undressing – He fell asleep at once, & slept like an infant – before 11 E. on her way to bed, went into his room & her attention was called by Garment to the singular calmness of his rest – his hands laying gently on the coverlet. She observed him breathe twice rather heavily – but neither she nor anybody in [the] room thought it anything unusual – but it was his last breath – & thus ended a long, laborious, useful & well spent life; without pain discomfort or any human drawback.
>
> Knowing his objection to sending 'old bones' as he called it, all over the world, I decided to bury him here – a Public funeral in Westminster abbey is not to be thought of – & the alternative wd. have been Nine Churches – But on every account, he is better here–

The funeral took place at Cannes on 10 May. All the English and most of the French in Cannes, and many from the Var area, came. Sometime after 5 p.m., Mero, mayor of Cannes, made an oration. Then the mourners went bare-headed under blazing sun to the church through a dense crowd. Two ministers, Rolfe and a Mr. Acland, performed the ceremony. Rolfe, wrote William, gave a short eulogy of Henry, dwelling 'on H.'s affection for Cannes, the place he had almost created' rather than his personality and achievements, and all was over by six o'clock.

After another funeral on 24 May, Henry was buried in a plot of land given by Cannes' mayor and council. William designed a simple monument and cross for it. On 10 June William proved Henry's will, which left under £2,000. On 26 June, supported by Lords Dacre and Vaux of Harrowden, he took his seat in the Lords so that he could take part in the Irish Church Suspension Bill Division. On 21 July William was back at Brougham. Though he missed Henry, he had long since become his family's commander. But on the horizon lay fresh troubles, despite the calmness of the sea.

1. John Cropper, *Notes and Memories* (Bateman and Hewison, Kendal, 1900).
2. Whellan, *History of Cumberland and Westmorland* (1860), p.166.
3. *R.I.B.A. Journal of Proceedings*, 3 February 1887, obituary by Thomas M. Rickman, the son of Hussey's professional partner.
4. Splays: sloping, chamfered surfaces which widened windows by slanting their sides.

Chapter 8

William and Henry Charles 1868-1927

On 26 September 1863 William wrote wearily in his diary: 'AET: 68!!! It is dreadful to think of it, & so much still for me to do, before I can comfortably wind up everything, so as to leave all 1 day for Henry ...'. Henry Charles' career had been undistinguished so far. Before Lord Brougham died, however, he began an 'apprenticeship' under William, learning to manage the family affairs.

Henry Charles had a sheltered childhood and leisurely youth. Born on 2 September 1836, he was William's favourite son: William's diary records lavish celebrations of his 11th birthday in 1847. In the octagon room at Brougham the German table was decorated with flowers and wreaths. 'To the King of the Day' was written in ivy. Grapes were laid out, as were presents for Henry Charles, for example a watch from Lord Brougham. Once these were opened, the children danced the bolero and tarantella by the southern staircase. The servants then danced, supper followed, and then another dance of 12 masks. The party's highlight was William clanking down the Great Staircase in armour to join in.

Henry Charles' academic career was disappointing. In July 1848 a Mr. Golding, a master of his, told William that his son had '... no want of ability but intolerable care-lessness producing the greatest inaccuracy'. He was a pleasure-loving and sporty youth. In 1849 he entered Eton as Captain of the New Boys. In autumn 1851 Henry Charles started mathematics, Lord Brougham ensuring that he received special tuition in it (and indulgently overlooking an incident at Eton when he was caught stealing). In 1852 Henry Charles played cricket for Eton, the greatest achievement of his school career. In 1853, though, his laziness gave his father anxiety, and William reproached him about others doing his work. On 20 November Henry Charles denied this was so. He admitted he had help with verses but wrote, '... you are quite mistaken, since I have been at Eton, I have always done all my own work myself'.

In autumn 1856 Henry Charles entered Trinity College, Cambridge, failed 'prelims' and was 'plucked'. He decided to do the Civil Service Examination while receiving coaching in statics and dynamics. On 6 March 1857 he wrote to his father from Trinity, saying that he had just done the Charity Commission's examination. Two friends (one of them Frederick Vane) helped his studies, but in late May he expected to fail the regular college examination. On 7 June Henry Charles told William that with his C.S.C. certificate passed with credit, he was going to the House of Lords the next day to be appointed a clerk by Sir John George Shaw-Lefebvre, Clerk of the Parliaments. On 13 June he told Emily he liked his work at the Lords committee office 'exceedingly', had Vane as a colleague, and would soon become a Division Clerk.

Though he enjoyed London, Henry Charles was happiest in the country. His letters to William abound with references to hare-coursing. On 20 February 1858 he tells of his dog, Bat, so enthusiastic a chaser that after a race near Kendal he pursued a hare and was found three hours later near Shap, exhausted and ill! His letters also contain family news and gossip about Brougham. On 25 June 1858 he tells Emily of a dinner at 4 Grafton Street the previous day, attended by the Dukes of Newcastle and Wellington, Lord and Lady Stanley, Lords Broughton, Ashburton, Glenelg, and Alfred Montgomery. On 19 August he wrote to tell William that good progress had been made on Brougham's waterworks.

Henry Charles' position was enviable, with a secure income, and access to London social life and country houses. He played only a small part in family management: on 29 November 1859, he reported to William that the recent change at Brougham from board wages to housekeeping money for servants had given them 'more than universal satisfaction'. On 26 March 1860 he wrote about the legal position of timber on the estate of his grandfather, Sir Charles Taylor, Bt. (d. 1857), under the latter's will. Henry Charles took a close interest in Brougham's gardens, writing of the plant store house being built with Wetheriggs bricks (in November 1861), and asking (in February 1862) that William buy tuberous bulbs for Brougham.

William believed Henry Charles, 'excellent with money and indeed in all respects', needed a much better job to sustain the family finances.[1] So in 1861-2 he tried, and failed, to get him a Registrarship in Bankruptcy, and in June 1863 the combined posts of Clerk of the Patent Office and Recorder of the House of Lords. On 13 June 1864 he wrote in his diary:

> Finished my testamentary direction for Henry ... so that in the event of my death he will know exactly what to do – He will have (while his mother lives) £2,542 to pay out of an Income of about £6,000 a year – leaving him after Taxes and expenses £3,700 a year – but this will increase as people, such as Joyce, die – he will then, if no further additions are made have about £4,000 a year. This is little enough, considering the expenses at Brougham, wch. are almost unavoidable – & proves that he must get money when he marries.

But William described Henry on 27 November 1865 as '... eaten up with selfishness, never moves a finger to help anybody, or to lessen the intolerable bore H. has become'. He was often away at gatherings ranging from an Appleby masonic lodge meeting to Edenhall house-parties. On 21 January 1866, William wrote bitterly: 'If he cares for either his mother or me he takes every pain to conceal it – & I see that E. is terribly wounded by this'.

After Lord Brougham died, Henry Charles did not realise his duty straightaway. But William had many problems to face, such as his brother's autobiography. He worked on it at Brougham in August and September 1868, and negotiated its publication with Longmans, enlisting Lord Truro's help with the manuscript's preparation. Selling Thwaites Farm (originally bought for £1,150) on 4 November for £1,350, William left for London on 11 November. He wrote in his diary on 31 December 1869: 'Debts & liabilities & Dentist litigation all in H.'s account have cost me upwards of £10,000 – so that it will take another year to bring matters round'. He had let out his London home, 21 Berkeley Square, and spent much of 1869 in Italy. To diminish the anxiety of Wilfred's profligacy, his new will of 7 October 1869 omitted him. Eventually Wilfred was left £800 per annum 'if not otherwise bankrupt' on William's death.

William was prepared to be even more ruthless. On 11 January 1870 he wrote of:

> ... the grave alarm both E. & I have had, that Henry has got into a third scrape, by committing himself [to] that atrociously vulgar girl, Dickinson, the daughter of a Sodomite! The Schusters wrote about this some months ago – & lately the Lenox's [sic] have had letters from England stating that he is engaged to her! as some confirmation of this, the girl writes to him almost daily from Florence! but this Lady Arthur thinks proves nothing – as it has been her habit to do this when ever she cd. lay hold of any man – as in Darrell's case at Nice last year – E. spoke to Henry – who denies it – but remembering how far he went with Madelin Agnew & still more with Miss Cowper – I cannot but feel greatly alarmed – shd. this go on, I shall write to Gilbert Elliot – & if in spite of all I say, they marry, I must disinherit him.

Both Miss Dickinson and her mother wrote that they were engaged, but Henry Charles denied this and there was no marriage. In early 1871, William again heard of his being near marrying (whom it is not clear) but Henry coolly denied this on 16 March: 'As to my marriage I hardly know to what you allude – I have heard nothing about it'.

William was in Italy until late April 1870. His stay in Rome (£250 a month), two tutors for Reginald and 'Tib' (Adela Mary), and the journey from Cannes and back cost £1,190. On 27 June William travelled to England with Wilfred in worse trouble than ever: at least £2,857 in debt. By February 1871 Francesca was trying for a legal separation from him, allowing her to take one of their daughters. In Brougham's 1871 census entry, Wilfred appears as a 'lodger' with his three children: Wilfred (six), Mabel (five) and Eva (three). The separation was acrimonious. On 14 December 1877, Henry Charles wrote to William that 'Mrs. W.' (Francesca) was to '... pay £300 now £600 after Vignati's death to Trustees for the maintenance of the children, on condition he [Wilfred] does not correspond with, or molest her. Considering what her income is I think this arrangement very liberal'.

Henry Charles' role in the family now increased. William spent most of his time at Brougham or Cannes. No. 21 Berkeley Square was let out from 1869 to February 1871, and in 1876 William was trying to let it again. In London Henry Charles kept an eye on his brothers and sisters, and in crises liaised with the astute James Rigg Brougham. He spent more time at Brougham, and by 1871 he was a J.P. in the Penrith Leath Ward division.

The Edmunds affair took a long time to die. It had already done real damage to the Broughams' reputation and rumbled on. On 21 November 1869, arbitrators decided that Edmunds still owed the Crown £8,544 18s. (including £3,033 16s. from fees and emoluments). His animus against the Broughams continued. In 1870 Edmunds published a 120-page book *The Case of Leonard Edmunds and The Crown* (price 3d.) attacking them. He was then languishing in Whitecross Street Prison. In the summer of 1872 he tried court action in the Queen's Bench, Westminster, against the Liberal politicians Gladstone, Robert Lowe and James Stansfield, for alleged libel in a treasury minute of 1871. Embarrassingly, William's diaries for 1863 and 1864 were subpoenaed by Chief Justice Sir Alexander Cockburn, Bt. He had to produce them and appear at proceedings on 13 June. But Edmunds' action failed (as did those he took against London newspapers) and he seems to have played no further part in Brougham family history.

In early August 1876 Sir Charles William Taylor, 2nd Bt., lay ill at Beaufort on the Welsh border. Lady Taylor sent Henry Charles a telegram: 'Your uncle is better though not out of danger – Most undesirable that anybody should see him: will write fully'. But he soon died. On 2 September Henry Charles told William of his arrangements for Hollycombe in Sussex. Henry Charles was paying annuities to Lady Taylor's old servants, and the jointure (a sole estate limited to the wife for her own life, taking effect on her husband's death) on the estate, of £1,200 a year. The land was under let and he was communicating with the agent, Mr. Garrod. Henry had told James Rigg Brougham that he wanted him to act for him. On 20 September Henry Charles wrote that he was going to Wells to negotiate an agreement with the Taylors' Somerset tenants who had been served with notice to quit. He was thinking of taking 18 Charles Street, Berkeley Square.

William's health worsened. In early summer 1873 he had become lame for a while after a fall at Cannes, and in early July 1878 (aged 82) he was suffering from a hernia and giddiness. William was not helped in May 1877 by having to pay Reginald's debts, beyond those Reginald could pay himself. But these small problems were probably outweighed by satisfaction at seeing the Brougham estates larger and more prosperous than ever. The

Taylor estates in 1876 doubled his landholdings, adding another 2,716 acres in Somerset and nine acres in Hampshire, valued at £4,587 per annum, in 1883.[2] In the last week of July 1877 James Rigg Brougham invested another £11,000 for William in the Metropolitan Railway, at a three and a half per cent return with a first dividend payable that October.

There were further minor developments at Brougham. In 1869 William bought £11 of glass from Salviati's, a shop in Venice. In 1878 he tried and failed to buy Brougham Castle from Lord Tufton. By 1877 he had also created Brougham's cricket ground in the field below St Wilfred's chapel. William had his own team, taking a proprietory interest. On 29 September 1877, he wrote in his diary, '... by the help of the darkness we beat the Penrith players – a black-guard fellow called Bewley, a cabinet maker, put out 3 of our men most unfairly – so had notice that he is never to come upon the ground again'. The first match between Cumberland and Westmorland was played there in 1879.

By the mid-1880s William's children had established themselves. Alice and Evelyn had moved away from Brougham and Wilfred was in London. Reginald had married Augusta Louisa Ward in February 1884. By 1886 he was an engineer and partner in Mackenzie & Brougham, 'consulting & electric light engineers & electricians' of 15 Great George Street, London, S.W.1. By 1878 Henry Charles was living at 18 Charles Street, Berkeley Square. In April 1885 William's favourite daughter, 'Tib', married the

40. Emily, Lady Brougham (1812-84).

barrister Charles Archer Cook. The absence of Tib and Emily's death in 1884 may have weakened William's will to live. On 3 January 1886 he died at Brougham, aged ninety.

In his will, proved on 15 February 1886, William left £116,165. In 1883 he had had some 5,076 acres of farmland valued at £7,138 per annum. Of this, 1,369 acres were in Cumberland and 985 in Westmorland, worth £905 and £1,646 per annum respectively. He had the Somerset and Hampshire land mentioned above, property in Sussex and London and interests in the Eden Valley Railway. He had an impressive set of houses: Brougham, Scales, High Head, and Château Eleanore-Louise.

Henry Charles' approach to management was neither the entrepreneur's nor the squire-farmer's. But he was, dour, intelligent and practical. In 1891, *World* magazine wrote of him that '... under a somewhat reserved exterior is concealed a deep fund of feeling and humour ... there are few men whose conversation is better worth listening to, or whose judgement is more trustworthy'. Few of Brougham's owners have loved it as Henry Charles did. One of his retainers commented that 'Nothing suited him better than to sit quietly in the shade of some of the trees by the lawn. He often said to me 'Brougham is my home ...'. He preferred it to London.

Henry Charles immersed himself deeply in local activities, later becoming a Deputy-Lieutenant of Westmorland. His interests included dog-breeding, and he was a Steward in the 1882 Brougham Hare-Coursing Trials. These awarded the Brougham Cup. Interested in wood-turning, he frequently visited Robert Pletts' Penrith workshop. Sir Richard Courtenay Musgrave, 11th Baronet, and his wife 'Zoë' (Adora Francis Olga), from Edenhall, were his close friends. A lively, attractive woman of 33, Zoë was the daughter of Peter Wells of Forest Farm, Windsor Forest, Berkshire and Adora Julia, daughter of Sir John Lethbridge, 3rd Bt. She was devoted to Sir Richard, having married in January 1867, when she was 19 and he twenty-eight. He wrote to her on 17 January 1873, their sixth marriage anniversary: 'Every year you are dearer to me and I hope we may have many happy years together. Without you life would be a blank'. When he died prematurely, aged 42, on 13 February 1881, leaving Zoe with their six children, Henry Charles' life was transformed.

On 18 April 1882, after a courtship springing from shared loss, Henry Charles married Zoë at St Paul's church, Knightsbridge. Now 45, he became stepfather to her Musgrave children, Dorothy (b. 1869), Zoë (b. 1871), Richard George (b. 1872, later the 12th Musgrave baronet), Philip (b. 1873), Thomas (b. 1875) and Joan (b. 1879). He also became guardian and master of Edenhall, a fine mansion designed by Sir Robert Smirke. In 1883 its horticultural genius, head gardener Busby, moved to Château Eleanore-Louise. When Henry Charles inherited the Brougham estates (whose executor he was), he became 3rd Lord Brougham and Vaux, in February 1886. He and Zoë had two children, Eleanor Mabel Valentine, born on 14 February 1883 and Henry, born on 26 May 1887.

Henry Charles was a conventional aristocrat. Giving up his House of Lords clerkship on inheriting, he took part in its debates as a Liberal Unionist. One writer noted that he spoke little, devoting 'his best abilities to committee work, where his experience, tact and good sense are of real service'. By 1891, when *World* magazine profiled him as an unlikely celebrity, he was also a noted shorthorn breeder and 'diligent and much valued member' of the Royal Agricultural Society. He spent two or three months a year in London at 36 Chesham Place, entertaining there a great deal. He was a member of Brooks' and Arthur's Clubs by 1894 and later the Marlborough, Bachelors' and Garrick Clubs. He spent winters with Zoë at Cannes where his neighbours included a close friend, the Count of Paris, King Louis-Philippe's grandson (later exiled by the French government). The Brougham Hall visitors' book for 1888-1915 shows that late summer or autumn were

41.   Henry Charles, 3rd Lord Brougham (1836-1927).

42. Zoë, Lady Brougham (1849-1925).

passed at Brougham, when house-guests were invited. By 1891 he was spending two months a year at Edenhall during Richard Musgrave's minority. This ended in mid-November 1893.

Henry Charles had a few obsessions, like real tennis. He proudly maintained that Brougham's court was 'the exact mean' of those at Hampton Court, Paris and London. He and Zoë bred dogs, and took two black poodles everywhere. Another sporting interest was fishing, and Henry travelled frequently to fish salmon at Mertoun Water near St Bothwells, rented from Lord Polwarth.[3] He was a great china collector, buying the deceased Earl of Airlie's fine collection of silver and Dresden china in 1881. Sèvres china soon adorned Brougham's Armour Hall. Henry supplied gravitas and steadiness, and Zoë, an accomplished socialite who loved china and flowers, brought charm and new connections.

Architectural changes at Brougham were subtle and insubstantial. So much had been done by William that there was little more to do, and Henry Charles was no student of architecture. Judge Hills' wanting High Head to live in, rather than to demolish, baffled him. So, naturally, changes at the Hall were few. In 1892, he spent £164 on a new window and casements in the print room. In 1895, he ordered a new housekeeper's room, window and cistern for £78. In 1902, he built a new dining room window for £130 and made other small changes in the following year.

Henry did, however, make considerable alterations to Brougham's gardens and park. By 1891, Zoë was growing winter cherries and anemone japonicas in the kitchen gardens. Peaches and grapes were also grown, while the Brougham irises gained an international reputation. In 1897 new machinery was built to pump water from the River Lowther to the gardens and in 1899 new byres were built. Ordnance Survey maps show other changes, too. The 1900 map shows three garden buildings in a line parallel to the north of the avenue, as one left the Hall from the guardhouse gate, with walled pleasure gardens in front of them. The 1920 map shows two new rectangular blocks, in front of the middle garden building.

According to Arnison's 1908 schedule of the estate, the Hall grounds (including a 17th-century sundial, and a fountain) covered 5 acres, 0 rods and 30 perches and the gardens 2 acres, 2 rods and 15 perches. The area of the deer park, once full of wapiti, fallow and red deer, was 25 acres, 3 rods and 7 perches. By the end of 1897 it was empty and the heads of some Brougham deer were in the armour hall. The big park, 61 acres, 1 rod and 37 perches was dominated by three large sweeps of trees, by the road to Lowther Bridge, by the ride from Clifton Cross to the Hall's south wall, and the great avenue of oaks leading up to the Hall's two north wall entrances.

The 1866 and 1899 Ordnance Survey maps reveal other changes. On the 1866 map a ride comes from the direction of the greenhouses into the arched tower of the stable courtyard, but this is not shown on the 1899 map. A dogs' cemetery was added in 1891 near the chapel. Its headstones had Latin inscriptions. *World* magazine piously recorded that of Punch, a pug: *Hujus domus nuper spes et solatium; nunc desiderium* (He who was recently the hope and solace of this house has now become its loss).

Henry Charles had neither the active, inquisitive genius of Henry nor the obsessive cleverness of William. Wanting to forget the past, he refused to let Aspinall examine the family papers, saying he had seen none of any value. He summed up his approach to the estates in brusque advice to Mr. W. Bainbridge, a former Brougham cowman, made Estate Bailiff[4] in 1900: 'Farm as you like. You know the farm better than I do myself. I farm for pleasure, but remember there is no pleasure in losing money'. Henry Charles knew his limitations, realising that the cardinal sin of landowning is spending thoughtlessly.

Some sixty indoor staff were on hand in the Hall itself. Mainly maids from the south, they worked seven days a week, and had to be in by 9.30 p.m. Paid £1 a month with free food, they (and every estate family) got firewood and a free roast of beef at Christmas. With efficient catering, Henry Charles could play host to London society in late summer and early autumn. He and Zoë were helped by the Hall's splendour, its nearness to Clifton and Lowther railway station and its position on one of the main roads to Scotland.

The Brougham Hall visitors' book for 1888-1915 records celebrities such as Lord Curzon of Kedleston (Viceroy of India and Foreign Secretary) in 1910, the 'Yellow' Earl of Lonsdale in 1889, James W. Lowther (later Speaker of the House of Commons and 1st Viscount Ullswater) in 1890 and the writer W. F. Rawnsley (1899 and 1900). Other local gentry came: Alice, Countess of Bective (of Underlay Hall, near Carlisle); the Grahams of Netherby; Lord and Lady Hothfield; the Markhams of Morland; and the Musgraves. Aristocracy arrived from further afield, including the Duke and Duchess of Argyll, the Earls of Sefton and Craven, Earl Howe, Lords Dorchester, Elphinstone, Barnard, Lough-borough, Baring and Somerton. Other visitors were Sir Bache Edward Cunard, 3rd Bt. (d. 1925), his wife Lady Maud Alice Cunard, and Sir Archibald Edmonstone, 5th Bt., C.V.O. (1867-1954), Groom-in-waiting to Edward VII from 1907 and his wife,

43.   The terrace front of Brougham viewed from the chapel side in 1899.

Lady Ida Edmonstone, later a Woman of the Bedchamber to Queen Victoria's daughter, H.R.H. Princess Helen (1846-1923) (also known as Princess Christian of Schleswig-Holstein). The Edmonstones came to Brougham between 1889 and 1910.

Broughams also visited: Diana Brougham (nèe Sturt) (in 1908 and 1910); Reginald Brougham (1890 and 1893), and Adela and her husband Sir Charles Archer Cook (from 1888 to 1907). But while Wilfred and Henry Charles' daughter Eleanor lived long periods at Brougham, Henry Charles' sisters Alice Eleanora (d. 1924) and Emily Evelyn (d. 1919) are notably absent from the visitors' book. But Zoë's daughters drew new visitors: Dorothy Musgrave married Henry Compton, M.P. of Minstead Manor, Hampshire. They came frequently from 1895 onwards. Zoë Musgrave married the very rich Aberdeenshire landowner Alex Farquharson, 14th Laird of Invercauld (1867-1936), a neighbour of the Royal Family at Balmoral. They, their children, Myrtle and Sylvia, and other Farquharsons came. Thomas and Edith Yorke visited between 1888 and 1892. But the greatest mark of approval came from royalty.

King Edward VII's visit in 1905 was a highlight of Brougham's history and Henry Charles' tenure. It is unclear exactly which of the Broughams' friends or relations drew the Royal Family to it. There were links: Eleanor Harbord, a Lady-in-waiting to Princess Victoria, married Zoë's son, Sir Richard George Musgrave, 12th Bt., Zoe's brother, Dr. Arthur Poulett Lethbridge Wells (who visited Brougham in 1890) lived at 48 Belsize Square, London, practising as a doctor at 83 Harley Street. In March 1889, he was treating 'Algie' (Alexander, Duke of Athlone) and his sister, Princess Victoria Mary of Teck (later Queen Mary and George V's consort). Dr. Wells' father, Peter Wells, had been a friend of Mary Adelaide, Duchess of Teck (Victoria Mary's mother) since at least 1887 and was invited to Victoria Mary and George's wedding breakfast at Buckingham Palace on 5 July 1893.

There was a trickle of Royal visitors to Brougham: George was the first, in September 1892; then Albert Edward in September 1894; then George again (October 1896); Mary Adelaide and her husband the Duke of Teck (October 1897); Alexander George of Teck ('Algie') on 8 October 1897; his sister, Princess Victoria Mary (30 August 1900); and brother Prince Francis of Teck ('Frank'). The most important and last royal visitor recorded in the book was King Edward VII.

The visit began on Thursday 14 October 1905. After the king had stayed two weeks at Balmoral, the royal train left Ballater Station at 9.50 a.m. that day, arriving at Carlisle at 4.06 p.m. to the cheering of thousands of onlookers. Policemen were on duty on the sealed off platform. A party of railway officials attended, including Sir Frederick Harrison, London and North-Western Railway's general manager. Driven by the engine *Aurania*, the royal train set off for Clifton and Lowther station. The platform had been covered with red carpet, the rails with red and white material, and a red and white canvas awning stretched from the entrance gate to the platform edge. Under this canopy there was a fine display of hanging baskets and exotic plants provided by Mr. Isaac Relph, of Herd Bros., Victoria Nurseries, Penrith. The road to Lowther was lined with Cumberland and Westmorland policemen, marshalled by Mr. C. de Courcy Parry, Chief Constable of both counties.

Lord Brougham had waited at Clifton and Lowther Station since 4.20 p.m., arriving in an open 'Sociable', driven by his coachman, William Walker. Two other carriages awaited the king's arrival. The king's two plum-coloured Mercedes (40 and 20 horse-power) had been driven down from Balmoral the previous day. The *Wordsworth* engine shunted the king's train in front of the awning at 4.45 p.m.. King Edward got out, was greeted by Lord Brougham, and got into the open-topped carriage. A policeman, Sergeant Phillips, led the way on a charger. The royal carriage followed. Then the court officials, Major-

44. Edward VII at Brougham Hall in 1905: others left to right are Lady Brougham, Mrs. Keppel and Eleanor Brougham

General Sir Stanley de A. C. Clarke, and the Hon. Sydney R. Greville, came after in an open carriage, the Chief Constable bringing up the rear. Receiving a warm reception they went to Clifton Cross, past Brougham Home Farm and Lodge, and into the Hall courtyard.

The king was welcomed by Zoë and Eleanor Brougham, and photographed by Mr. G. Reed of Penrith. An official message was sent to London by a specially built phone line from the Hall to Eamont Bridge: 'His Majesty's slight cold is passing away. It does not prevent him travelling, and keeping engagements. Equerry-in-waiting'. The house party at the Hall (ringed by policemen) consisted of the king's friends and officials, including Lord Elphinstone, Sir Archibald Edmondstone, the Hon. Mrs. George Keppel, the Hon. Mrs. Ronald Greville, Mrs. Vyner, Sir Stanley Clarke, the Hon. Sydney Greville and Eleanor Brougham.

Friday was fine and the king visited Raby Castle at Staindrop, on the first royal motor journey in Cumbria. After being photographed by Charles Fearnsides of Penrith, the king and Mrs. Keppel got into his 40 horse-power Mercedes. Clarke and Lord Brougham drove the king's small car. Lady Brougham, Eleanor and the others used two more cars, with an additional emergency one provided. The Chief Constable had placed 60 police-men at the Hall and at every road junction, corner and bridge between Brougham and Stainmore (the county boundary). The County Surveyor, Mr. J. Bintley, had organised the sweeping away of all stones from the 40 miles of road over which the royal motorcade would pass, up to the border with Yorkshire.

At 11.25 a.m. Lord Brougham's car left the Hall and the rest followed, going towards Temple Sowerby and Kirkby Thore. They drove through Appleby, where all work was cancelled and the church bells were rung, and just after 12 o'clock entered Brough, where a brass band played the national anthem. Then they went up Stainmore (1,500 ft. in six miles), through Startforth and Stainton, reaching Staindrop just after 1.00 p.m. At Raby Castle the king and his party lunched with Lord and Lady Barnard, her sister Lady Louisa Cecil, and Colonel and Lady Catherine Vane. He left after two and a half hours, at 3.20 p.m. Amid 'glorious sunset' he travelled back to Brougham Hall, reached at 5.30 p.m. Before dinner he made Lord Brougham a K.C.V.O. (Second Class) and presented a Victorian medal each to his lordship's house steward John Hodgson and coachman, William Walker.

On Saturday morning, after his visit to the Brougham shorthorns was cancelled, the king and his party had to leave. He liked the Hall's terrace, which reminded him of Windsor Castle's. Promising to return, he took his leave of Zoë and Eleanor Brougham at 11.20 a.m. The king left in his 40 horse-power Mercedes for Clifton and Lowther railway station, where the same preparations as for his arrival had been made, with Sir Frederick Harrison again in charge. The Lord Lieutenant of Westmorland, Lord Hothfield, the Chief Constable of Cumberland and Westmorland and Lord Brougham bade him goodbye. The king and his party left, reaching Euston at 5.05p.m.. Though it had been an arduous public relations exercise, the Hall and the Brougham family had never received a better compliment.

Magnificence can deceive. The Broughams owned an impressive amount of property, but it provided a disappointing income. Their management, too, left something to be desired. Henry Charles did not have a close eye for detail: the Brougham estate papers, now at University College, London, are very extensive until 1886 but then tail off markedly. The estate did not grow much after the Taylor lands came to the Broughams in 1876. Although they had minor commercial property, such as Wetheriggs Pottery (prospering under the Schofields and Thorburns, related dynasties of potters, from the 1860s) and the estate saw-mill just north of Brougham, these and the urban property

45. Captain Hon. Henry Brougham (1887-1927): the heir who never inherited.

were not developed. The next generation would have to manage and develop them if the family was to prosper.

The heir was the Hon. Henry Brougham. On 13 July 1908 he married Diana Isabel Sturt at St Paul's church, Knightsbridge. She was 24, he twenty-one. She was the eldest daughter of Humphrey Napier Sturt, 2nd Baron Alington and Feodorovna Yorke, eldest daughter of Charles Yorke, 5th Earl of Hardwicke. Made K.C.V.O. in 1908, Alington was M.P. for Dorset East from 1891-1904. In 1904 he had inherited the title and around 17,500 acres in Devon and Dorset (worth £24,000 a year in 1883), a valuable estate in Hoxton, Middlesex, and the fine Crichel House near Wimborne, Dorset. Both Diana and Henry were talented. She served the Red Cross Society in both World Wars, gaining an O.B.E. in 1919 and worked as a staff officer from 1939-49. Educated at Eton from 1901 onwards, Henry, a career soldier, had joined the Coldstream Guards in 1907 and was a Captain in the Coldstream Guards Special Reserve in the First World War. His health may have been poor and in 1917 he had a serious operation. He became at some stage a Knight of Grace of the Order of St John. Despite three children, Victor Henry Peter (b. 1909), Eileen Millicent Eva (b. 1912) and Anthony Charles (b. 1915), the marriage failed. In 1919 it was dissolved on Diana's petition, a decree nisi later being made absolute on 13 January 1920.[5]

The Hon. Henry Brougham was little involved in management of the estate and lived at Lansdown Place, Hove, and 10 Oxford Square, London. Gregarious, he had four London clubs – White's, the Carlton, Pratt's, and St James'. Diana was also little involved with the Brougham estate and in 1910 she signed the visitors' book. In June 1931, her daughter Eileen signed the book for the first time. On 24 April 1923, in Budapest, Henry married an Austrian, Micheline, Baroness Hengelmüller, daughter of Ladislaus, Baron Hengelmüller von Hengevar. (Her family had been ennobled in November 1859, when Michael Hengelmüller, a King's Councillor, and son of Franz Hengelmüller (1806-41), a butcher in Enns, Austria, was made Lord von Hengevar. The title was inherited by his son Ladislaus Hengelmüller, a Doctor of Law, an Imperial and Royal Councillor and Austro-Hungarian ambassador to the United States. In December 1906, he was granted a Hungarian peerage and became Baron Hengelmüller von Hengevar.)[6] Henry's second marriage was childless.

Henry Charles must have been relieved that his son escaped the First World War alive, but he had a severe blow when, on 17 December 1925, Zoë died in Middlesex. She was not wealthy, leaving only £368, but she had given Brougham and Henry Charles happiness and gaiety. As 1927 drew on, the 90-year-old Henry Charles sickened, too. In 1934, the Hall's last disconsolate retainer, the caretaker and handyman, Mr. H. Clark of James Street, Penrith said: 'I remember him leaving Brougham for the last time. His Penrith doctor went with him from Brougham to London, and all the way down the drive his Lordship waved his hand as if in farewell to Brougham'.

1. William Brougham's diary, 31 December 1859.
2. In George Edward Cockayne's *The Complete Peerage* (1912), p. 343.
3. Walter Hugh Hepburne-Scott, 8th Baron Polwarth (1838-1920) succeeded to the title in 1867 and lived at Harden, Roxburghshire.
4. Bainbridge stayed until 1920, living at Brougham Home Farm, representing Lord Brougham in the Penrith Association of Shorthorn Breeders, and becoming a member of Westmorland County Council in 1918.
5. Diana died in June 1967.
6. This is according to *Adelslexikon Band* Vol. V (1984). Ladislaus, Baron Hengelmüller wrote *Hungary's fight for National Existence, or the History of the Great Uprising led by Francis Rakoczi II, 1703-1711* (1914). He was dead by 1927.

Chapter 9

High Head (1820-1956): Grandeur and Neglect

In 1820 Henry Brougham purchased from Robert Baynes' executors his moiety (share) of High Head Castle and manor.[1] The financial advantage gained was small. In addition, the castle's history over the previous 71 years had been strewn with squabbles against a backcloth of increasing dereliction. It looked a far from promising situation.

After Henry Richmond Brougham's death in 1749, his executor, John Gale of White-haven (bap. 1730, d. 1814), a merchant and sometime High Sheriff of Cumberland, had lived in half the house. Susanna Richmond, an unmarried daughter of Isabella Richmond (d. 1739), lived in the other half, held by her as 'tenant for life'. When she died, aged 87 in 1774, it was abandoned. Neither her executor Isabella Curwen[2] (John Gale's sister), her husband, Henry Curwen of Workington Hall (d. 1778), nor their trustees did much to prevent a series of legal battles over it. These, between John Gale[3] and Robert Baynes of Cockermouth (d. 1789), eventually reached the Court of Chancery. They made the house uninhabitable and reinforced its division, splitting the 18th-century building and even the drive in two. Meanwhile, the castle stagnated. In the eighth edition of Daniel Defoe's *Tour Through The Island of Great Britain* (1778), William Hutchinson moralised gloomily on Henry Richmond Brougham's '... lessening his estate in building a superb mansion, the upper part of which was soon to be inhabited by the birds of the air, and the lower apartments by noxious animals, which tear each other to pieces for want of better prey'.

This ridiculous situation was unchanged when Robert Baynes left his share of High Head in trust to John Birkett of Portinscale and his heirs on his death in 1789. Around 1800, High Head was used as a storehouse and granary. In 1803 Birkett leased the Baynes moiety ('All that part of the Old Tower or old House adjoining to the New House called Highhead Castle ... and the Dove Coat') to one George Bell for £166 per annum in rent.[4] Though Henry Brougham managed to purchase this share in 1820, the rest of the estate proved elusive. He did not lose interest, though. According to an 1826 entry in James Losh's *Diaries*,[5] Henry wanted to buy it, but the owner (Thomas Richmond-Gale-Braddyll of Conishead Priory) had no power to sell because of the entail of Isabella Miller's will. Apparently a visit by Henry Brougham and his friend John Temple Leader M.P. to High Head in mid-October 1839 ended in the carriage accident from which it was rumoured Henry spun the tales of his own death.

By the late 1820s High Head was a farmhouse. But this did not prevent its decay. On 27 July 1846 William Bragg, Steward to Colonel Braddyll's estates, reported to his master that he had met the tenants, Mr. George Rayson and Miss Blamire, there earlier that week. He wrote: 'I ... at their parlous desire went thro' and over all the buildings and land. The buildings are in a state of utter ruin ...'.[6] Though the land was in good order, the income gained from the Richmond-Gale-Braddyll share, the land opposite Broad Bank, was probably not very big. The Broughams' income from theirs was not large either. In 1848 they owned 216 acres, 2 rods and 27 perches of land. Their tenant, a Mr. Jefferson, paid an annual rent of £230. The 1851 census records that John Thornbarrow and his wife Peggy (both 55) occupied High Head with their unmarried children (six sons and a daughter ranging in age from 10 to 33) and their maidservant, one Jane Armstrong (20). The castle was surrounded by a small farm of 207 acres.

46. The Braddyll Family (1789) by Sir Joshua Reynolds. Left to right are: Wilson Gale Braddyll (1756-1818) of Conishead Priory, Lancashire; Jane Braddyll (d. 1819) his wife; and their son, Thomas Gale (later Thomas Richmond-Gale-Braddyll) (1776-1862).

In July 1853 the Richmond-Gale-Braddylls threatened to demolish High Head. William Brougham immediately obtained an injuction preventing this. On 30 November he wrote of the subsequent legal adjudication in his diary: '... we get the half castle & all the ground about it, amounting to 1¾ acres & given 11½ acres of bad land at a distance'. Exchanging land for the castle, William Brougham finally acquired the Richmond-Gale-Braddyll 'moiety' of High Head Castle and estate.[7] On 21 April 1854 the deeds to High Head were signed and sealed. The same day William Brougham acquired land in the parish of Dalston from Frances, Margaret Frederica and Sarah Jane Braddyll, spinsters, and Clarence Braddyll, Esq. What followed, however, was an anticlimax.

In 1854, on acquiring the second half of the castle, William Brougham blocked a window in the Tudor wing and cut a door through a blocked window. Some restoration was done to make the main block habitable, though in 1858 panelling was removed from the castle to Brougham Hall. The family's continuing interest in the castle is evinced by the proud alteration of Henry's title from 'Baron Brougham and Vaux of Brougham, Westmorland' to 'Baron Brougham and Vaux of Brougham and High Head Castle, Cumberland', in March 1860. In 1862 William Brougham purchased nearby Beacon Hill Farm for £1,800. But High Head remained a tenanted farmhouse.

This state of affairs did not have to continue. In 1863, William Brougham tried to return it to a country mansion. His diary tells how his decision to restore High Head was precipitated by his footloose and extravagant son Wilfred's announcement, in March 1863, that he was marrying Francesca Vignati, a none-too-wealthy Irish-Italian girl in May. On 18 April William wrote that at High Head it was '... practicable to put 4 or 5 rooms into habitable repair & he [Wilfred] may live here & *agitate* on £750 a year – what a future to look to! at barely 21! It is a wretched business ...'. Wilfred, then a 2nd Lieutenant. in the 10th Light Dragoons, resigned his commission later that month, and got married the next. But by mid-September work was well advanced, with the stonework nearly done and plain plasterwork nearly complete. By 24 December the bill for repairs stood at £900: £260 for masons' work, £400 for carpentry and £240 for plastering and work on the dining room ceiling. High Head now stood ready to be revived. Unfortunately, this did not happen. On 25 September 1868, William wrote in his diary of settling 'the Dining Room Chimney Pannel and the apple tree planting in the Garden ...'. But despite all the work no Brougham lived in it, and an excellent opportunity to renew High Head was lost.

William, 2nd Lord Brougham, died aged 91 in January 1886. In his will he made his eldest son, Henry Charles (b. 1836), first tenant for life of High Head. Like so many second country houses, High Head now became a likely candidate to be sold off, since the Brougham family now relied heavily on farms in Somerset, Cumberland and Westmorland. In the face of agricultural depression from 1870s onwards, retrenchment was likely and common.

Renting country houses was particularly popular from *c.*1870 to the First World War. Many, where there was good shooting, fishing or hunting had declined to the status of summer lets. Beatrix Potter's photographer father, Rupert Potter, easily obtained Lake District mansions like Wray Castle and Fawe Park, near Windermere, to rent for his holidays. Other visitors, falling in love with the surrounding landscape, wanted to stay more permanently. One such was Herbert Augustus Hills, a Judge of the International Courts of Appeal in Alexandria, Egypt.

Hills had a somewhat idiosyncratic background. Born in 1837, the only son of John Hills, Recorder of Rochester, he had been called to the Bar in 1864 after taking a degree at Balliol College, Oxford. Later his career flourished in the unlikely setting of Egypt, then a British vice-royalty. From 1875 to 1882, Hills was Judge of First Instance of the

International Tribunals, then Judge of the International Courts of Appeal in Alexandria from 1882 to 1894. Attracted by country house life in England, he became tenant of Corby Castle, Cumberland, in the early 1890s. He was well liked in the area and became a local J.P. His eldest son, Brigadier-General Edmond Herbert Grove-Hills, C.M.G. (b. 1864), strengthened these local ties by marrying Juliet, youngest daughter of local squire James Spencer-Bell of Fawe Park, Keswick. Judge Hills' wealth seems to have come from his legal career and his wife Anna, the daughter of the wealthy judge and physicist, the Rt. Hon. Sir William Grove Q.C., P.C., F.R.S. (1811-96). The couple fell for and decided to buy High Head Castle.

After Henry Charles had agreed to sell High Head to Hills in mid-September 1902, events moved swiftly. On 20 November Hills' solicitor wrote to Lord Brougham's:

> Since completion is so near and it is only delayed by reason of the absence of Mr. James in France would you allow Judge Hills' builder to have possession of the House on Monday next? Mrs. Hills is anxious for work to begin so that the house can be ready for occupation by the Summer.[8]

On 26 November the sale, by private treaty, was completed. Judge Hills paid £18,000 for the castle along with two other estates (one of them Beacon Side) which had been entailed on Henry Charles by his father, William, 2nd Lord Brougham. So the tenants, farmer Thomas William Armstrong and Joseph Wilson moved out. The builder, William Grisenthwaite of Penrith, started work.

Using designs by local architect J. H. Martindale F.R.I.B.A., Hills made only minor modifications in existing work, restoring the rest. He introduced new wooden entrance gates made of corkscrew uprights and in two pieces. They were modelled on those at the poet Dryden's family seat, Canons Ashby, Northamptonshire. Hills made no outstanding alteration to the 18th-century block. He did two minor things, though, which much improved the look of the castle. One was to complete the north wing, finishing off the work facing the entrance drive and adding a balustrade, thus making it uniform with the rest. Up against it he built a small, squat servants' wing with a roof at the main block's first floor level. The front entrance side he embellished with his coat of arms and the inscription 'H.A.H. 1903' above. Hills made other changes in the castle grounds, which must have been a mess. He replaced a wilderness between the entrance gates and the front door with a charming rose garden. He also got Grisenthwaite to build an entrance lodge, designed by Martindale, at the head of the drive. Within a year, Hills had turned High Head back into a country mansion, injecting the necessary resources.

On 11 November 1907, Judge Hills died at High Head. He left the castle not to his eldest son Edmond but to his second son, John Waller ('Jack') Hills. Jack Hills was easily the most dynamic and interesting man to live in the castle since its 18th-century rebuilding. Born in 1867, he was educated at Eton and Balliol College, Oxford. Qualifying later as a solicitor, he practised as a partner in his firm Hills, Halsey and Lightly in London. When he inherited High Head he was M.P. for Durham City. This he had won by standing as a tariff reformer in 1906. His opponent was a Unionist Free Trader, Arthur Elliot. A Liberal Unionist, Elliot had resigned as Financial Secretary to the Treasury in September 1903. In January 1905, Hills was adopted as Conservative and Unionist candidate and Elliot was disowned. Hills, in addition had the support of the formidable Colonial Secretary Joseph Chamberlain, supporter of tariff reform and 'imperial preference'.

47.   Mrs. Anna Hills at High Head Castle.

48.   John Waller Hills, M.P. (1867-1938).

The historian Professor Richard Rempel wrote in *Unionists Divided: Arthur Balfour, Joseph Chamberlain and the Unionist Free Traders* (1972):

> In the struggle to capture the Liberal Unionist party, Chamberlain had found Elliot a most determined foe. To destroy Elliot, Chamberlain sent one of the most gifted tariff reformers, Jack Hills, to contest the Elliot seat at Durham. In the *National Review* of January 1906 Maxse described 'the direst confrontation of Tariff Reform and free trade' at Durham as a key fight in which tariff reformer must defeat 'one of the ablest and most respected members of the House of Commons'.

Hills won despite starting as a stranger to County Durham. High Head now proved a useful retreat from constituency work.

The pre-First World War battle between free traders and tariff reformers had first drawn Hills into politics. But the Great War itself had the greatest impact upon him. Serving as an officer may well have given him a deeper insight into the concerns and feelings of working men under his command, but it was also a chilling and bizarre experience. Deciding to enlist, aged 47, Hills entered the army in October 1914 as Captain of the 4th Battalion of the Durham Light Infantry. In France, losses were tragically high and opportunities for promotion correspondingly plentiful. Hills distinguished himself and rose rapidly. In October 1915 he was made Major of the 20th Battalion of the Durham Light Infantry; in July 1916, Acting Lieutenant-Colonel.

In September 1916, in a case of mistaken identity, Hills was reported by some English newspapers as killed in action. The Durham Cathedral bell was solemnly tolled in mourning. Hills, told of his death, telegraphed *The Times*, which had not carried the report: 'Was never better in my life'. But this may have been tempting fate too much. Hills was severely wounded a few weeks later and, though mentioned in dispatches, invalided home. He spent the rest of the war working in the Ministry of Munitions. It seems he found time to visit High Head, since Grisenthwaite was working on the lodge to Martindale's designs in 1916.

Re-elected M.P. for Durham City, as a Coalition Unionist in 1918, Hills became unhappy about retaining High Head. On 16 September 1919, the *Carlisle Journal* announced its sale, with 500 acres. On 19 September it announced the sale of 'the greater portion' of the castle's old pictures, china and furniture, to be handled by J. S. Castiglione of 24 Haymarket, London. Not surprisingly in view of the property market's lack of interest in country houses at the time, the first sale did not take place. It is unclear, though, whether the sale of the contents happened. With no buyer, Hills let the castle, from 1921 to 1929, to T. R. Cavaghan, head of the Carlisle meat firm of Cavaghan and Gray, bacon curers. Hills went on living in part of the house since the *Country Life* feature on the castle (21 October 1921) describes it as his seat, and he served locally as a J.P.

Hills spent much of the year at his London home, 2 Palace Gardens Terrace, W.8. A large array of parliamentary and business interests would have required his attention. As an M.P., he was interested in the budget and government finance, the status of the legal profession, housing and labour conditions.[9] He supported women's equality and their entry to the learned professions. On the left wing of the Conservative party, to which he was intensely loyal, Hills was made Financial Secretary to the Treasury in Bonar Law's cabinet in October 1922 because of his deep knowledge of government finance. He seemed on the threshold of eminence. But in May 1923 Bonar Law, dying of throat cancer, resigned, and Hills lost office. Then came worse humiliations. He lost his seat at Durham (in November 1923) and then lost a by-election at Liverpool Edge Hill.

But Hills was never idle for long. He was a brilliant fisherman, loving the open air and clear, swift waters, like those of the Ive, a fine trout stream. He also had a long list of commercial interests including directorships in the London and Scottish Railway, Imperial Airways and the chairmanship of the Legal Insurance Co. He was also deputy-chairman of the British Match Corporation Ltd., vice-chairman of Stern's, and a member of the London Board of the Colonial Mutual Life Assurance Society and the Council of the Law Society. Fellow council member, Robert C. Nesbitt, recalled that Hills was 'of the greatest assistance to his profession', and 'the chief unofficial means of communication between the legal profession and government departments' when legislation affecting it was considered. He and Samuel Garrett (later Law Society President) were once in a minority of two supporting the appointment of women as solicitors when the society's council discussed the issue.

In semi-exile from politics, Hills wrote two books, *A Summer On The Test* (1924) and *The Finance of Government* (1925), on parliament's control of public expenditure and government finance. The former was on trout-fishing on the River Test and one of a series of fishing books he wrote. The subject matter of others included the history of fly-fishing for trout; Lunn, the famous Stockbridge river keeper; and wild South American river fishing. Hills' obituary in *The Times* called him 'the best writer on fishing since Lord Grey of Falloden'.

In December 1925 Hills became M.P. for Ripon, Yorkshire, succeeding Ernest Wood (later 1st Earl of Halifax) who had been appointed, as Baron Irwin, Viceroy of India.[10] In 1929 he was made a privy councillor (a recognition that he was now one of 'the great and the good') and awarded an honorary D.C.L. degree by Durham University. As a back-bencher, Hills supported Baldwin's governments of November 1924-May 1929 and June 1935-May 1937 in their attempts to achieve industrial peace at home, and appease a resurgent Italy and Germany abroad. He continued to work hard, becoming a member of the Departmental Committee on Housing and of the Royal Commission on Land Drainage. He presided over the Credit Insurance Committee and the Committee on the Export of Horses, and also chaired the Committee on Export Credits and the Inter-Departmental Committee on the Prices of Building Materials.

John Hills seems to have remained hale and hearty after his return to Parliament. In 1927, aged 60, he took a holiday, stalking stag in the Scottish Highlands. In 1931 he got married for the second time. His bride, Mary Grace Ashton, aged 22, was a novelist and daughter of Leon Dominic Ashton. She produced his only son, Andrew Ashton Waller Hills, in 1933.[11] The Hills family now seemed set to become a Cumbrian squire dynasty based at High Head, but this was not to be. In 1934 John's brother, Judge Eustace Gilbert Hills, K.C. of Tolson Hall, Kendal, died. He had been a local judge and Chairman of Cumberland Quarter Sessions from 1930-3. His death, though he left five children who visited High Head, may have loosened the family's ties with Cumbria. In June 1934, Hills enthusiastically welcomed a Cumberland and Westmorland Archaeological Society visit to High Head. But despite his fondness for the house and his retention of Ripon with a 21,688 majority in the 1935 General Election, he decided to sell the castle that year, to fund the education and career of his son Andrew.[12]

In 1935, Alan Vincent Gandar Dower (1898-1980) bought High Head. Educated at R.M.C. Sandhurst and Oxford University, he had fought in the First World War in France as a 2nd Lieutenant in the Royal West Surrey Regiment and then the 2nd Dragoon Guards, before transferring to the R.A.F. in 1918. In 1928 he had married Aymée Lavender, daughter of a Scottish laird, Sir George James Robert Clerk of Penicuik, Bt. and was M.P. for Stockport from 1930-5. Dower became Conservative M.P. for Penrith and Cockermouth in 1935. An all-round sportsman, he enjoyed hunting, big game

49. Colonel Alan Gandar Dower, M.P. (1898-1980).

shooting, polo, tennis and golf. He seems to have found the castle a convenient retreat with relaxing surroundings. He had a good Second World War, as Lieutenant-Colonel commanding the 36th AA Battalion (1938-40), then as Commander of the 39th Lancashire Fusiliers Regiment from 1940. His brother, a war reporter and keen squash player who lived in Nairobi, was drowned in the Indian Ocean when his ship was sunk by enemy action. On the Public Accounts Committee of the House (1945-50), outside the Commons, Alan Gandar Dower was a Liveryman of the Barbers' Company and was made a Freeman of the City of London. He was a typical Conservative backbencher with many interests. Unfortunately these did not include property and estate management.[13]

In 1935, Gandar Dower had settled at High Head. He had some affection for it, resisting suggestions in 1941, from RAF Maintenance 50 Wing, that he let it to them as a possible alternative headquarters. But in 1950 he lost his seat. Defeat naturally hurt and on 9 June 1950 he tried to sell the castle (given a Grade II star listing that year). The 301-acre Home Farm and two cottages, 386 acres in all, were offered with it. The sale, in Carlisle's *County Hotel*, was a fiasco. For sale in lots or as one, it failed to meet its reserve price, and had to be withdrawn.

That High Head should remain unsold was not surprising. Cumbria was only beginning to revive economically, and the country house world in general was in decline in a time of austerity. The issuing of building licences in wartime had deterred owners from building anew or restoring mansions. The '40s, '50s and '60s saw a gale of brutal destruction of often restorable mansions. Some were already in long-term decay by the mid-'50s. In Cumbria these included the Curwens' spectacular Workington Hall (much of it by John Carr of York c.1777-82) and the Briscos' handsome Crofton Hall (demolished in 1958). Bolton Hall (demolished in 1951), Brayton (demolished in 1940) and Morland Hall (made roofless in 1949) had already been lost. In December 1950 Gandar Dower,[14] who it seems had already bought Newington House, near Warborough, Oxfordshire, unwittingly eased High Head nearer destruction by selling it to Gordon Robinson, a Penrith pork butcher.

In 1972, Colonel Gandar Dower told *Cumbria* magazine: 'I stressed that, if I sold it, the house must be preserved. This was agreed to; so I let it go ...'. The house, however, was not preserved. The 1954 Cumberland Directory lists Charles H. Robinson as living in it, but the castle seems to have become dilapidated. There are no records of repairs and maintenance being done. On the night of 11 December 1956, fire broke out in the castle's east wing while Mr. and Mrs. Gordon Robinson (Gordon was Charles' brother) were in occupation. According to one account this was put out by the fire brigade, but not before it had been whipped up by gales into 100-ft. high flames which destroyed the roof. The next day, it is said, fire started again in the castle's smouldering shell. The fire was eventually put out by lunchtime that day, but it was too late.[15]

For the next few years High Head resembled a Verdi opera set. Roofless and open to the weather, it was pillaged by vandals and bounty-hunters. It next changed hands in 1959, for £800. The buyer, William Dickman, had recently retired from the Pay Corps and had dreams of running a market garden in its grounds. He lived in the one habitable piece of the castle (apart from its stable block) that remained. This, ironically, was the Hills' servants' wing of 1903.

1. He was the son of Robert Baynes (d. 1789), and died unmarried.
2. Died 1776. Susanna Richmond's will was dated 5 September 1773.
3. Edward Hughes' *North Country Life In The Eighteenth Century Vol. II Cumberland and Westmorland 1700-1830*, (O.U.P., 1965) mentions John Gale's commercial interests which included iron

smelting and the West Cumberland coal trade. His eldest son, Wilson Gale-Braddyll (1756-1818) of Conishead Priory, Lancashire, succeeded to High Head on his cousin Thomas Braddyll's death, assuming the name Braddyll by Royal Warrant on 15 August 1776. Groom of the Bedchamber to George III, he was a Colonel in the Lancashire Militia and an M.P. His only son was Thomas Gale-Braddyll, later Thomas Richmond-Gale-Braddyll (1776-1862), who was High Sheriff of Lancashire in 1821, and a Lieutenant-Colonel in the Coldstream Guards. He assumed the surname and arms of Richmond by Royal Licence on 18 October 1819. Extravagant, Thomas gothicised Conishead Priory with the help of architect Philip William Wyatt (d. 1835) from 1821-36, but had to sell it c.1837.

4. D/BEN/Highhead Box 1, Cumbria Record Office.
5. Quoted in Hughes, op. cit. p. 391-2. Losh would have been in a good position to know. His daughter, Cecilia Isabella, had married a grandson of John Gale, William Gale of Bardsea Hall (1788-1865) in April 1820.
6. D/BEN/Highhead Box 1, Cumbria Record Office.
7. The seller in 1854, according to *Burke's Landed Gentry*, Vol. III (1972) was Thomas Richmond-Gale-Braddyll's grandson, Henry John Richmond-Gale-Braddyll (b. 1837, d.s.p. 1886). Aged about seventeen in 1854, his legal representatives in both sales were probably his maiden aunts and bachelor uncle. They handled the 1854 sale of land in Dalton parish. These (Clarence, d.s.p. 1867, Frances, d. unmarried 1876, Margaret Frederica, d. unmarried 1894, Sarah Jane, d. unmarried 1895) were the brother and sisters respectively of Henry John's father, Edward Stanley Bagot Richmond-Gale-Braddyll (1807-74).
8. Cumbria R.O. D/AR/53. Mr. A. H. James was the 3rd Lord Brougham's agent. Later, along with Sir Charles Archer Cook, he was one of Henry Charles' executors.
9. He chaired the cross-party British Association for Labour Legislation.
10. Edward Frederick Lindley Wood, 1st Earl of Halifax (1881-1959), Viceroy of India (1926-31), Foreign Secretary (1938-40), and ambassador to the U.S. (1941-46), was created Earl in 1944.
11. Hills' first wife, Stella (b. 1869), the glamorous daughter of barrister Herbert Duckworth of Orchardleigh Park, Somerset, and stepdaughter of Sir Leslie Stephen, died of peritonitis after only four months of marriage in July 1897. Her half-sisters were the remarkable Vanessa Bell, the painter, and Virginia Woolf, the novelist, who visited High Head.
12. Hills' health began to fail in April 1938. Still M.P. for Ripon, he died on 24 December 1938 at his London home, aged 71, and was buried in Kensal Green Roman Catholic Cemetery. The baronetcy gazetted for him was instead conveyed in February 1939 to his son, Andrew Ashton Waller Hills. Andrew sadly died, childless, in 1935, in a street accident in Oxford, aged twenty-two. Lady Hills died in 1980.
13. After Dower's ownership of 1950-80, Newington House, a mansion near Warborough, Oxfordshire was suffering from timber infestation, a leaking roof, flooding basements and dry rot, requiring more than £600,000-worth of restoration under two subsequent owners. This neglect was not due to the owner's poverty: according to *The Times*, 4 October 1980, Gandar Dower left £490,472.
14. According to *Who Was Who 1971-80*, he was later Master of the South Oxfordshire Hunt (1950-3), and Joint-Master of the Old Berkeley from 1953 onwards. He was Deputy-Lieutenant of Middlesex 1961-5 and of Greater London from 1965 onwards.
15. *The Cumberland News*, 20 January 1984.

Chapter 10

Victor's Trail of Havoc 1927-1967

'The aristocracy has three successive ages: the age of superiority, the age of privilege, the age of vanity; once it has left the first behind, it degenerates in the second and expires in the last.'

Chateaubriand: *Mémoires d'outre-tombe* (1841).

'You know I disapprove of education altogether, and think it is a perfect injury to the country; what I always ask is, who is to black my boots?'

Henry Charles, 3rd Lord Brougham

The inter-war years saw crisis and decline for country houses, their owners and the once-dominant country house culture. Families and houses with industrial or banking connections or urban property to support them often survived, but their properties were sometimes rationalised. Others, with agricultural incomes, were not so lucky. The price of agricultural land, depressed since the 1870s, did not revive until the 1950s. Many landed families had undergone a terrible crisis of confidence before and after the First World War. For many of its survivors the future seemed bleak. They had lost their right to take part in local government in the County Councils Act in 1888. Personal sacrifice in the First World War had sometimes brought crippling death duties and disillusionment with landed life. It made some want to enjoy themselves frantically in careless gaiety and relief. 'I broke the bank at Monte Carlo' (inspired by Harry, 5th Earl of Rosslyn, thrice bankrupt by 1926 and loser of £250,000) was a hit music-hall song. But good living often could not hide the fact that many were uncertain of their role and became demoralised. With the rise of a welfare state, they were not the caring, traditional squires of Fielding's and Jane Austen's novels, or entrepreneurs like Galsworthy's Soames Forsyte. They were often not the politicians who previously had made parliamentary seats in the shires into virtual family fiefs or even controlled matters from behind the scenes in the Lords. The 1911 Parliament Act took away the Lords' veto of Commons' bills. Many families just lost their way – the melancholy context of Evelyn Waugh's *Brideshead Revisited* and *A Handful of Dust*, and Isabel Colegate's *The Shooting Party*. Many gentry families, like Waugh's Flytes, were psychologically and educationally ill-equipped to find a new role, let alone survive.

Against this backdrop, in summer 1927, the Broughams found themselves in some trouble. Henry Charles, 3rd Lord Brougham died on 24 May at 36 Chesham Place, London at the age of ninety. Unfortunately his only son, Capt. Hon. Henry Brougham, had died prematurely three weeks earlier at Hove on 4 May, aged thirty-nine. The 3rd Lord, an unspectacular, unintellectual country squire had seen the estates' value rise from above £116,000 in 1886 to about £500,000 in 1927, despite the selling of High Head Castle and two other estates in 1902. Henry Charles left 11 properties, including some in scattered but well-sited areas of London and Sussex and Château Eleanore-Louise. He retained 3,500 acres in Cumbria, including Wetheriggs Pottery and the Somerset estates. His son Henry left a substantial £5,795 but had taken little part in business. After his grandfather and father had played 'caretaker' roles in the family firm, Victor Henry Peter, only 18 on his father's death, became heir to a large land and property portfolio.

Victor's personality and the powerlessness or unwillingness of friends and relations to influence him ensured trouble. He was the son of a broken marriage. His mother's family, race-horse owners, had much more land and money than the Broughams and far less need to economise. These two factors perhaps shaped Victor's attitude, which was like an immature adolescent's. He was handsome, reputedly the tallest peer in the House of Lords (at 6 ft. 7 in.), extravagant, frivolous and unbalanced. No sooner did he acquire something than it ceased to satisfy him: for example, he owned one of his four-and-a-half litre Bentleys for only five months.

Victor inherited in a family vacuum. The 3rd Lord's brothers and sisters, Wilfred, Reginald, Alice and Evelyn had all died by 1927. Another sister, Adela Mary Grenville (1847-1933) had married the Surrey barrister Sir Charles Archer Cook, K.C.B., Chief Charity Commissioner from 1909-16. Cook was one of the 3rd Lord Brougham's executors but, after failing to restrain Victor's extravagance, died in 1934. There were no financially skilled people of his father's generation or his own to help, either. The 4th Lord's aunt, Eleanor Mabel Valentine Brougham (1883-1966), was a novelist. In 1940 Victor's sister, Eileen, married Colonel Francis Davies of the Grenadier Guards, of solid gentry stock, son of George V's much-decorated A.D.C. General, Sir Francis John Davies K.C.B., K.C.M.G., K.C.V.O. (1864-1948) of Elmley Castle, Worcestershire. But by then Victor had lost much of the Brougham fortune. Tragically no friend or relation emerged as the highly proficient businessman required at Brougham.

In 1927 Westmorland and Cumberland were already in some economic disarray. Towns like Maryport and Whitehaven had been declining since the 1880s, as a result of lack of investment in local industries such as mining, chemicals and textiles. In West Cumberland in the '30s, unemployment reached 70 per cent. In rural Cumbria some estates were slowly collapsing. The Briscos moved from their seat, Crofton Hall, Thursby, near Carlisle, in 1908, unable to live on its £4,000 a year income, but retaining the estate. The Lowther estate was in poor shape under the extravagant 'Yellow' Earl of Lonsdale, who was spending, not re-investing, £180,000 per annum in mineral royalties by 1910. The Wilsons' neo-Grecian Rigmaden Hall near Kirkby Lonsdale was reduced to a shell in 1923, and Edenhall was demolished in 1934. But Victor's approach did not reflect much recognition that the lavish lifestyle of Edwardian times was over.

According to *The Times* of 29 July 1927 the 3rd Lord Brougham left 'unsettled property of the gross value of £70,259 with net personalty £69,398'. He left bequests of £300 to his butler John Hodgson 'if still in his service and not under notice' and £300 to Busby, his gardener at Cannes. More substantially, he bequeathed a further £208,290 in settled lands, mentioned in a *Times* report of 9 January 1928. Victor had to reach his majority at 21 before inheriting. But he was forever getting into avoidable, thoughtless scrapes that sullied the family name and boded ill for the future. In May 1930, for instance, he was had up in court for speeding along the Kingston bypass – his fourth driving offence – while learning estate management at the Duke of Norfolk's estate at Arundel. This was typical of Victor's impulsiveness. By 1930, for instance, he had had three four-and-a-half litre Bentleys specially built, each with Reginald Phillips' sports concealed-hood bodies. In 1928, he had commissioned a conversion of the stable block at Brougham from the local architect Morton Rigg, to accommodate his cars.

Victor started well but later met disaster. On 23 October 1930, a lunch at Brougham Hall celebrated his coming of age. All the tenants and people connected with the Brougham estates were invited. The family proudly displayed a gold cup presented to Lord Chancellor Brougham for securing parliamentary reform, paid for by subscriptions in London and the Metropolitan districts. Victor's health was proposed by the oldest estate employee. Its oldest tenant, Mrs. Schofield (of Wetheriggs Pottery), presented him

50. Victor Henry Peter, 4th Lord Brougham (1909-67) on the *S.S. Bremen*, January 1937.

with a silver cigar box and cigar cutler. The Somerset tenants and the Hall's indoor staff gave him a pair of silver salvers, the Brougham parish residents a gold-mounted walking stick.

The Broughams had quite substantial non-agricultural assets which could have been used to offset the relative fall in farming income. There is some evidence that Victor realised that a change was needed. In 1932 he commissioned Dickinsons Nurseries Ltd. of Chester (landscape gardeners to the Royal Family) to draw up specifications for a raspberry canning factory on 31 acres at Brougham. In October, Dickinsons gave him three schemes outlining the initial outlay on machinery and buildings needed, costed at £13,929 2s. 2d.; £10,728 12s. 2d. and £11,535 12s. 6d. Unfortunately, after much intelligent work from Victor and the Dickinsons, the Brougham trustees rejected them. Despite Victor's attempts at maintaining continuity by altering the Hall, holding the coming of age lunch, doing an agricultural course at Arundel, trying to develop the estate and joining the Scots Guards in 1929, something changed. He decided to gamble professionally.

Victor could have squandered all his assets without gambling, such was his spending. For instance, in 1931 he spent some £1,500 on a lily pond in the Hall grounds, then under the care of the head gardener, Joe Grisedale. Victor also built tennis courts with a nine foot-high boundary fence. Around £300,000 was left, after death duties, in April 1931. On 21 April at the fashionable London society church of St Margaret's, Westminster, in front of his estate workers, relatives and Penrith traders with whom the Broughams had business, Victor married Violet Valerie French, daughter of Major Hon. Gerald French, D.S.O. and granddaughter of the 1st Earl of Ypres (Field Marshal Sir John French), commander of the British Expeditionary Force in the First World War. Pipers of the Scots Guards flamboyantly played the bride and bridegroom from church, and flowers were flown in by the municipality of Cannes. There were festivities at Brougham Hall and a dance for the estate workers in Penrith Drill Hall. The marriage, however, did little for the Hall, which was disliked by Victor's wife. The financial arrangements he made that month did little for it either. He seems, on his own rather vague account, to have split the remaining £300,000 of his grandfather's bequest in two, putting £150,000 into a settlement. Of the rest he gave £25,000, for no obvious reason, to his mother. He gave another £25,000 to his sister and brother, leaving himself with about £100,000 in liquid assets. By 1932 he was gambling with this.

The story of the collapse of the Brougham finances is still not totally clear. In August 1931 Victor may already have been in trouble, selling Scales Hall and land around it. He sold an 87-year lease on a property in Culross Street, Mayfair, for a ground rent of £165 a year in October. But this was nothing to the débâcle that followed. He seems to have broken the bank (taken the day's winnings) at Monte Carlo casino twice around that time. Subsequently he paid a third visit, probably in spring 1932. This time the casino had its revenge, taking a large part of his fortune.

By 26 April 1932, when *The Times* reported that arrangements for the sale of Brougham Hall's furnishings were now 'in progress', it was obvious that the Brougham estates had had a shattering blow. The report mentions family treasures shown to its writer: a 1797 pastel of Caroline, Princess of Wales and her daughter Princess Charlotte; the silver salver William IV had given the 1st Lord as a stand for the Great Seal; the 1820 Lonsdale portrait of Henry Brougham commissioned by his Westmorland supporters; and the Gold Cup he was given when Lord Chancellor. Victor was seeing what he could sell.

On Tuesday 21 June and the four following days, auctioneers Garland-Smith and Co. of 100 Mount Street, London W.1, sold most of the Hall's contents in some 1,319 lots.

But blanks in the sale catalogue suggest that items were bought in private views on 17 and 18 June. The sale was not conducted very professionally, and the catalogue has factual errors, some vague entries, such as 'Portrait of a Gentleman', and abounds with unattributed paintings. A remarkable array of furniture was sold. On Tuesday the contents of 18 bedrooms were sold; next day those of another twelve. The latter included a Sheraton semi-circular card-table (25 guineas) and a 15th-century carved oak bedstead (£8). Thursday cleared away rare carpets, tapestries and pictures at knockdown prices: an old Flemish tapestry (valued at £1,350) for £28, a Gobelin panel £19. Though a Persian Ispahan carpet, dating from Shah Abbas the Great's time (14 ft. by 6 ft. 2 in.) was sold for £1,500, so depressed was the market that a Gobelin tapestry (valued at £3,600) was withdrawn when bidding reached only £500. A Gainsborough landscape went for £270, an oil attributed to Titian for £120. On Friday the contents of the dining room, armour hall, library, billiard room, and Lord Brougham's study were swept away, and on Saturday those of the minor bedrooms, service and servants' rooms followed them. The sale raised £4,450 in its first three days. At its end a collection including Jacobean, Queen Anne, Hepplewhite, Chippendale, Louis Seize and Empire furniture, Persian carpets, fine tapestries, a set of fine old grandfather clocks and Sèvres, Bloor Derby, Dresden and Worcester china was no more. The Hall was empty and desolate.

Victor had already sold large portions of Westmorland and Cumberland family land. 'The Outlying Portion of The Brougham Estate near Penrith', handled by the solicitors S. Pearman Smith and Sons of 147 Litchfield Street, Walsall and Arnison and Co. of St Andrews Place, Penrith, some 712.558 acres of land were auctioned by John D. Wood of 23 Berkeley Square, London W.1, in early 1932. The sale included useful small properties such as the Brougham family's laundry house, the blacksmith's shop, the *Crown Hotel* in Eamont Bridge, and Wetheriggs Pottery (then held on a tenancy of £44 per annum) with six acres. But the bulk of it was made up of: the Home Farm at Eamont Bridge (88 acres, 1 rod, 22 perches), Hospital Farm (141 acres, 1 rod, 18 perches), Clifton Dykes (111 acres, 2 rods), Moorhouse's Farm (142 acres, 3 rods, 24 perches) and Wethericks Farm (55 acres, 2 rods, 33 perches). In early June 1932, Victor sold nearly 800 acres in the Penrith area through the estate agents H. Liddington & Co. of Duke Street, London, retaining a rump of 160 acres, 2 rods and 2 perches around the Hall. The Brougham Estate was now stripped to the bone.

Victor soon wanted to sell the triptych (at that time attributed to Dürer but actually made by Guild of Antwerp craftsmen in 1490) which William Brougham had placed in the chapel in 1869. Ostensibly he wished to use the sale money to maintain the chapel. It seems to have needed £250 in repairs and £100 for the repainting of crests in its ceiling (according to an appeal circular). The triptych was even more valuable than was then realised. By mid-September 1932, *The Times* reported that Victor was applying for permission from Carlisle Consistory Court to sell it for an estimated market price of £3,000. Week by week things disappeared with a dizzying speed. By October 1932 he was selling the German and Swiss 16th-and 17th-century stained glass from six Hall windows through Messrs. Garland-Smith of Mount Street. Valued for probate at £6,000, they were sold to an Italian firm.

The dismantling of the Brougham estate went on apace and its Cumberland and Westmorland property was sold off. The Broughams' neighbours, especially their personal enemies and middling local farmers and local squires, profited from Victor's folly, buying up bits of the estate, Hall or contents. Even the local diocese benefited. On 1 October 1932, with ridiculous partiality, H. B. Vaisey, K.C., Chancellor of the Carlisle Consistory Court, authorised sale of the triptych by private treaty, on terms he decided. The proceeds, he ruled, were to go to the Carlisle diocese. The previous month he had talked Victor into agreeing to apply to the Court for the right to sell something almost certainly his own. In early June 1934, Victor renounced all rights to the triptych. The affair was typical of how Victor, throughout his life, allowed himself to be outwitted in business and talked into situations in which he would be the sole loser. There was, enemies saw, no need to deceive Victor. He deceived himself.

Unfortunately not even the birth of a son, Julian Henry Peter Brougham, on 5 October 1932 at 5 Aldford Street, London, changed Victor's approach or situation. The decline in the Broughams' fortunes went on unchecked. On 20 December 1932 a third of the Hall library went under the hammer at Sotheby's. A real public humiliation followed on 2 October 1933, as West Westmorland Rural Council summoned Victor at Hackthorpe Magistrates Court, for £102 18s. in rates arrears. A distress warrant was issued against him, as he had not appeared in person to answer the charges. Things became even more bleak when Victor's wife successfully petitioned for divorce in late February 1934

51. A family snapshot of Julian Henry Peter Brougham (1932-52) trying on peers' robes he was never to use.

on the grounds of his adultery with actress Marion ('Betty') Seton the previous May. He did not defend the suit, had to pay the legal costs and saw his ex-wife get custody of their son Julian.

After Messrs. Thornbarrow & Co. of Penrith had sold its 'surplus contents' (without even a catalogue) on 1 February 1934, by 3 March Victor had sold Brougham Hall. It was an ignominious end of 208 years of Brougham family ownership. The buyer, Major Geoffrey Thomas Middleton Carleton Cowper, J.P., was a local 'nouveau-riche' squire whose nearby Carleton Hall estate adjoined the Broughams'. His deep hatred of the Broughams had started with a dispute with them over shooting rights. Unlike Cowper (who had added the name Carleton to his own by deed poll), the Broughams had 'old' money, which he resented. His intrigues helped Vaisey relieve Lord Brougham of the 'Dürer' triptych and ultimately of Brougham chapel. Apparently he said that he wanted an oak tree to grow in the Hall's dining room. Under such vindictive ownership, destructive revenge was swift. The *Times* printed a report on 16 June 1934 that the Hall was 'to be sold for demolition'. Cowper made half-hearted attempts for appearances' sake to let the Hall for use as a house, school or hotel. Then on 18 July a demolition sale of its fittings was conducted by Mr. F. D. Roach of Messrs. Perry and Philips of

52.   The Mansion House being stripped and demolished in autumn 1934.

Bridgnorth. They specialised in demolition sales and had already disposed of Edenhall's fittings that April.

The sale on 18 and 19 July was reported by a local newspaper, *The Herald* in an understated, deadpan way which failed to mask its sadness. In a period of recession bidding was unenthusiastic, especially the first day. The prices of the splendid pieces of architectural salvage were low, even ridiculous. Seven hundred square feet of drawing room pine flooring went for £2, while the rest of its fittings reached a total of £55, a panelled oak sliding door having a top price of £18 10s. The old oak panelling William Brougham scoured Britain and Europe to buy was sold off in lots (including some of High Head Castle's best panelling and more from Scales Hall). The library fittings went for £110, including oak bookcases (£9) and carved oak linenfold doors (£13). According to *The Herald* a set of marble statues in the billiard room, which had 'nothing of any consequence', went for a mere five guineas. The miserable prices were repeated in Lord Brougham's study where the plaster masks of statesmen (Brougham, Wellington, Chatham, Pitt, Cromwell and Bonaparte) went for 5s., the Brougham organ (albeit not working) disappeared for £4 to one Frank Lynn, and some 22 ft. 6 in. of carved oak bookcasing, adjustable shelves and carved and panelled doors were sold to the owner of a house near Bassenthwaite for only £8.

The Hall's oak fittings, according to *The Times,* made the 'best prices', most of them in four lots. Some of the armour hall's beautiful old Jacobean panelling (200 sq. ft.) went to a Mr. Metcalf Gibson from Ravenstonedale for £30. A smaller lot went to the Rev. W. Kewley for £7. According to *The Herald*, 'buyers from a distance' bought other lots of oak panelling for £43 and £11. Typical of the bargains was an Italian carved oak screen which fell into their hands for £30. In the dining room, a London dealer got all the fine linenfold oak panelling for £130. Mr. G. H. Pattinson of Gossel Ridding, Windermere, Chairman of Westmorland County Council, worked with a will, acquiring panelling from the dining room lobby (£50), an oak Gothic staircase (£32), the staircase hall's linenfold panelling (£80) and its matching oak balustrading (£10).

Many of the Hall's stone fittings were sold on 19 July. Mr. Clark, who had packed many of the furnishings, books, armour and Italian stained glass into crates in the last days of Victor's ownership, watched crestfallen. *The Herald* says that some items bought the first day were resold and that bidding was brisker and prices twice the previous day's. It would be more true to say that they were still ridiculous: all the red stone paving in the courtyard was sold for £12 15s., the whole of the clock tower with its stone work and bell for £30, and three folding garage doors with metal runners for £20. The Mansion House's oak panelled and studded entrance doors went for a crazy £4 5s. 0d.! Victor's lily pond, with lead figure fountains and stone paving surrounds was broken into three lots and bought by Lord Lonsdale's agent, R. S. Woof for £50. A raised flag platform, symbolically, received only £4. From the lawn, the attractive sundial of 1660 with a Latin inscription was carried off for £18 after 'spirited bidding'. Victor's tennis court fencing went for £11, his combined tennis pavilion and garden house for £10.

It was then discovered (to the consternation of some) that a large amount of bees' nests were underneath the Hall's eaves. One last farce ended the sale: all the Hall's stonework (bar items of stone coping, sold in separate lots), its roof joists and roof timbers, 25 tons of its lead roofing, its heating pipes, steel girders and its staggering number of 17,000 Westmorland slates constituted the last lot, no. 600. Its conditions of sale were that its buyer demolished the building within nine months. Bidding started at £100 and did not excite those present. Eventually a Mr. H. Pearson of Coventry triumphed with a £380 bid. A family of 'demolition specialists', the Pearsons counted amongst their 'achievements' demolishing, in 1931, the splendid classical Haggerston

Castle, Northumberland (a 1770s house added to by Richard Norman Shaw and rebuilt in 1911 by Dunn of Edinburgh), Leatham's Flour Mill, York and the classical Warwick Gaol. Despite his impressive pedigree, Pearson's cheque bounced. The sale was a financial flop, raising only £1,479.

It seems that Cowper had more than one sale of all the Hall's wood fittings, and that the Harkers of Brooklands (owners of the *Glenridding, Patterdale* and *Lodore Swiss* Hotels) bought tiles, woodwork and sinks from it. By September 1934 Carleton Cowper, obeying a bizarre Westmorland County Council ruling that the Hall's outer walls should be preserved and the inner ones knocked down to their level, was employing J. J. King and Co. of Redheugh, Newcastle to demolish it. The demolition men (whom Carleton Cowper accommodated in two rooms in the Hall's servants block) smashed their way steadily through Cottingham and Hussey's splendid architecture in the Mansion House until they got to Lord Brougham's study. There, on 29 September, occurred another Brougham Hall tragedy.

James Maughan of Byker, Newcastle, and Thomas Alexander were demolishing the area of Lord Brougham's study. The wall above it was roped but would not fall. When they removed a quoin at the corner of the wall it fell, taking their scaffolding and poor Maughan with it. Alexander leapt out of danger but Maughan fell 20 ft. and was covered with masonry, dying instantly. The Major, perhaps now superstitious, decided he had had enough and demolition was abandoned. Roughly one third of the Hall was gone, but parts like the servants' quarters and Tudor hall were still roofed and some early 17th-century panelling still remained on an upper floor. The rest, a large part of William Brougham's life-work, remained a ruined shell.

Within seven years Victor had literally wrecked his inheritance, squandering assets which would now be worth millions of pounds. Unlike the 19th century, there was to be no successful family revival. Over the next 51 years the Hall's remaining contents were dispersed. Victor had a further financial collapse, then went bankrupt in 1950. At the same time Brougham Hall's future became increasingly bleak.

In June 1935 Victor had remarried. His bride was Jean Follett, of Devon gentry stock and daughter of Brigadier-General G. B. Spencer Follett D.S.O. (1878-1918), who had fought in South Africa with the Coldstream Guards and, achieving the French Croix de Guerre, dying in action in the First World War. Through her mother, Lady Mildred Murray, Jean was a granddaughter of Charles Murray, 7th Earl of Dunmore (1841-1907), a Scottish grandee, explorer and Lord Lieutenant of Stirlingshire. But unfortunately the marriage did not change Victor's situation or approach to life. He went on running up debts and borrowing from friends and relatives. He had, he later claimed, an income of £1,500 a year before this was reduced by bombing in the Blitz. But even before the war Victor seems to have been strapped for cash: in May 1939 Sotheby's was ordered to sell a large batch of Brougham papers. These were some of the 1st Lord Brougham's books and manuscripts. In 20 packing cases, they included material on the anti-slavery agitation, the trial of Queen Caroline, the 1832 Reform Bill and the founding of London University. They went to Mr. C. K. Ogden, a bookseller, for only £205. In 1953 some of these were acquired by University College, London, in whose Manuscript Room they are kept. Two years after the Sotheby's sale Victor's second marriage broke up, despite the birth of two sons, Michael John (in 1938) and David Peter (in 1940). On 20 October 1941 Victor's wife Jean divorced him on the grounds of adultery.

Brougham Hall, ironically still owned by Carleton Cowper, was lying ruinous, but in 1941 it was taken over by the 35th Royal Tank Brigade, which became part of 79th Armoured Division in October 1942. The 35th's headquarters was at Clifton, and they also used nearby Greystoke Castle as a base. Brougham now became part of one of the most secret British war projects: the Canal Defence Light tank. It formed a satellite station for the Royal Armoured Corps' base and C.D.L. 'school' at Lowther Castle. Then it was used by the R.E.M.E. service unit, formed of other regiments in 1941-2. From March 1942 to April 1944, a re-organised 35th Tank Brigade also used it as a tank brigade workshop. Three officers and six sergeants were trained in Sherman and Grant Tank engine mainte-nance at Boving-ton Camp and then passed on their knowledge within the battalion. At Brougham the

53. An M3 Grant C.D.L. Tank.

35th repaired Churchill, Covenanter, Matilda, Grant and Sherman tanks and also converted them into C.D.L. tanks. These C.D.L. tanks (the Matildas were eventually axed from this group) were tested with a 13-million candle-powered strobe light fitted in their turrets to confuse the enemy. The C.D.L. turret was in two sections, the optical equipment on the right side with the operator sitting on the left side. The beam of light (dispersed at an angle of 19 degrees from the turret) came from a carbon arc. It was mounted on a cradle, its power provided by a 9.5 kilowatt generator. A 'scatter' function created a nightmarish and disorientating flicker effect as the light went on and off on a moving tank's turret. The tanks were tested in conditions of great secrecy, with all C.D.L. personnel signing the Official Secrets Act once a month. One man went to Durham jail after it was discovered that he had written in a letter to his parents that he was 'working on tanks', which were operating during the night. Recently, though, two servicemen, Lt. Col. J. J. Dingwall, (retd.) and Mr. B. Stacey of Sheffield D.S.O., have provided details of operations at the Hall.

Mr. Stacey arrived, aged 21, as a WO2 armament artificer in July 1942, and was in a team of 135 men, staying until June 1944. He has clear memories of his time at Brougham. In that period the Brougham tank workshop was part of the 35th Tank Brigade servicing its tanks. The workshop was joined by men of the 1st Tank Brigade on its return from North Africa in March 1944. The 35th Brigade comprised the 152nd Regiment of the Royal Armoured Corps (built from a Liverpool infantry regiment), the 155th Regiment from the D.L.I. (Durham Light Infantry, Newcastle) and the 49th Royal Tank Brigade, a genuine specialist tank regiment. The 35th was made up of 154 tanks arranged in three Regiments. These comprised 50 conventional tanks, 50 C.D.L. tanks, 50 conventional tanks, and four headquarters tanks for the Commanding Officer.

To convert the Hall into workshops, nissen huts were installed in the courtyards, and concrete roadways were built on the avenue for tank exercises. When Stacey arrived in July 1942, everyone lived in canvas tents just outside the main gate of the Hall. In addition to everyday training locally, between August and October 1943 there was intensive C.D.L. training and firing on the Linney Head range in Pembrokeshire. By late 1943, nissen huts had been built on both sides of the Hall's avenue and two large work-shop hangars at its end. Other more destructive changes were made. The library end of the mansion house opposite the carriage arch was levelled to allow tank movement. A two-room air raid shelter was created in the cellars, but there was never an air raid. A lot of stone was removed from the Hall and became hard standing for tanks in Lowther Park. This continued until a young, recently appointed staff-officer, now Lt. Col. J. J. Dingwall and, fortuitously, a great-grandson of James Rigg Brougham, stopped the destruction. The hinterland of the Hall and the mansion house area were now a mess.

In 1942-4, the Tudor hall's first floor (without electric light) was used by Stacey and WO2. Thomas Tucker, both armourers, as offices because the roof was sound. The work was arduous for both of them. Stacey was in charge of the 75 mm Woolwich guns. He also made the C.D.L.'s dummy barrels with tubular steel from Carlisle and serviced the American 75 mm guns of Grants and Shermans. He also tended British tanks, Churchills, Covenanters and Matildas, too. Tucker worked on Beazer machine guns, revolvers and rifles. It is clear that the Brougham site resembled a military laboratory. The authorities kept its use and especially the C.D.L. tank a closely guarded secret. In 1942-4 the land from the Clifton end of the avenue up the hill to the unused chapel was a restricted area, guarded by a sentry in the chapel's gate and another man by the gardeners' cottages at the bottom of the avenue. Neither of the Hall's big doors facing the road was ever opened, entry being instead by the little lych gate by the billiard room.

Away from the Hall, C.D.L. training was done in 1941 on ranges above Knipe Scar, fells above Ullswater and on high ground up to the Emperor's Lodge at Lowther Castle. In September 1942, the authorities requisitioned farmland in the Highfield, Woodhouse, Winder Hall and Celleron areas for more practice. Tank testing went on for 24 hours at a time, in 12-hour shifts. Crews were able to manoeuvre the C.D.L. with a high degree of skill, but found keeping the beam near its target tiring and the heat in the cramped C.D.L. turrets uncomfortable.

The C.D.L. experiments at Brougham impressed distinguished and secret visitors such as General Sir Oliver Leese (Montgomery's successor as 8th Army Commander in Italy). The first major C.D.L. demonstration took place on 5 May 1942 when the C.I.G.S. Viscount Alanbrooke, the Chief of Combined Operations, Earl Mountbatten, and Sir Oliver Lucas (of the Ministry of Supply) visited Lowther to see the C.D.L. tank in action. In December 1942, George VI, Eisenhower and Churchill (accompanied by his daughter, Mary, a 2nd Lt.) arrived by train at Penrith station and proceeded to Lowther to see a C.D.L. tank demonstration. During it, all roads between Penrith and Lowther were closed off. The spectators saw tanks, whose crews had been trained to attack in V-formation, shielding the infantry coming up behind them and blinding the enemy in front. These demonstrations, which always included No. 7 troop of 'C' Squadron, had one major effect. Eisenhower, much taken with the weapon, ordered that U.S. troops were to be trained in its use at Linney Head.

In March 1944, after the 1st Tank Brigade's return, men from the 35th Tank Brigade either joined it (as Stacey did) or went as a 'feeder' unit to Lockerbie. After D-Day, the 1st Brigade departed from Gosport to Avromanches. They first saw a big engagement in the Wessel Valley in Germany, but did not use C.D.L. tanks. Most of 35th Tank Brigade departed from Brougham in March-April 1944. The C.D.L. Tank now began its active service. Though Montgomery's lack of enthusiasm for it meant that its use in the Second World War was restricted, it was first used by British troops after the Normandy landings in the assault on the town of Rees on 24 and 25 March 1945, when 'B' Squadron of 49th APC Regiment gave 'movement and direction light' for Buffalo amphibious vehicle crossings, illuminated Rees and protected the Highland Division from floating mines and underwater sabotage attempts when the town fell on 25 March. Thirteen C.D.L.s had been used at the crossing of the Rhine at Remagen on 7 March (by the U.S. 738th Tank Battalion). When the Elbe was crossed at Artlenburg (on 29 and 30 April), 'B' squadron of 49th APC (now with 8th Corps) gave British and American troops good movement light from C.D.L.s. After the War the C.D.L. was used in Africa and India (it was effective in Calcutta in 1946). In an improved form, it was adopted by the U.S. army and called 'The Xenon Searchlight'.

Though 49th RTR's operations went well (the regiment lost only two tanks, an officer and 13 other ranks), the Brougham C.D.L. project was not properly used in combat. In the whole C.D.L. project, 1,850 tanks were converted and 6,000 British officers and men, and 8,000 American troops, trained to use them. £20 million was spent on the C.D.L. Tank project at Lowther alone. The over-cautiousness of commanding officers on the battlefield, however, rather than technical flaws in its design, meant that C.D.L.s were usually deployed in the War just as mobile search-lights. The skilled and highly-trained C.D.L. crews ended the War manning Armoured Personnel Carriers and amphibious vehicles like Kangaroos and Buffalos instead. This lost opportunity annoyed the C.D.L.'s supporters. A 1967 article in *After the Battle* magazine, entitled 'The C.D.L. Tanks of Lowther Castle', quoted Sir Giffard Martel, chief of the British Army's tank forces and a tank designer, as saying it was a 'great misfortune the tanks were never properly used' and that they could have been used at Caen with a tenth of the casualties suffered there, and 'cleaned up' in North Africa. Major-General J. F. C. Fuller, the world's leading authority on tank strategy, said in 1949: 'I regard the failure to use this tank as the greatest blunder of the whole war'. Marcel Mitzakis, manager of the first C.D.L. tank project in 1933, blamed extreme secrecy for the generals' ignorance about its capabilities. The nature of the regime at Brougham lends weight to that charge. In Spring 1945 the tanks left Lowther and the R.E.M.E. left Brougham. Concrete nissen huts' bases were built outside its stable block that year and Brougham became a Polish displaced persons' camp.

Victor, Lord Brougham (despite an embarrassing court summons in January 1942 for £25 unpaid solicitors' costs) served with distinction in the war. By 1942, after being a 2nd Lieutenant in the Scots Guards, he was a Major in the Middlesex Regiment of the Territorial Army, fighting in North Africa in the Desert Campaign. He was mentioned in dispatches for his conduct in the run-up to the allied victory in Tunisia ending in German surrender on 9 May 1943. He left a perceptive, meticulous account of the campaign, now owned by his son Michael, the present Lord Brougham. In June 1942 he had married for a third time. His new wife was Edith Ellaline Hart-Davis, daughter of Leonard Teichman. But when Victor was discharged in 1945, his old pre-war problems returned. By 1942 he had been earning £300 to £400 a year from property, of the £1,500 per annum he had previously received. But his extravagance brought an inevitable, humiliating reckoning. In September 1949, four months after his brother Anthony

Charles went bankrupt, Victor too filed for bankruptcy. He had farmed at Sheldon Manor, Chippenham, Wiltshire, on behalf of Grazing Estates Ltd. for £8 a week since 1947 and lived at Allington Grange nearby. On 30 May 1950, his affairs went into the hands of a receiver.

A hearing in Bath in December 1950 was told that Victor had unsecured liabilities of £21,021 and £543 worth of assets. He said he had lost through gambling and speculation in 1932 all 'free' money he had inherited and things had never been right since. He had sold jewels to the value of £1,376 by auction, heirlooms or trustee property of which he was custodian, not telling the other trustees, and pawned 'a few bits of silver'. He admitted spending £1,600 or £1,700 on personal pleasure and owing £648 to small tradesmen. Another hearing, in March 1952, established that he had run up house-keeping and personal expenses for 1950-51 of £4,205. Of the £21,016 debts, £12,700 was owed to friends or relatives. He was also in debt to Wiltshire Farmers Ltd. Then came further disasters. Victor's eldest son, Julian Henry Peter Brougham, serving with the 12th Royal Lancers in Malaya was killed by terrorists, on 8 May 1952. Things got worse and worse. On Thursday 9 October, both Allington Grange and the herd of cattle established in 1948 by Grazing Estates Ltd. were sold by the receiver, acting for the company's creditors. In early 1953 Victor was made homeless. By August he owed £4,000 to Wiltshire Farmers and £14,562 to friends and relatives. His gross liabilities were £23,070, his gross assets £2,043. At a hearing that month he mentioned an unsuccessful £39,000 property investment and gifts of expensive jewellery to his second wife as contributory reasons for his bankruptcy. It was 1963 before he was discharged on payment of £1,000 to the trustee in bankruptcy, stumped up by friends. On 20 June 1967, Victor died. The Broughams' brief age of vanity had, however, long since ended.

After the Polish refugees had been moved out, Brougham Hall languished, unused. Around 1948 a London company, Evans Belhouse (mainly interested in felling the 265 oaks in the park), bought it for £7,700. In 1967 it was purchased by Beacon Builders Ltd. of Penrith for £4,500, who proposed a motel, trade union education centre and caravan site at the Hall. Soon afterwards the involvement of Christopher Terry, a wealthy businessman, was to reverse the decline of Brougham Hall and also of High Head.

Chapter 11

Twilight into Dawn 1968-1992

I: Christopher Terry

Christopher Terry, committed to conservation, had experience of historic building work, restoring 11 of 42 houses in Nash's Chester Terrace, in Regent's Park, and Turners, near Farnham, Surrey, Britain's largest ironstone mansion. He had an unusual background for this work, born in 1938 of Southern Irish extraction, a country noted for destroying mansions. When his father, an army officer in Combined Operations, returned from the War, petrol rationing restricted movement. Terry recalls only four or five days with him. One had a profound influence, when they went in a Morris 10, registration number DED 844, to Wells and Glastonbury. They glimpsed Wells' ruined Bishop's Palace, through its Great Gate's keyhole. Moated and mysterious, it seemed an ideal medieval castle. The boy Terry also saw Glastonbury Abbey and found a scale model and plan of it. That evening he announced that he would restore it! Packed off to boarding school, Terry heard, on 8 May 1952, that DED 844 had crashed into a Gloucestershire dyke, killing his father.

Unable to afford a car, Terry cycled far from home to see old buildings. Archaeology fascinated him. He dug on Iron Age, Bronze Age, Roman and Medieval sites, his imagination fired by Antoinette Powell-Cotton whose family owned archaeological sites and a very important museum at Quex Park in Thanet. He also had luck, finding a Roman brooch on his first day's digging, and at Reculver, a tile inscribed 'CIB'. This redated many of the Saxon shore forts by 150 years. He was in a team that revised the scale of the 'Notitia Dignitatum' at Brenley Corner, near Faversham, on Watling Street, six gallic leagues west of Canterbury and which discovered Walter and Matilda's tomb at Faversham Abbey and the Painted House at Dover. Terry trespassed with Barry Cunliffe (then an undergraduate) on a duck farm near Chichester and saw the latter prove the existence of Fishbourne, the finest Roman palace north of the Alps.

After public school at St George's, Terry read Architecture and Estate Management at London University, which he entered as Kitchener Scholar. He later had senior management, finance and marketing posts with Birmingham small arms maker Sir Bernard Docker, a Dunlop subsidiary, Imperial Tobacco, and with Ireland's Industrial Development Association. He also searched for a Roman fort to excavate and open to the public. Brancaster Roman Fort, Norfolk, built like Terry's beloved Reculver by the first Cohort of the Betasi, ('CIB') was available but too expensive to buy. Later, when Terry had the necessary money, a new owner would not sell. Silchester (Caleva Atrebatum), Hampshire, had a rare contemporary theatre. Excavated in the 19th century on the Duke of Wellington's estate. Stafford Castle attracted but eluded him.[1]

Terry stumbled upon Brougham, in March 1968, while recovering from a bad illness. He stayed near Patterdale. Lake Ullswater flooded the road, and snow blocked mountain passes. Terry was forced on to an unfamiliar road from Brougham Castle to Brougham Hall, the latter unmarked on the Ordnance Survey map. He visited the chapel, but the stone bridge to the Hall was blocked with trees, barbed wire and a scaffold board fence. The two great Hall doors were chained and padlocked. He saw through the huge keyholes a tantalising, forbidden area. For Terry, it was Glastonbury re-visited, and its restoration was somewhat more feasible. Notices threatened to prosecute trespassers and a badly-typed paper on the door said that the Hall would become a caravan park. Outraged that, with 1,682,592 largely useless Cumbrian acres, Brougham should be chosen for such a fate, Terry decided to prevent the Hall's destruction.

Terry asked Beacon about purchasing Brougham. The price was 10 times his Sussex home's, and more than five times what Beacon had paid. He could not raise this but dragged out the correspondence to postpone the caravan site threat. Working in Scotland for the next three years, Terry kept an eye on the Hall.

Beacon's scheme for 25 houses, five within the Hall's curtilage and four on the line of the south wall and billiard room was given full planning consent in 1984. Terry, seeing the first house built late that year, knew he had to act fast. With considerable overseas earnings, as Managing Director of a Belgian-based security firm and assistant to a British politician with Aegean interests, he returned to Britain. He wrote a last letter to Beacon asking if they would sell. It transpired that the majority shareholder, past retirement age, had no natural successor and was in favour of selling the company. Negotiations with this shareholder's accountants, who greatly overestimated Beacon's worth, soon became difficult. Later that year, in July 1985, Terry found demolition continuing, despite his insistance that he would not purchase Beacon if any further vandalism occurred. The then directors promised to stop and reinstate. They stopped, but did not reinstate. In August 1985, however, a deal was struck to buy 75 per cent of the shares at a third of the original asking price, provided that the Hall's destruction ceased.

All seemed well. Terry came north, buying essential equipment and vehicles and recruiting staff, including his personal assistant, Dawn Tyler. Three clearing banks were interested in lending the acquisition capital. Largely at the insistence of one of their partners, solicitors Theodore Goddard were engaged to handle the deal. A famous City practice, they worked as a team of specialists under senior partner Andrew Bingham. He advised Terry that, because of potential tax liabilities for Beacon, the deal should not be a simple share transaction, financed by high street banks. So, Theodore Goddard provided the client finance. There was a shock for Terry in September 1985: Beacon's junior partner (who owned 25 per cent of the company's shares) tried to sell Beacon to another party. He used the same solicitors who were negotiating with Theodore Goddard. Terry then sued for breach of contract and the second deal fell through. Eventually Terry's purchase of Beacon was concluded (at a much higher price than he had offered earlier) on 26 November 1985. Terry wrote to Michael, Lord Brougham telling him about the proposed restoration of the Hall and inviting his help. This began a close friendship between them and Lord Brougham became the project's patron, taking a close interest in the restoration.

In the next two and a half years all went well. The housing scheme was abandoned, and an agreement made with Eden District Council under Section 52 of the 1971 Town and Country Planning Act ensured the Hall's preservation. Restoration began in early 1986. In July 1986, the D.O.E. upgraded the Hall, on Terry's petition, to Grade 2*. The English Tourist Board, C.O.S.I.R.A. (later renamed The Rural Development Commission), Cumbria County Council and Eden District Council gave restoration grants. (When Terry saved High Head, Bingham proffered the finance and the vehicle for its acquisition.)

Within six months of the transfer, Beacon made its first profit for three years, and in the next financial year it made more than in its previous 25 years taken together. Terry modernised and relocated the company, a move paid for within 15 months. Turnover tripled in the next trading year. The 26 inherited staff rose to 108, while staff employed indirectly also increased. Local master craftsmen were attracted by Beacon's quality work in stone, slate, wood and lead. Fifteen trainees were taken on, studying stone-masonry and other skills at centres like York. Offers were received for Beacon and Terry, now a millionaire and well-placed to complete Brougham's restoration, considered selling the company and restoring the Hall with the sale money. He discussed offers with Bingham, who had left Theodore Goddard (expelled, it later transpired, for fraud in July 1986) and set up his own London firm in Duke Street. Bingham suggested the sale price, requested and was given his fees on account.

In April 1988 (during Easter all building companies and builders' merchants are mandatorily obliged to shut), Terry was doing a 'work in progress' audit with the firm's auditors at Beacon's offices when a businessman, Theodore B. Wynne and David Frank Taylor, a newly-qualified barrister, arrived. They announced that they were taking control of Beacon for Bingham. Now on the run, Bingham had converted Terry's 10,200 shares (worth about £75 each), while at Theodore Goddard, into a company of which he was managing director. Wynne and Taylor suggested that Bingham claimed Brougham and High Head, too. Working unpaid, building up 'Bingham's company' was bad enough, but to have Brougham at risk too was unbearable. Terry flew into a violent rage. Shaken, the visitors left. Wynne resigned his commission the next day, but Taylor persevered, threatening defamation writs.

Unknown to Terry, Bingham had been covertly altering Beacon's memorandum and articles of association, appointing a new board of directors and altering the bank mandates. He told the company's auditors of a change of emphasis. He had used similar tactics in July 1986 against Theodore Goddard, syndicating confidential papers (entrusted to him as a partner there) to the Inland Revenue, D.S.S., and H.M. Customs and Excise. By July 1988, Terry had obtained a Chancery Court order prohibiting Bingham and his associates' interference. Bingham now ran his solicitor's business by fax from Switzerland with Taylor as his London mouthpiece. The Law Society refused to strike Bingham off although the Vice-Chancellor Sir Nicholas Browne-Wilkinson pronounced him a fraud in the action of Walters and Others v. Bingham (Consolidated) in the Supreme Courts. As late as 16 September 1988, the Law Society was still inviting him to functions, even though a bench warrant had been issued for his arrest and he had been sentenced to six months' imprisonment for contempt of court.

Such had been Bingham's standing that many, from Barclays Bank to Sir Ian Collett of Westhorp Ward & Catchpole, were prepared to treat with or act for him. Terry meanwhile despaired. His provincial solicitors took six months to produce their first badly-written junior opinion and could not deal with Bingham's manoeuvres. Three and a half years later, with nothing left to fight over Terry persuaded a Master in Chambers to end this. During that time he was advised not to work or he would be liable for some or all of the huge legal aid bill. Terry had paid thousands of pounds of fees before his money ran out.

Bingham re-entered Britain as 'Arthur Davis', was seen by detectives and, after resisting with CS gas and a Stanley knife, was arrested in Bath, on 28 June 1989. On 23 July 1990, charged with 23 specimen counts of theft and fraud, he pleaded guilty to 11, involving just under £1 million, plea-bargaining the rest. He was sent to prison for six years, the judge indicating he could face more charges when released. In the event, he escaped from H. M. Prison Weylands and was on the loose for five weeks. He was only re-arrested following complaints from the public that he was at liberty.

In 1988, Barclays pressured Terry to resolve Beacon's ownership. He allowed them a debenture (a formal charge over its fixed and floating assets) knowing that it would rank ahead of any of Bingham's claims. Although the company was £150,000 within its facility, and £50,000 within the local bank manager's discretion, they exercised the debenture to recover the debt. On 26 October 1988, receivers Peat Marwick McLintock (Ferranti's advisers when they acquired fraudulent Californian firm I.S.C.) took control of Bingham's 62nd and last victim.

Finding Bingham more 'plausible' than Terry, Peat's questioned his ownership of Beacon. This bias was not surprising, as Bingham's employers, Theodore Goddard, had been the most powerful legal firm in the land and never less than ninth largest. Using Taylor and Collett, Peat's negotiated with Bingham. Peat's had two partners acting as directors in four of Bingham's companies. Bingham was in none of Peat's public reports on Beacon. Terry's presence in these reports affected the Brougham Hall Charitable Trust, and Peat suggested that it owed them a staggering £290,792. Then the Customs and Excise claimed he owed £203,034, the Inland Revenue £68,321. No claim was pursued but Terry did not know this would be the outcome, and was naturally worried as the Establishment closed ranks.

Perhaps prompted by Taylor, Peat's attacked Terry. On 30 November 1988, exceeding their remit, they wrote asking the English Tourist Board to suspend their £48,600 grant for Brougham, £27,000 of which had been received and spent. Under Nicholas Ridley's instructions to phase out Section Four grants anyway, they obliged. In 1992, having made their own enquiries the E.T.B. restored the grant. In January 1989, the National and Provincial Building Society withdrew £650,000 announced for High Head. Peat's had told the press that Terry owed them £210,000 and a 'well-wisher' had sent the reports to the National and Provincial. Peat's, in petty spite, told B.T. to cut off Terry's home telephone over Christmas 1988. B.T. obliged, even though Terry's guest, a local medical supervisor, needed a telephone to contact patients. The most senior Penrith lawyer and normally impartial local magistrate told Terry that no Penrith legal practice would help him.

Terry complained to the Chairman of Barclays and Peat's senior partner. He reported Peat's to the Institute of Chartered Accountants for unprofessional conduct, but no satisfactory response came, although the personal attacks stopped. In July 1990, Beacon (owned by Valuemarket Ltd., a wholly-owned subsidiary of 3M Construction of Carterton, Oxford) again went bankrupt, together with its parent company. With more receivers appointed for Beacon, Peat's wrote to Terry, on 11 July 1990, suggesting an interim discount of £156,437. 44 on their earlier bill.

Terry tackled Theodore Goddard. Before retiring, Michael Walters, senior partner, was evasive. On 20 February 1989 he wrote that it was 'not correct ... to suggest that my partners and I knew of Bingham's activities', until '... after detailed research and investigation following Mr. Bingham's departure from this firm'. Bingham left them on 7 July 1986. But in 1984, Dennis Cope of Fairview Estates, had complained to Walters about the conduct of the Salmanaza Trust, a company Bingham set up for the firm's clients. On 11 March 1985, Walters wrote to Bingham: '... it could reasonably be construed as a tacit admission that we had acted incompetently or improperly. This is the kind of problem that could turn into a real and expensive problem'. On 7 April 1985, Walters wrote again to Bingham: 'I confess it makes me more than a little uneasy that Jack Davis [an Isle of Man-based friend and business associate of Bingham], who is now getting quite old and over whom we have no control, appears to be in possession of about £300,000 of our clients' money'. Walters received similar clients' letters. One, from a family of four, told him of Bingham's theft of £280,410. 30 from two children between 31 May 1984 and 3 April 1985. On 25 July 1985, he told them that he had 'instituted an enquiry and hoped to be in touch in a few days'. On 30 July 1986, Mrs. Marie

Stacy (number two partner) told them that 'the prospects of recovering any of the mis-appropriated funds were remote'.

Terry met expensive, timewasting irrelevancy. Stacy told him to report Bingham to the Attorney-General because he could 'investigate bodies established for the public benefit'. The latter had no such interest. In April 1989, Walters told him that Lovell White Durrant were acting on Theodore Goddard's behalf. Tery took Lovell's 21 files on Bingham's activities. By November 1989, they had referred part of the matter back to Theodore Goddard. Anthony Heald, Walters' successor, then refused to discuss anything. A letter of 14 November 1989 said: '... we are not prepared to accept liability for your claims and nor are we prepared to enter into tendentious correspondence with you'. Lovell White Durrant wrote: '... we do not consider the responsibility for the failure of Beacon Builders can be ascribed to Mr. Bingham or to our clients'. Lord Brougham discussed the affair with Lord Mishcon. Preserving professional etiquette, Lord Mishcon kindly asked Terry whether he could help as an intermediary. On 25 May 1988, Lord Mishcon stated '... you have been the victim of fraud. Your shares have been stolen as a result of steps, taken by you, on the advice of a partner of Theodore Goddard'. Sir David Napley, introduced to Terry by Sir Clement Freud, wrote: '... at all material times he [Bingham] was a partner in Theodore Goddard and Co., was active throughout in the capacity of a partner, and the liability of that firm is beyond question'. This situation remains unresolved. Christopher Terry has received no compensation at all for the demise of Beacon at the time of writing.

II: Brougham Hall (1975-92)

Despite the upgrading of Brougham Hall from Grade 3 to 2 in 1975, Penrith building surveyor Peter Armstrong later examined it in 1978, for an abortive housing development, requiring partial if not total, demolition of the Hall. Five buildings Armstrong thought dangerous to enter. Meanwhile, 'protected' by law, Brougham suffered. By 1978, Beacon had taken much of the south wall to build houses. They built bungalows on concrete platforms in the avenue. The north wall turrets were pulled inwards, taking six feet of coping off a 60 yard, 50-ft. high wall. The listed building officer acquiesced, persuaded that the wall was unsafe. It was found to be sound on restoration. The terrace's doorway went. The terrace steps were cut to make fire surrounds. From the mansion house went coping stones, flags, ironwork and decorative figures. By July 1985, it was barely head-height. Roofs and much of the servants and stable blocks' inner walls vanished.

Saplings grew through the Hall's floors, undermining walls. The south-east tertiary archway was cut to its carved medieval keystone. Three tunnels were thought unsafe in 1978. The lily pond's remains disappeared in about 1984.

Supervised by architect Brian Lowe, restoration had already begun when Lord Brougham and his son Charles laid a foundation stone outside the office tower, on 30 May 1986. The 13th-century gateway had been rebuilt by the time a Community Programme (set up by Cumbria County Council and the M.S.C.) began on 27 August 1986. By 1 December the bridge had been restored. The south wall and stonework to the right of the office tower were now being repaired. The kitchen area near the bridge, and a stable block well (where a medieval spearhead was found) were cleared. A passage under the road was uncovered. On 30 December 1986, the Hall was transferred to the Brougham Hall Charitable Trust.

Stonemasons worked, sometimes with stone found on site, using a sheltered makeshift workshop under the carriage arch. In May 1987, the first unit, a smoke-house run by ex-careers officer Rona Newsom, opened. In late January the stable block's rebuilding

54. The stable block from inside the courtyard in the early 1960s.

started. The mansion house, billiard room, guard house, two stable rooms, office tower and the woods beneath the terrace were cleared. The kitchen area and nearby pheasant pens were dug out. A three-feet-wide courtyard well was found and cleared to a depth of 18 feet in March 1987. In April, the Hall was put on the telephone. Craftsmen worked in intervals between other projects and even in their spare time. In May, master mason David Fawcett restored, from a photograph, the garden archway in the south wall, itself completed as far as the billiard room. New bridge gates were made in Penrith and the guard room was re-floored. In July the stables and ice-house walls were rebuilt. There was further clearance in the mansion house and Bird's Tower. The digging out of the billiard room revealed bits of its ribbed ceiling, and foundations of a massive earlier tower.

From August to November, archaeologists David Cranstone (Director) and Chris Richardson (Site Assistant) led an excavation, with Supervisors Mike Treece and Lee Barry, and the Project Cumbria Team. Funded by Cumbria County Council, Project

Cumbria and the B.H.C.T., it dug four areas: (1) the interior of Bird's Tower; (2) an area extending north along the front of the mansion house; (3) a north-south corridor inside those walls and (4) a large room east of this within the mansion house. Although a separate report and finds analysis is still required, the major findings, in Mr. Cranstone's 1987 interim report, can be mentioned. It found that the tower (11 ft. square internally) had not originally been an external structure. Poorly constructed of rubblestone and originally cobbled, its first floor may have been reached by ladder or timber stair. Demolished masonry at its base showed it had been heightened. The tower seemed entirely domestic and not older than the 17th century. Dendrochronology dating of an 18-ft. long oak first-floor beam by Dr. Michael Baillie at the Palaeocology Centre, Queen's University, Belfast, revealed that it was from a tree planted in 1425 and felled in 1586. Perhaps the tower, or at least its internal timber, was James Bird's work. Elsewhere, cobbled floors (perhaps 17th-century) and three east-west walls were found. Rougher, lower floors to the north may have been a yard or roadway and (2) was perhaps byres or stables. Three sub-phases of 19th-century construction were indicated. The west wall was built straight on to cobbles of a demolished block. Later, a plinth-wall was built between (3) and (4). Finally an alcove was made in (3), eliminating the east-west corridor, and an above-ground partition wall was built between (3) and (4). Cranstone concluded it was unlikely that the north wing of the mansion house incorporated earlier work.

Meanwhile the main gateway tower was restored, mostly by trainees, by mid-December. The stable block windows were inserted in early December. David Fawcett cut a limestone archway for the area above the ice-house, and in November the billiard room's spiral staircase was cleared. A room east of Bird's Tower was found, along with pieces of gold-leafed stonework that it is hoped one day will be displayed or re-erected.

Brougham's training and job opportunities had reduced Penrith's unemployment by one per cent. With wide publicity, visitors arrived. The first Friends of Brougham Hall meeting took place on 19 December 1987. In 1988, Robert Stewart's book *Henry Brougham: His Public Career 1778-1868* appeared. Lord Hailsham reviewed it on Radio Four, and there seemed increasing interest in its subject.

1988 saw progress, despite the difficulties. Young trainee masons and carpenters under Fawcett and Geoffrey Bowerbank completed the stable block walls by mid-January. Chimneys were built by young mason Paul Grundy and the roof was timbered and complete by April. In early June, it had finishings, such as window frames, made by a City and Guilds trainee, Andrew Barclay. The artesian well was restored and dedicated to Dennis Warwick (1932-88) the first mason to have worked on the restoration.

In Spring 1988 a woodland path was made beneath the terrace, with a stone 'viewing' balcony with wooden railings. In September the steps beneath the terrace were cleaned. A cobbled path was started from the entrance gate to the billiard room by a retired Royal Artillery officer. He laid new grass lawns and flagstone paths. A sunken garden was made enclosing the 17th-century cobbles in front of Bird's Tower. Syd Walker tidied and rebuilt the tops of the guard house and Tudor hall in May and June. An Italian stone-cutting machine was installed in the stable block. Part of the terrace wall was rebuilt, and the ice house was cleared of hundreds of tons of rubbish.

The M.S.C. workers, led by Lee Barry, did great service. They discovered the foundations of a gazebo, 225 ft. south of the billiard room and excavated the passage from mansion house under the terrace. In the armour hall they found ceiling plaster, wood, marble and six lions' heads, two roses and an acorn, all gold leafed, and a bell-pull. The splendid armour hall fireplace (smashed into more than 20 pieces) was put in storage. In September the team found gold-patterned armour hall floor-tiling of 1848 carrying the

55. The restored stable block at Brougham Hall in April 1989.

56. The renovated office tower over the main gateway at Brougham, August 1989.

57. Rebekkah Wright and Dave Johnson's model of Brougham, made in 1988, showing the massive task of restoration remaining.

Brougham crest, probably made at Wetheriggs. They then cleared the south-west corner and mansion house cellars.

In June 1988, Rebekah Wright and David Johnson completed the B.H.C.T.'s model of the Hall and grounds. It showed the task ahead, one of this century's most ambitious British country house restorations. It is a rolling programme, with restored elements paying for more restoration. It means rebuilding two-thirds of Cottingham and Hussey's E-shaped mansion house: the 'down-stroke' from kitchen to octagon room, the top 'cross-stroke' from kitchen to ice-house, the middle one from just beyond the carriage arch to the tudor hall, and the bottom one from octagon room to billiard room.

In 1989, the B.H.C.T. restored parts of the E's top cross-stroke. Three stable block doors were made and an information board put up. In April, Penrith's Midland Bank donated their old oak panelling. More came from Appleby Courthouse, from the room where the Broughams' 1843 case against the Birds was heard. In early July the terrace was cleared and grassed over, and part of its top wall was rebuilt. This restoration was for Christopher and Alison Terry's wedding reception on Saturday 15 July.

58.   Christopher and Alison Terry at Brougham, July 1991.

After a blessing in St Wilfred's chapel, the reception took place on the terrace in sweltering afternoon heat with 150 guests. A marquee had been set up with a splendid spread of food and wine. Best man, Canada-based businessman Mr. Tony Karawani, a staunch Friend of Brougham, made a polished speech singling out the bride for special praise. As guests socialised, explored, drank or danced at the disco in one of the restored units, they sensed a little of what the Hall was like before its pillage. In 1990, the author examined the Brougham Hall visitors book: its last entry was in April 1933.

The wedding was a happy and entirely positive event. Christopher and Alison had a child, Jonathan, born on 31 August 1990. Alison had an immediate effect on the Hall. She has great affection for it, and the advantage of being a Cumbrian. Daughter of Mr. and Mrs. George Smailes of Highways, Cliburn, she boarded at Queen Elizabeth School, Kirkby Lonsdale, did a B.Tec Diploma in Sciences at Hull College of Further Education, and then worked for the well-respected Kendal land agents, Fisher Hogarth. She has brought to the Hall a shrewd, business-like common sense and charm.

By August 1989, rubble was cleared from the coach house and adjacent bakery. A passageway was found beneath the ice-house floor joists, and mid-19th-century tiles with red, yellow and black flower patterns were found in the floor of buildings in front of the stable block. However, on 22 August, the Cumbria Training Company's Brougham Hall Project was axed, ending on 29 September. The site was now largely cleared. In September a Brougham Hall information centre was set up in the office tower. Visitors could now buy information on Brougham and High Head, a print of the Tudor Hall and an exciting range of pottery embossed with the B.H.C.T.'s lion's head logo, of the head in the porch of the billiard room.

Ten tons of stone were delivered for more restoration in 1990. The pantry was slowly rebuilt and, in June, John Harrison moved in his metal-working equipment. By August the roof trusses and timbering of the Tudor hall (to become the Children's Lakeland Museum) were installed. The rampart area was sealed and flagged to waterproof the guard house, whose parapet was rebuilt in June and interior painted white. The site's main features were labelled with brass plaques. In August the guard house, now 'The Brougham Cupboard', opened as the Hall shop and reception centre.

The ice-house's first floor was made into an art gallery, with a large reconstructed mullion window using a hitherto unknown 1843 watercolour brought to the Hall by a visitor. David Fawcett (who runs his own stonemasonry company) returned to work in late June. In July (when Walker returned) the steps to the clocktower were rebuilt. A small round-headed window was created, and beneath, a plaque marked 'BHCT MCMXC'. The walls and battlements were complete by the end of July. The 1,000 square feet gallery, the 12th tenanted unit, opened in October.

After the art gallery's opening, restoration progressed purposefully, moving from the Hall's least damaged to its most devastated areas. Outside the walls, trees on the south lawn were replanted. Inside, the Tudor hall was roofed, floored and equipped with its own electricity supply. The opening of the museum was planned for July 1992. Malign fate seemed to strike, however, during the Penrith Horse Show on 9 April 1991. A 20-ton lorry smashed into the stair-bridge by the chapel, raising it five and half inches from position. The police eventually arrested the driver on the A66. The bridge then needed £25,000-worth of repairs and the B6262 was closed until 12 July while the damage was repaired. Much of the bill was met by the Norwich Union.

In 1992, the Brougham project has entered its toughest phase: the reclamation of areas left as stumpy, incongruous fragments by years of demolition. One of those, the tower in the north-west corner nearest the bridge, is being rebuilt as a temporary library

59.   The ice-house and clock tower area during its rebuilding and conversion into an art gallery, August 1990.

and strongroom for valuable exhibits. Another section, against the carriage arch and stretching across the courtyard in the direction of the 13th-century gateway, is being rebuilt from old photographs as the first complete unit to the east. The rebuilding of Bird's Tower is now a really urgent priority. This and the museum's opening, the unveiling of a memorial to the men of 79th Armoured Division who served at Brougham during the Second World War, and the publication of this book are all small stages in the regeneration and even re-invention of Brougham. A hard struggle, though, to revive it completely remains to be won.

The Hall's best security is a sustainable economic base and the enthusiasm and commitment of those who care about it. It may have led an exhausting, roller-coaster life of prosperity and ruin, but its supporters hope its revival is only just beginning.

III: High Head Castle (1956-92)

> I wanted to pull it down, and until I made an application for demolition, nobody seemed to care. Suddenly it becomes the most important place there is.

William Dickman, in *The Cumberland News*, 9 January 1987.

High Head, a major loss, was mentioned in the Victoria and Albert Museum's 'The Destruction of The Country House' exhibition of 1975.[2] This persuaded public opinion

that the country house was
a common heritage to be
cherished, not a 'white
elephant'. Country house
restoration became a
flourishing crusade. Cum-
bria did see restorations like
Appleby Castle (completed
in 1975) but its conser-
vation record as a whole was
poor, though it had the
lowest ratio of residents to
acres in England and Wales,
and plenty of space for new
building. Eden District
Council had twice the
number of listed buildings
the 1971 Town and Country
Planning Act recommended
for a listed buildings officer.
An unqualified, part-time
officer spent 20 per cent of
his time on them.

Masonry fell from the
castle's east and south sides
in 1956. Two earthquakes in
1979 and 1980 caused the
collapse of the east façade,
part of which moved almost
90 degrees from true. Old
cars by the walls gave the
castle a look of hopeless
desolation. Dickman would
not sell, despite interest

60. High Head Castle's entrance front in 1988.

from people including Kit Martin, the leading country house restorer in the north and
Scotland. In mid-November 1984, he applied for listed building consent to demolish.
The local authority consented, but Patrick Jenkin, Secretary of State for the Environ-
ment, ordered a public enquiry for July 1985.

On 2 May 1985, Mark Blackett-Ord of Warcop Hall appealed in *Country Life* for
an enterprising restorer to buy High Head. On 16 July, architect and surveyor
Mr. F. E. Palmer chaired the public enquiry in Penrith Town Hall. All parties gave
evidence: seven heritage bodies, including the Georgian Society, opposed Dickman.
Skelton Parish Council and Eden District Council did not oppose him. The enquiry
found that the castle was not dangerous or near collapse as he claimed, recommending
that its Grade 2* listing be retained and that it should be stabilised as a ruin. In October,
the Secretary of State refused Dickman consent to demolish, giving heritage groups 12
months to stabilise it.

Not having to sell, Dickman had an incentive to ensure more decay. Eden District
Council supported him, arguing that with Dalemain and Hutton-in-the-Forest open, the
area did not need a third attraction. They would not serve a compulsory purchase order

on him. By 1 August 1986, despite the Georgian Group, English Heritage and Eden District Council's plans, Dickman applied to demolish. He was refused. Removing timber frames in the parapet behind the servants' wing caused a stone fall. He applied for a Dangerous Structure Notice. Dickman planned to demolish the castle and sell the stonework, rejecting professional advice on the cost of stabilising the damaged wall. Neither well off nor fit, he had a sick wife and children aged from seven to 22 living in an insanitary two-bedroom wing.

61. The Venetian window in High Head Castle's south front overlooking the Ive.

In Summer 1986, the Georgian Group commissioned a feasibility study, written for the British Historic Buildings Trust by Hannah O'Grady (on secondment studying for an M.Sc. degree in Historic Preservation at Columbia University, New York). It outlined three options: (1) demolishing the main block but retaining the rest; (2) stabilising the castle as a ruin; and (3) restoring and converting it for domestic use. Arguing that an economic or commercial use was unsuitable, it concluded that (1) was the simplest, involving selling the stone to pay for the Tudor wing's repair. But it would destroy most of the house's architectural interest and Dickman could not maintain the rest. Option (2) would cost some £50-70,000 (assuming an H.B.M.C. grant for 40 per cent of costs) but would be financially unproductive. The grounds would need continued expenditure and Dickman was unhelpful. The report called (3) the most risky, involving substantial expenditure on the grounds to increase the castle's attraction. A grant of 40 per cent of costs could not be assumed. It would create a large deficit and need 'hitherto unheard of benefactors'. It said that the ownership problem could be solved by buying the castle and giving Dickman £30-35,000 of housing near Carlisle.

One day in November 1986, Dickman waited at High Head to receive the Dangerous Structure Notice the Council had told him to expect. Meanwhile Christopher Terry, who had tried to buy High Head, had a telephone call from a council official at home in Lowther, telling him to be at the castle in an hour if he was still interested in it. Collecting architect Brian Lowe in Penrith, he drove there. Architectural Salvage Ltd. were already on site, and were about to demolish the castle. Terry talked Dickman, initially hostile, into selling. Architectural Salvage left, while Terry promised to stabilise the castle within 24 hours, and did so. Dickman could now buy himself a good Cumbrian house with the sale money.

After Christopher Terry had bought High Head, in May 1987, raising funds to begin its restoration was problematic. Delay and frustration followed, mainly because of the project's estimated cost. The 1986 British Historic Buildings Trust had presented Carlisle architects Roy Nicholson Becker and Day with the task of assessing this. Accordingly, they costed the castle's re-roofing, the provision of floors for it at principal and first levels, the introduction of special 'hip trusses'. The calculations excluded the costs of windows, doors, ceilings and 'second fixing' items. The essential items of conversion above were calculated at £1,302,271. This figure included a contingency fund of five per cent of known costs (£54,261) and 15 per cent for preliminaries (£162,784). The company also drew up a list of 'desirable' features: a 50-space car park and landscaping for the grounds, a lift, a 700-metre road with drainage and passing places, and the reconstruction of garden and grounds. Including these costs, an allowance for structural repairs and fees (at 16.5 per cent of expenditure), the restoration and conversion's total costs came to £1,748,981.

Roy Nicholson Becker and Day also prepared a second, cheaper cost schedule. This included a provision for preliminaries, a contingency fund and the cost of installing windows. This cheaper scheme came to £970,445. In both schedules there was a significant problem. Even after an estimated £79,600 in grant aid had been allowed, neither produced a profit. The first provided a return of £1,079,600 and a £669,381 loss; the second a £954,000 return and a £15,845 loss. To be restored, it was clear that the castle would need much more grant aid.

English Heritage had been so delighted by the saving of High Head, that, even before the completion of the purchase, they had invited Terry to see them in London. After the purchase, he applied to English Heritage for their maximum grant of £400,000. By November 1987, obtaining it had become pivotal in the restoration plans. After some weeks of deliberation and inspections, English Heritage's Historic Buildings Advisory Committee recommended that he receive this grant. They cited Terry's 'good track record' of restoring houses and his enormous task at High Head. In early 1988, this decision was ratified by Lord Montagu of Beaulieu, the Chairman of English Heritage. The grant was made conditional on Terry's raising another £600,000 from the private sector before starting work. After he had cleared this £1,000,000 hurdle, they could reward him with another £100,000 of grant aid. Until he had raised £600,000 he was unable to start work.

The conditions English Heritage attached to their grant may have meant that the project looked vulnerable to potential backers. Its cost rose because of building industry inflation (around nine per cent per annum) and high interest rates. Borrowing became hazardous, since the site would actually produce nothing financially until after its two-year restoration. It did not help the project that the site remained empty while money was being sought. In addition it promised, as Brougham's restoration had been, to be an unpredictable business in which unexpected difficulties could arise. Some banks and institutions are worried about such schemes. They insist that costs are minutely itemised before work starts and expenses meticulously accounted for on a day-to-day basis. An unexpected discovery of an unsound wall can send such discoveries haywire. There were, in addition, the problems at Beacon.

Though the story of Beacon's collapse has been dealt with in large part earlier in this chapter, its effects at High Head have only been touched on. It ensured firstly that Terry had to direct Beacon employees towards non-B.H.C.T. projects, so that, by 14 June 1988, less than £1,000-worth of work had been undertaken at the castle. Volunteers started to clear the gardens and woods from spring onwards, and in the summer the Trust bought the rest of the western woods, more of the River Ive and a reversionary interest in part of the stable block, all for £28,000. (This was in addition to the £70,000 loan from Midland Bank, which had been taken out to buy the castle from Dickman.) The Trust also obtained a Countryside Commission grant towards restoring the formal avenue. On 22 December 1988 it seemed that, finally, there had been a breakthrough: the National and Provincial Building Society told the B.H.C.T. it wished to fund the first part of the castle's restoration with £660,000.

Unfortunately, in circumstances explained earlier this offer was withdrawn, a crushing blow for Terry's plans to revive High Head. Every month which passed added to interest payments for which he was personally liable. Work continued, however, and by the end of 1988 the castle was equipped with a new gravel forecourt (paid for by the Trust). The Trust had gained a further £38,000 from various sources including the Edmund Hodge Trust (a foundation specially established in memory of a landowner who lived at Elterwater Hall and loved Cumbria). But Peat Marwick McLintock, the sequestrators, soon removed all the scaffold battens from the castle. These had been paid for, in fact, by the National Heritage Memorial Fund on behalf of the Edmond Hodge Trust and were worth around £500. The sequestrators also tried to charge the B.H.C.T. £2,140 for site huts at the castle, but the worst blow came when they secured the suspension of the whole project with their public announcement in February 1989, that Terry owed them £210,000. As a result, no work was done at High Head in 1989.

In September 1989, after another offer to restore High Head Castle had fallen through, Christopher Terry placed the castle on the market, with estate agents Arnison and Co. of Penrith, once the Brougham family's local solicitors and estate managers. At the same time, he sought funding for the project to make the sale unnecessary. A year later, after this campaign had failed and no buyer had been found, it was decided to auction the castle.

The well publicised sale of a ruined mansion can attract the interest of a wide range of people, from committed restorers to dubious businessmen and incompetent amateurs. High Head was no exception. It attracted 640 potential bidders for its auction, planned for 7 February 1991 at Lords Cricket Ground. Unfortunately, the auction never took place.

On 16 January a man styling himself 'Richard Melville', of 'Vega Investments, Bethnal Green' offered to buy the castle for £160,000 on three conditions: that the auction was cancelled, the other 639 potential bidders were told that the castle had been sold, and that the Trustees' solicitor and stake-holder, Malcolm Hooker of Fleet, Hampshire, would return deposits he had received from potential bidders. Unfortunately Terry, hoping that it would bring a final end to the financial pressure High Head exerted on him 'bought' the deal. Its immediate conditions were that Melville paid over a £20,000 deposit, that contracts were exchanged on 19 January and that completion was achieved on 8 February. On 17 January, Melville insisted that the deal depended on Terry working as site supervisor and security officer for 20 months (the anticipated length of the project). Melville then started a company, High Head Castle Ltd., incorporated on 4 February, and published a public share offer. The share offers were dispatched from the address of a partnership which did not exist. This set the tone for what was to follow.

Soon after the exchange of contracts on 23 January, it became clear that despite their completion on 4 March, Melville could or would not pay the £160,000 purchase money. He could only come up with £136,000. Nor, it seemed, did he have enough money to pay Christopher Terry (promised a £3,000 salary per month) or his brother Hugh Terry, a Surrey-based professional builder who came north to help. On 16 March, work started on restoring the servants' quarters but the brothers had to suspend operations on 3 April and again on 10 April. Eventually on 11 April (warned by a former friend and business associate that Melville was crooked) the Terrys served him with a statutory demand for £26,083 (£2,083 of this being interest at the Law Society's rate of 15 per cent). Melville made more empty promises to pay this, and still unpaid, the Terrys again abandoned the site on 17 May. A £5,000 first payment arrived for them on 14 June, a sum of £3,000 on 3 July and another £3,000 on 5 July. As the servants' quarters neared completion, it became clear that Melville had not followed up Terry's introductions to sympathetic potential lenders like Canada Life. He had a mysterious lack of capital and an odd lack of enthusiasm for borrowing to make up the shortfall. Soothing assurances of payment were seldom followed by concrete results. On 25 July, a Colchester company, Black Crouchman & Co., tried to serve a bankruptcy petition on Melville at his Colchester address. His common law wife, Hermina Mary Day, denied ever meeting him.

After visiting High Head with Hermina Day (who had claimed not to know him at all the previous day!) Melville arrived on 27 July at Brougham Hall with her. He attended the Friends of Brougham Hall meeting there and was served with a bankruptcy petition by Christopher Terry and Lord Brougham. Melville (it was subsequently discovered that his real name was Richard Hastings Melville Smith) then fought an intricate but seemingly doomed rearguard action in the courts against bankruptcy. First he acknowledged the debt owed to Terry (£24,000 for completing High Head's purchase and £12,003 to Christopher and Hugh Terry), then he repudiated it. Later, in November 1991, he submitted a long late affidavit which postponed the proceedings until January 1992. On 18 February, the case was concluded but judgement was reserved, and later

62. High Head in 1921 from the north, showing the 1744-9 entrance front.

postponed until 5 March. Three large banks took action against Melville between January and March. On 13 April, four days after his solicitors had abandoned him, he submitted another affidavit and was put to proof by 28 April. Melville defended himself, and was given a further adjournment until 6 June. This depressing affair sadly continues at the time of writing. It marks a further destructive episode in High Head's sad history.

Just as this book was going to press, at 3.03 pm on 2 July 1992 Richard Smith (Melville) was made personally bankrupt in the Supreme Courts of Justice, upon the petition of the Trustees and other creditors.

* * * *

A restored High Head Castle and a reconstructed Brougham Hall would be fitting tribute to the past generations and families who lived in and cared for them. There has already been too much damage and destruction of the heritage left to Cumbria by the talent, enterprise and taste of families like the Musgraves, Curwens, Wilsons, Senhouses, Atkinsons, Lowthers and Briscos, and the gifted architects, craftsmen and gardeners they employed. A decayed Cumbrian country mansion like the fine, little-known Shaw End, a classical house near Grayrigg, which was burnt down c.1978, should not just be left to rot. The revival of old buildings that past squires and entrepreneurs have left us revitalises and enriches areas and communities. One local woman said, in 1989, of Crofton Hall's demolition: 'It was an absolute tragedy ... we really should have done something'. But now we have a second chance with the buildings, gardens and landscapes that remain. We can do something to stop their needless decay and destruction. For two such buildings this book has been an attempt, however imperfect, to help preserve and understand them.

1. Since well excavated, interpreted and stabilised with its gardens restored, it is now a successful tourist site.

2. *The Destruction of The Country House 1875-1975* (Thames and Hudson, 1974), picture no.57, and pp. 98 and 188.

BROUGHAM OF EAMONT BRIDGE AND BLACKHALL

CHART 1

```
PETER BROUGHAM OF EAMONT BRIDGE¹  = = Jane .........
   b: ca.1520                          b:
   d:    1581                          |  v:1581
                        _____|
                       |
HENRY BROUGHAM OF BLACKHALL²  =     = 1. Jane Wharton
   b: ca.1560                      |
   d:    1622                      |-----→ Jane = = Edward Aglionby

                       = 1602 = 2. Katherine Fallowfield  =   = 2. Toby Eden
                  _____|       b:              = 3. 1651 = Abraham Hawkins
                 |                               v:1651
                 |
THOMAS BROUGHAM OF EAMONT BRIDGE³ = 1638 = Mary Fleming
   b: 1619                                  b:
   d: 1648                        |         d:1654
_____|_____
|            |                              |    |      |                        |            |
HENRY⁴ =1660=Mary Slee   John⁵ = = 1. Margaret Allison   Thomas⁶=??  |   Agnes = Anthony       |   Toby⁸
b: 1638         b:        b:                 b:1642  |    b:      Wybergh          |   b:
d: 1698         d:1730    d:                 d:      |    d:                       |   v:1658
                         |                           |                        William⁷ = ??
-- SEE CHART 2 ----      |    =1716= 2. Susannah du Caster                        b:
   |                     |         b:                |                            d:
   |                     |         d:1726            |
___|_____       ____|_____      Christopher = = Margaret ...
|     |       |     |                |                    |
| O.I.   Mary = = Daniel     2 O.I.            Dudley =1730= Grace Carr
                 ↓                                    ↓
Brougham of New Hall, Newcastle & Cockermouth    Brougham of Askrigg and Kirkby Stephen
      ---- SEE CHART  4 ----                            ---- SEE CHART  5 ----
```

NOTES

1. Will dated 11 August 1581 refers *inter alia* to his wife Jane, his son Henry, and his sister's son, Roger Salkeld.

2. Bought 'land in Skelton Scales' from Robert and John Southwycke and Christopher Harrison 28 July 1618.

3. Born 17 years after his father's marriage to Katherine Fallowfield. Nothing is known of his life, and he died intestate. Admon. P.C.C. 6 July 1655 to John Fleming.

4. Generally known as Henry Brougham of Scales, where, according to Edmund Sandford 'he built a very fine house'.

5. Sometime High Constable of Kendal, referred to as John Brougham the Elder to distinguish him from his nephew, Commissioner John Brougham. His elder daughter, Agnes, married George Mounsey of Patterdale, and John the Elder was buried in Patterdale churchyard 6 May 1730. His younger daughter, Mary, married Richard Benson.

6. The only one of Thomas Brougham's sons for whom there is a parish register record of baptism: 16 January 1642/43 The BT for Skelton (the register is missing) shows the baptism of William, son of Thomas Brougham, 21 November 1663

7. Barton parish register shows the baptism of Agnes, daughter of William Brougham of Bridge, 20 November 1668

8. Known to be living in London in 1658, when he wrote to his uncle, John Fleming, from the 'Woolsack' in Bucklersbury on 10 October. Nothing more is known of him.

CHART 2   BROUGHAM OF SCALES AND BROUGHAM

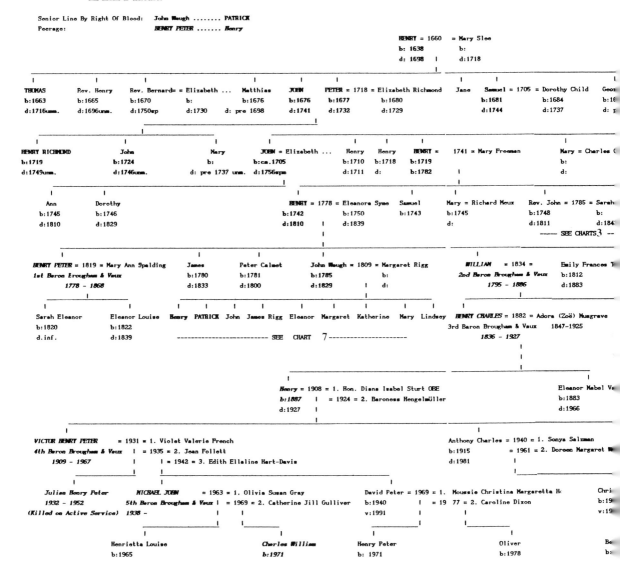

THE HOUSE OF BROUGHAM

Senior Line By Right Of Blood: John Waugh .... PATRICK
Peerage: HENRY PETER .... Henry

HENRY = 1660   = Mary Slee
b: 1638   b:
d: 1698 | d:1718

THOMAS   Rev. Henry   Rev. Bernard= = Elizabeth ...   Matthias   JOHN   PETER = 1718 = Elizabeth Richmond   Jane   Samuel = 1705 = Dorothy Child   Geor
b:1663   b:1665   b:1670   b: b:1676   b:1676   b:1677   b:1680   b:1681   b:1684   b:18
d:1716unm. d:1696unm.   d:1750sp   d:1730   d: pre 1698   d:1741   d:1732   d:1729   d:1744   d:1737   d: p

HENRY RICHMOND   John   Mary   JOHN = Elizabeth ...   Henry   Henry   HENRY =   1741 = Mary Freeman   Mary = Charles C
b:1719   b:1724   b: b:ca.1705   b:1710   b:1718   b:1719   b:
d:1749unm.   d:1746unm. d: pre 1737 unm. d:1756spm   d:1711   d: b:1782 | d:

Ann   Dorothy   HENRY = 1778 = Eleanora Syme   Samuel   Mary = Richard Meux   Rev. John = 1785 = Sarah
b:1745   b:1746   b:1742   b:1750   b:1743   b:1745   b:1748   b:
d:1810   d:1829   d:1810 | d:1839   d: d:1811   d:184
                                                                                        ----- SEE CHARTS 3 --

HENRY PETER = 1819 = Mary Ann Spalding   James   Peter Calmet   John Waugh = 1809 = Margaret Rigg   WILLIAM   = 1834 =   Emily Frances T
1st Baron Brougham & Vaux   b:1780   b:1781   b:1785   b: 2nd Baron Brougham & Vaux   b:1812
1778 - 1868   d:1833   d:1800   d:1829 | d: 1795 - 1886   d:1883

Sarah Eleanor   Eleanor Louise   Henry PATRICK John James Rigg Eleanor Margaret Katherine Mary Lindsey   HENRY CHARLES = 1882 = Adora (Zoë) Musgrave
b:1820   b:1822   3rd Baron Brougham & Vaux   1847-1925
d.inf.   d:1839   --------------------------- SEE   CHART   7 ----------------------   1836 - 1927

                                              Henry = 1908 = 1. Hon. Diana Isabel Sturt OBE   Eleanor Mabel Va
                                              b:1887 | = 1924 = 2. Baroness Hengelmüller   b:1883
                                              d:1927 | d:1966

VICTOR HENRY PETER   = 1931 = 1. Violet Valerie French   Anthony Charles = 1940 = 1. Sonya Salzman
4th Baron Brougham & Vaux | = 1935 = 2. Jean Follett   b:1915   = 1961 = 2. Doreen Margaret W
1909 - 1967 | | = 1942 = 3. Edith Ellaline Hart-Davis   d:1981 |

Julian Henry Peter   MICHAEL JOHN   = 1963 = 1. Olivia Susan Gray   David Peter = 1969 = 1. Moussie Christina Margaretta H   Chri
1932 - 1952   5th Baron Brougham & Vaux | = 1969 = 2. Catherine Jill Gulliver   b:1940 | = 19 77 = 2. Caroline Dixon   b:19
(Killed on Active Service) 1938 - | | v:1991 | v:19

                Henrietta Louise   Charles William   Henry Peter   Oliver   Be
                b:1965   b:1971   b: 1971   b:1978   b:

```
|                        |
Agnes = John Forster    Mary =      = Daniel Brougham
b:1661                  b:          b:1679
d: ca.1740              d:1754      d:1717
                        — SEE CHART 4 —

          |              |
        Dorothy        Dorothy
        b:1709         b:1713
        d:1710         d:

          |              |
mas Aylmer   Charles    Rebecca = = Richard Lowndes
           b:1750      b:1753    b:
           d:          d:1828    b:


|                                            |                        |                              |                            |
ancesca Vignati  Reginald Thomas Dudley = 1884 = 1. Augusta Louisa Ward   Alice Eleanora          Emily Evelyn              Adela Mary Grenfell
                 b:1853                        b:1860                     b:ante 1839            b:1839                    b:1847
Maria Faunce     d:1925sp                      d:1902                     = Rev. Hon. Thomas Edwardes   = Francis Sandys Dugmore   = Sir Charles Archer Cook
T 4 ------                                     = 1900 = 2. Isabella Schuster
                                                       b:
                                                       d:


thia Millicent Eva = 1940 = Col. Francis Thomas Davies
                          b:


|                           |
Elizabeth Goldridge    Adrian Charles =   !1967= Jan Westhorpe
                       b:1945             b:
991                    v:1991             v:1991

          |
        Guy Christopher
        b:1975
```

CHART 3 BROUGHAM OF BALLYHAISE AND LISMORE

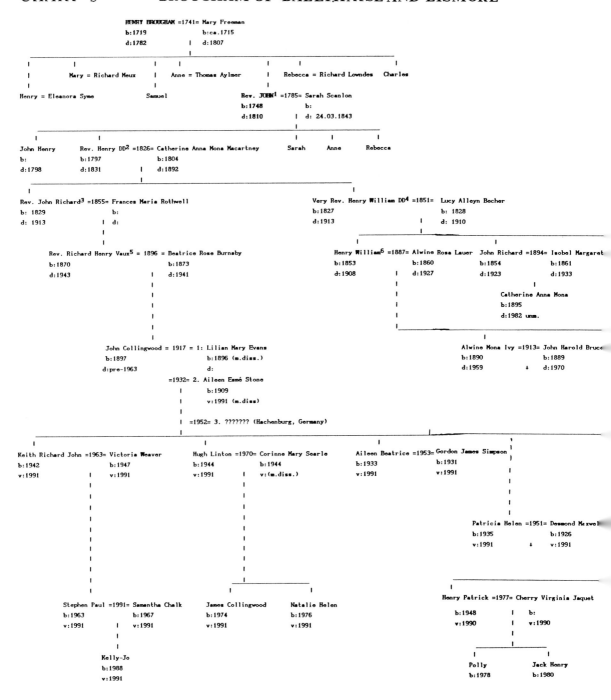

HENRY BROUGHAM =1741= Mary Freeman
b:1719   b:ca.1715
d:1782   d:1807

Mary = Richard Meux   Anne = Thomas Aylmer   Rebecca = Richard Lowndes   Charles

Henry = Eleanora Syme   Samuel   Rev. JOHN[1] =1785= Sarah Scanlon
b:1748   b:
d:1810   d: 24.03.1843

John Henry   Rev. Henry DD[2] =1826= Catherine Anna Mona Macartney   Sarah   Anne   Rebecca
b: b:1797   b:1804
d:1798   d:1831   d:1892

Rev. John Richard[3] =1855= Frances Maria Rothwell   Very Rev. Henry William DD[4] =1851= Lucy Alleyn Becher
b: 1829   b: b:1827   b:1828
d: 1913   d: d:1913   d: 1910

Rev. Richard Henry Vaux[5] = 1896 = Beatrice Rose Burnaby   Henry William[6] =1887= Alwine Rosa Lauer   John Richard =1894= Isobel Margaret
b:1870   b:1873   b:1853   b:1860   b:1854   b:1861
d:1943   d:1941   d:1908   d:1927   d:1923   d:1933

Catherine Anna Mona
b:1895
d:1982 unm.

John Collingwood = 1917 = 1: Lilian Mary Evans   Alwine Mona Ivy =1913= John Harold Bruce
b:1897   b:1896 (m.diss.)   b:1890   b:1889
d:pre-1963   d: d:1959   d:1970
=1932= 2. Aileen Esmé Stone
b:1909
v:1991 (m.diss)

=1952= 3. ??????? (Hachenburg, Germany)

Keith Richard John =1963= Victoria Weaver   Hugh Linton =1970= Corinne Mary Searle   Aileen Beatrice =1953= Gordon James Simpson
b:1942   b:1947   b:1944   b:1944   b:1933   b:1931
v:1991   v:1991   v:1991   v:(m.diss.)   v:1991   v:1991

Patricia Helen =1951= Desmond Maxwell
b:1935   b:1926
v:1991   v:1991

Stephen Paul =1991= Samantha Chalk   James Collingwood   Natalie Helen   Henry Patrick =1977= Cherry Virginia Jaquet
b:1963   b:1967   b:1974   b:1976   b:1948   b:
v:1991   v:1991   v:1991   v:1991   v:1990   v:1990

Kelly-Jo   Polly   Jack Henry
b:1988   b:1978   b:1980
v:1991

NOTES

1. Educated at Eton and King's College, Cambs: BA 1771; MA 1775: Fellow 1770-1778. Dean of Ely Cathedral 1771 priest 1773: Rector of Ballyhaise and Bailleborough, Diocese of Waterford, Ireland.

2. Rector of Tallow, Diocese of Lismore. His wife, Catherine, was the daughter of Sir John Macartney of Lish, Bt., by his second wife, Catherine, daughter of the Rt. Hon. Walter Hussey Burgh, Lord Chief Baron of the Court of Exchequer in Ireland.

3. Rector of Monkstown, Co. Cork, and Canon of Christ Church, Dublin. He was a witness at the marriage of his 2nd cousin, James Rigg Brougham to Isabella Eliza Cropper in Liverpool, 6 October 1854.

4. Educated Trinity College, Dublin. Classical Moderator and Gold Medallist 1847. Dean of Lismore from 1847

5. Was in Adelaide, South Australia, in 1908. Died at Freshwater, Isle of Wight.

6. Educated St. Columba's College, Ireland, and Keble College, Oxford. All-round sportsman and horseman. Housemaster of Wellington College, Berks. His wife was the daughter of Judge Lauer of Krefeld, Germany.

7. Married and died (date unknown) in Queensland, Australia. His only son, Roland, died young.

8. QC, 1988 and a Registrar in Bankruptcy.

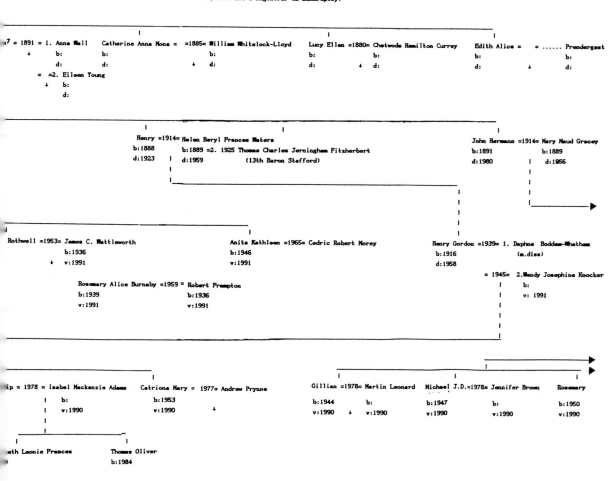

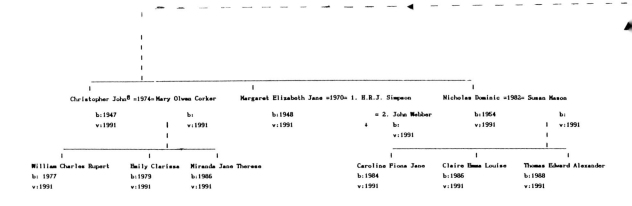

Christopher John[8] =1974= Mary Olwen Corker
b:1947   b:
v:1991   v:1991

Margaret Elizabeth Jane =1970= 1. H.R.J. Simpson
b:1948   v:1991
                                = 2. John Webber
                                b:
                                v:1991

Nicholas Dominic =1982= Susan Mason
b:1954   b:
v:1991   v:1991

William Charles Rupert   Emily Clarissa   Miranda Jane Therese
b: 1977   b:1979   b:1986
v:1991   v:1991   v:1991

Caroline Fiona Jane   Claire Emma Louise   Thomas Edward Alexander
b:1984   b:1986   b:1988
v:1991   v:1991   v:1991

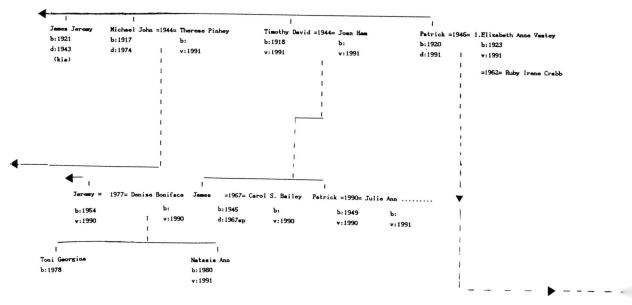

James Jeremy
b:1921
d:1943
(kia)

Michael John =1944= Therese Pinhey
b:1917   b:
d:1974   v:1991

Timothy David =1944= Joan Ham
b:1918   b:
v:1991   v:1991

Patrick =1946= 1.Elizabeth Anne Vestey
b:1920   b:1923
d:1991   v:1991

               =1962= Ruby Irene Crabb

Jeremy = 1977= Denise Boniface
b:1954   b:
v:1990   v:1990

James =1967= Carol S. Bailey
b:1945   b:
d:1967sp   v:1990

Patrick =1990= Julie Ann ....
b:1949   b:
v:1990   v:1991

Toni Georgina
b:1978

Natasia Ann
b:1980
v:1991

CHART 4   BROUGHAM OF NEW HALL, NEWCASTLE AND COCKERMOUTH

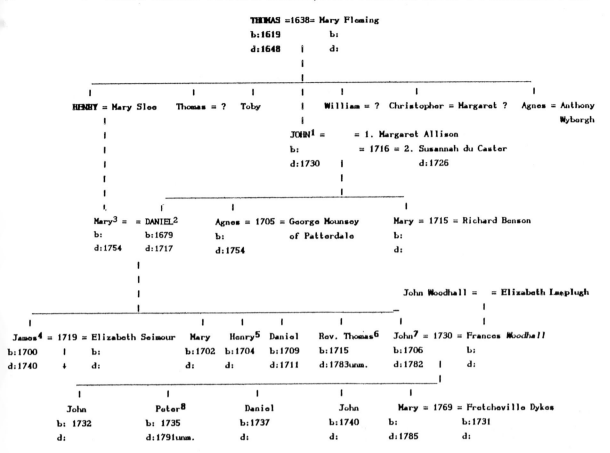

1. John Brougham the Elder was of New Hall, Fairbank, Westmorland

2. Daniel Brougham was appointed Collector of Customs, Carlisle, in 1709, and Port Surveyor of Newcastle in 1713 at a salary of £60 pa.   He was a godson of Daniel Fleming.

3. Mary Brougham inherited New Hall, Fairbank (Staveley), from her brother, Commissioner John Brougham, who had purchased it from Daniel's father, sometime High Constable of Kendal.

4. James was the father of an illegitimate son by his cousin, Grace Brougham, whose grand-daughter, Grace Idle, married Dr. James Brougham. He married Elizabeth Seimour, by whom he had two sons, at the Fleet Prison.

5. Carlisle Grammar School 1712; Queen's Coll. Oxford 1720; BA 1727, MA1728. No further information.

6. Rev. Thomas Brougham was vicar of Kingsey, Bucks.   He received the news of the death in London of his nephew, Daniel Seimour Brougham, 25.12.1778

7. John Brougham was an attorney of Cockermouth.   He married Frances Woodhall, whose mother was the former Elizabeth Lamplugh, at Lorton.

8. Peter Brougham took the name and arms of Lamplugh, and succeeded to the estates of his father, his uncle (Rev. Thomas Brougham), and his great-uncle (Rev. Bernard Brougham); and bought Scales from his cousin, Henry Brougham the Younger. He died unmarried, and his niece Mary Dykes, who had married her cousin Joseph Dykes Ballantyne, carried the estates of Dovenby (inherited from the Lamplughs) and Scales to the family of Dykes.

CHART 5

BROUGHAM OF ASKRIGG

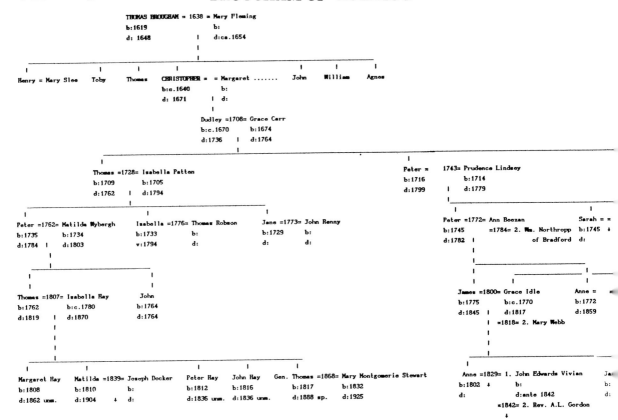

```
                                                                |
                                                            Grace =1730= George Monkhouse
                                                            b:1710  |   b:
                                                            d:1778  |   d:
                                                                    |
                                                       _____|_____
|            |                                         |                                                      |
Isabel    James =1776= Mary Lindsey   Samuel        Dudley         Mary           Grace =   = Christopher Idle      11 O.I.
:1747     b:1750      b:1747          b:1751         b:1754         b:1757         b:    |  b:
:1748     d:1837  |   d:1801          v:1800         d:1754         d:1831         d:    |  d:
                  |                                                                      |
                  |                                                                      |
                  |                                                                      |
          (Rev.) Samuel Lindsey =1814= Anne Banks
                  b:1778               b:1794
                  d:1835         |     d:1863
                                 |_____▶

                     |                                      |        |                        |                            |
v. Thomas Austin  Georgiana =1836= Rev. George  Drummond  William  Grace =1847= Capt. Martin Irving  Mary Ann =1854= Rev. Sparks Byers  James Peter =1843=
                  b:1805          b:                       b:1803   b:1807      b:              b:1812          b:              b:1816
                  d:1879          d:                       v:1845   d:          d:1855          d:              d:              d:1890   |
                                                                                                                                        |
                                                                                                                                        |
                                      |                        |                          |              |            ▶
                                  Marion =      = Col. Geo. Osborn   Grace Edith =    = .... Bryden   Matilda    Matilda Irmah =
                                  b:1848       b:                    b:c.1850       b:               b:c.1849   b:1850
                                  v:1888    ↓  v:1888                v:1888         d:ante 1888      d:1850     v:1888
```

```
←

Adele Fraser née de Momet    James Lindsey =1841= Mary Skelton              Mary =1837= Thomas Parke    Sarah Lightfoot    Anne = 1841 = Edward Thompson
b:1820                       b:1815            b:1816                        b:1817       b:            b:1819             b:1826        b:
d:1903                       d:1847      |  2. =1853= Edward Wood Davidson   d:1891 ↓    d:             d:1820             d:    ↓     d:
                                         |
←                                        |
        |                      |         |           |                    |
C.T. Thomas   Annie =     = ......MacDonald   Jean Margaret   James Webb =1883= Helena Grace Stewart   Joseph Skelton   Agnes Anne        Mary Isabel
b:            b:c.1845    b:                  b:c.1851        b:1860            b:1864                  b:1842           b:1844            b:1847
v:1888        v:1888      d:ante 1888         d.1909 unm.     d:1909      |     d:1923                 d:1875 unm.      d:1849            d:
                                                                         |
                                                                         |
        Helen Marion =1916= Francis Fraser Shepherd Douglas     Maud Adele = 1916= Tom Barry
        b:1884              b:1880                               b:1890           b:1889
        d:                  d:                                   d:               d:


                                                     James =1877= Elizabeth Montagu Shawe
                                                     b:1845       b:1847
                                                     d:1924   |  d:1938
                                                              |
                                                              |
                                                     Auriol Margaretta =1913= William Henry Alfred Fitzroy, Viscount Ipswich
                                                     b:1886                   b:1884
                                                     d:1938             ↓     d:1915

                                                              2. =1929= Lt. Col.G.R.V. Hume-Gore
```

CHART 6   BROUGHAM OF GUERNSEY AND CANADA

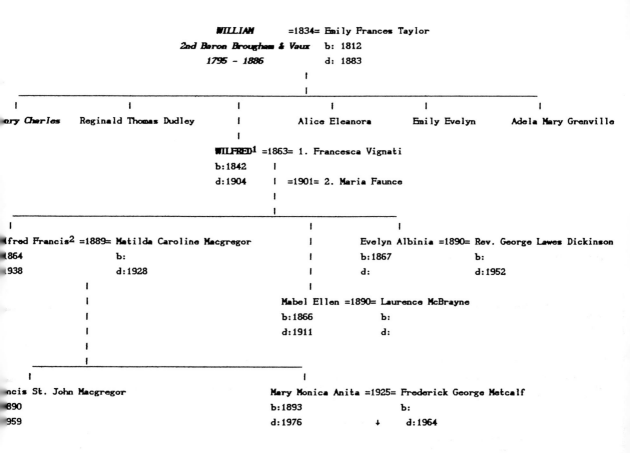

WILLIAM   =1834= Emily Frances Taylor
2nd Baron Brougham & Vaux   b: 1812
1795 - 1886   d: 1883

ory Charles   Reginald Thomas Dudley   Alice Eleanora   Emily Evelyn   Adela Mary Grenville

WILFRED[1] =1863= 1. Francesca Vignati
b:1842
d:1904   =1901= 2. Maria Faunce

fred Francis[2] =1889= Matilda Caroline Macgregor   Evelyn Albinia =1890= Rev. George Lawes Dickinson
864   b: b:1867   b:
938   d:1928   d: d:1952

Mabel Ellen =1890= Laurence McBrayne
b:1866   b:
d:1911   d:

ncis St. John Macgregor   Mary Monica Anita =1925= Frederick George Metcalf
890   b:1893   b:
959   d:1976   ↓   d:1964

1. Hon. Wilfred Brougham was of Grangehill, Guernsey. He was commissioned into the 10th (Prince of Wales's Own) Hussars in 1859 (Cornet, 18.02.1859; Lieutenant 10.05.1861), and transferred to 17th Lancers 12 December 1865. He resigned his commission in this regiment in 1865, and his father bought him a commission in the Westmorland Militia which so incensed the senior subalterns that they threatened to resign. Wilfred himself resigned in 1868, and was in 1869 Lord Brougham noted in his diary that he had made a new will, 'omitting Wilfred'.

2. Educated Charterhouse and Pembroke College, Cambs. (Admon. pens.1 October 1885), BA 1888. Solicitor, (Messrs. Day, Russell & Brougham of Norfolk St., Strand, London). Solicitor of the Supreme Court of British Columbia: Assistant Solicitor to Canadian Pacific Railways

BROUGHAM OF'EDINBURGH, LONDON AND AUSTRALIA

CHART 7

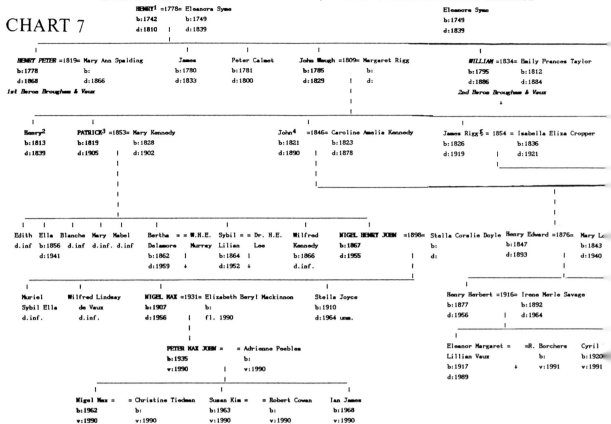

NOTES

1. Lived in Edinburgh from c.1770 until 1790, when he retired to Brougham Hall. It is doubtful if he had ever lived at the Hall prior to ca.1770. Existing documents show him as of Castle Yard, Holborn, Co. Middlesex.

2. Was an Addiscombe Cadet in 1830, but transferred to the Bengal Cavalry 1832. Died at Karnaul 10 October 1839.

3. Went to Australia (NSW) in 1838 and was subsequently disinherited by his uncle. His early years as a pastoralist were very successful, but a run of bad seasons and rash decisions ended his land-owning dreams. His final years (1876-1905) were spent as a Police Magistrate, and he died at Gunnedah NSW 23 August 1905.

4. Followed his elder brother to Australia in 1839, and in conjunction with Patrick and their Kennedy relatives had early success; but he, too, failed and was bankrupted in 1870. He died at Poolamacca Station, then owned by his son, John Waugh Brougham, 18 September 1890.

5. James Rigg Brougham was also born in Edinburgh, but completed his training for the Bar in London. He was appointed Registrar in Bankruptcy at the Liverpool court in 1848, and following a subsequent move to London in the 1860s was appointed Senior Registrar in Bankruptcy at the High Court in 1891, a position he held until his retirement in 1917. He died at Boathwaite Green (Levens), Westmorland 5 March 1919.

Patrick Rigg	Eleanor =1845= Henry Mowbray	Katherine =	=1875= John M. Douglas	Mary =1855= Rev. William Davidson	Lindesay	William
b:	b:1816 b:	b:1817	b:	b:1822 b:	b:1824	b:1828
d:	d:1887 d:	d:1884	d:	d:1876 ↓ d:	d:1845	d:1829

Eleanor	John Waugh =	= Blanche Desailly	Alice	Patrick William	Ada	Ethel =	= Robert MacDonald Chapman
b:1848	b:1849	b:	b:1850	b:1851	b:1852	b:1864	b:
d:1858	d:1923	d:	d:1858	d:1889unm.	d:1858	d:1939 ↓	d:

Alan Evans	Cyril Casey	Lilian Mary	Alfred Clive	Eileen =	= Dr. Dobbyn	Keith George =	= Katherine Langloh Parker	Beatrice =	= T.H. Palmer
b:	b:1881	b: ?1885	Desailly	b:	b:	b:1883	b:	b:	b:
dsp.	d:1919.unm.	d: unm.	d:inf.	d:	d:	d:1967	d:	d:	d:

nette =	= E.E. Healy	Henry John	Betty Lillian =	Leslie Coats	Loine =	= James Bryant	John Frederick	Kenneth Langloh = 1949 = Pamela Thwaites	Barbara Eleanor
b:	b:1922	b:1928	b:	b:1931 ↓	b:	b:	b:1913	b:	b:1918
↓ d:	v:1991	v:1991	↓ d:	v:1991	v:1991	d.young	d:1985	v:1990	v:1990 unm.

Timothy Langloh =1979= Jane Baker Douglas	Ann Heather =1977= Duncan Thomas Young
b:1950 b:	b:1956 b:
v:1990 v:1990	v:1990 ↓ v:1990

Georgina Jane	Annabel Eliza	Angus Langloh	Jane Langloh =1970= John Sidney Ayers	Sam Kenneth = 1986= Joan Tania Hill
b:1981	b:1983	b:1987	b:1951 b:	b:1961 b:
			v:1990 ↓ v:1990	v:1990 v:1990

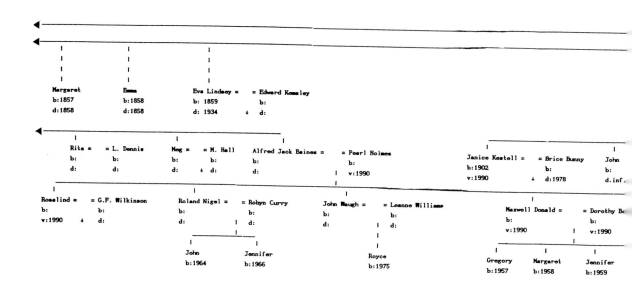

Margaret
b:1857
d:1858

Emma
b:1858
d:1858

Eva Lindsey =
b: 1859
d: 1934

= Edward Kemsley
b:
d:

Rita =
b:
d:

= L. Dennis
b:
d:

Meg =
b:
d:

= M. Hall
b:
d:

Alfred Jack Baines =
b:
d:

= Pearl Holmes
b:
v:1990

Janice Kestell =
b:1902
v:1990

= Brice Bunny
b:
d:1978

John
b:
d.inf.

Rosalind =
b:
v:1990

= G.F. Wilkinson
b:
d:

Roland Nigel =
b:
d:

= Robyn Curry
b:
d:

John Waugh =
b:
d:

= Leanne Williams
b:
d:

Maxwell Donald =
b:
v:1990

= Dorothy Be
b:
v:1990

John
b:1964

Jennifer
b:1966

Royce
b:1975

Gregory
b:1957

Margaret
b:1958

Jennifer
b:1959

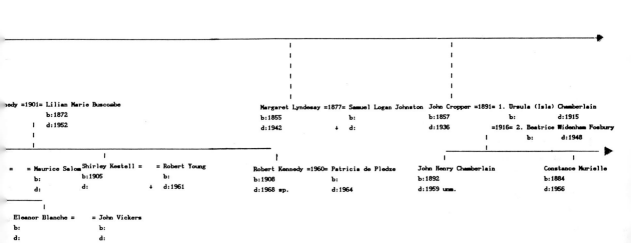

...edy =1901= Lilian Marie Buscombe
        b:1872
        d:1952

Margaret Lyndesay =1877= Samuel Logan Johnston   John Cropper =1891= 1. Ursula (Isla) Chamberlain
b:1855   b: b:1857   b: d:1915
d:1942   d: d:1936   =1916= 2. Beatrice Widenham Fosbury
                                                               b: d:1948

= = Maurice Salom Shirley Kestell = = Robert Young   Robert Kennedy =1960= Patricia de Pledze   John Henry Chamberlain   Constance Murielle
b: b:1905   b: b:1908   b: b:1892   b:1884
d: d: d:1961   d:1968 sp.   d:1964   d:1959 unm.   d:1956

Eleanor Blanche =   = John Vickers
b: b:
d: d:

Harold de Vaux =1893= Dorothy Elizabeth Puckle
b:1858   b:
d:1930 | d:

Kate =1890= Sir John Weston MP
b:1865   b:
d:1927 ↓ d:

B
b
d

=‡ 1912= Oswald Wells
b:
dsp.

Gwendoline Isla =1913= Gilbert Huggins
b:1892   ↓ b:
d:1974   d:

Thomas de Vaux
b:1894
d:1982 unm.

Annie Wakefield =1891= Jacob Wakefield
b:1860   b:
d:1951   ↓ d:

Mary =1897= Gerrard Pow
b:1872   b:
d:1956 ↓ d:

Bibliography

Primary Sources

Hill MS. Collection, Carlisle P.R.O. (in synopsis).

Ballantine Dykes Papers, Carlisle P.R.O.

Croker J. W., MSS., William Clements Library, Ann Arbor, University of Michigan (correspondence between Viscount Lowther and Croker).

Excise Minute Books, Kew P.R.O. (synopsis of entries on the Brougham family by Peter Brougham Wyly).

The wirrll of Hon. Diana Isabel Brougham (d. 1967).

Letters of 1836 from Henry 1st Lord Brougham to William Blamire, MP (1790-1862), in the possession of Dr. C.H. Maycock.

Deeds and papers belonging to Michael, Lord Brougham.

Brougham Papers in the Library of University College, London. These include: L. N. Cottingham's letters to William Brougham; letters from Richard Charles Hussey to William Brougham; letters from George Shaw to William Brougham; letters from Brougham employees to William Brougham; Mrs. Eleonora Brougham – William Brougham; Henry-William Brougham letters; correspondence on the dispute with the Bishop of Carlisle and the rector over St Wilfred's chapel, 1847; Brougham estate papers and maps, tax surveys; William Brougham's notebooks; William Brougham's Diary (1847-70 and 1877); letters from Henry Charles Brougham to William Brougham (1849-76); and from James Rigg Brougham, William Ewart Gladstone and Leonard Edmunds to William Brougham.

Bill of Complaint submitted in Chancery by Leonard Edmunds against William Brougham to Lord Chancellor Cranworth, filed 15 March 1866.

Brougham Hall Visitors' Book (1888-1933).

The Diary of John Cam Hobhouse, British Library (Additional MSS).

1871 Census Records, Carlisle P.R.O.

Ordnance Survey maps (1860, 1899, 1900, 1920) for the Brougham area, Kendal Record Office.

Markham Family Records, Morland House, Morland, Cumbria.

Atlantic House, Holborn Viaduct, London: bankruptcy records in the Public Search Room of 4th Lord Brougham and his brother Anthony Charles Brougham.

George Shaw's Diary, Hewkin Collection, Saddleworth Museum, Oldham.

Papers and correspondence of Christopher Terry.

Appeal for funds to repair Brougham Chapel, unpublished (1932).

The National Monuments Record for Brougham (1935).

Site survey and location plan of proposed housing development at Brougham Hall by Peter Armstrong, M.C.S.I., for Beacon Builders, Penrith (1 November 1978).

Bentley Drivers Club, Ltd.: records of four and a half litre Bentley chassis SM 3912.

Letters from ex-C.D.L. Tank crew members to Lt. Col. George Forty, Director and Curator of the Bovington Tank Museum (1991).

Unpublished books and pamphlets

Alisdair Ayscough: 'Brougham Hall – News Sheet for the Brougham Hall Community Programme' (1 December 1986).

'Lady Zoe Brougham (1849-1925)', extracts from Wells family papers, etc.

Chronology of High Head Castle's History, by D. B. Perriam (and Dr. Henry Summerson, Bruce Jones, David Bowcock, Jim Robinson, John Huggon, Steven White, Alec Dewhurst, Andrew Humphries and Mike Jackson).

David Cranstone: Interim Report on 1987 Excavations at Brougham.

The Friends of Brougham Hall newsletters.

Itinerary and service booklet for the 4th Lord Brougham's wedding, Tuesday, 21 April 1931.

Guide to St Cuthbert's church, Clifton.

Janet Myles, 'L.N. Cottingham (1787-1847) architect: his place in the Gothic Revival', PhD. Thesis, Leicester Polytechnic (1989).

Hannah O'Grady/British Historic Buildings Trust: 'High Head Castle, Ivegill, Cumbria' (1986).

Peter Brougham Wyly: 'The Brougham Family: An Extension' (1986).

Secondary Sources

Adelslexikon Band, vol. V (1984).

The Annual Register (1865).

Aspinall, A., *Lord Brougham And The Whig Party* (Archon Press, 1972).

Atlay, J. B., *The Victorian Chancellors*, vol. 1 (Smith, Elder and Co., 1906).

Bailey, R. N., 'A Cup-mount from Brougham, Cumbria', *Medieval Archaeology*, vol. 21 (1977), pp. 176-80.

Brougham, H., *The Life and Times of Henry, Lord Brougham* (Longmans, 1871).

Buddle Atkinson, R. H. M. and Jackson, G. A., eds., *Brougham and His Early Friends: Letters to James Loch 1798-1809*, 3 vols. (privately printed, 1908).

Brougham Castle (English Heritage, 1975).

Brougham, W., 'Report of the Cases of Robinson v. Bird And Others, And The Queen v. Birds. Held At Appleby Assizes, on Friday, 11th August, 1843' (James Ridgeway, 1843).

Brougham, W., 'The Tombs of the De Broham Family', *Archaeological Journal*, vol. IV (1847).

'The Outlying Portion of The Brougham Estate near Penrith For Sale by Auction 1932', published on behalf of Arnison and Co., St Andrews Place, Penrith, Cumberland.

'Brougham Hall, Penrith. Catalogue of the Valuable Contents. To be Sold by Auction, on the Premises ... on TUESDAY, JUNE 21ST, 1932 and Four following days, at 12 o'clock precisely each day.

Auctioneers: GARLAND-SMITH & CO., 100 Mount Street, London, W.1.'.

Bulmer, *Directory of Cumberland and Westmorland* (1906).

Burke's Family Index (1976).

Burke's Landed Gentry, vol. I (1863).

Burke's Landed Gentry, vol. I (1969).

Burke's Landed Gentry, vol. III (1972).

Burke's Landed Gentry (1937).

Burke's Landed Gentry (1970).

Burke's Peerage (1938).

Burke's Peerage and Baronetage (1940).

Burke's Peerage and Baronetage (1970).

Burke's Peerage, Baronetage and Knightage (1953).

Burke's Peerage, Baronetage and Knightage (1970).

Burke's Peerage, Baronetage, Knightage and Companionage (1963).

Burnett, T. A. J., *The Rise and Fall of a Regency Dandy: The Life and Times of Scrope Berdmore Davies* (John Murray, 1981).

Cannon, P., Fuller, Major-General J. F. C., Hordern, Colonel P. H., 'The C.D.L. Tanks of Lowther Castle', *After The Battle*, no. 16, pp. 50-53 (1977).

Carlisle Journal.

Carlisle Patriot.

Chateaubriand, Duc de, *The Memoirs of Chateaubriand* (Penguin, 1965).

Cockayne, G. E., *The Complete Peerage* (St Catherine Press, 1912).

Cockayne, G. E., *The Complete Baronetage*, vol. II, 1625-49 (1902).

Colvin, H., *Biographical Dictionary of British Architects 1600-1840* (John Murray, 1978).

Costin, W. C. and Watson, J. Steven, *The Law and Working of the Constitution: Documents 1660-1914*, vol. 2, 1784-1914 (Adam and Charles Black, 1952).

Cropper, J., *Notes and Memories: being selections from a book of Notes together with recollections of men, and their sayings* (Bateman and Hewitson, 1900).

The Cumberland and Westmorland Herald.

Cumberland News.

Curwen, J. F., *The Castles and Fortified Towers of Cumberland, Westmorland and Lancashire North of the Sands* (Titus Wilson, 1913).

The Daily Mirror.

The Daily Telegraph and Morning Post.

Davies, H., *A Walk Around The Lakes* (Hamlyn, 1983).

Davies, H., *William Wordsworth* (Hamlyn, 1983).

Debrett's Illustrated Peerage (1913).

Dictionary of National Biography (1975).

Disraeli, B., *Vivian Grey* (Bradenham edn., Peter Davies, 1926).

Finley, M. I., ed., *Atlas of Classical Archaeology* (Chatto & Windus, 1977).

Friedman, T., *James Gibbs* (Yale University Press, 1984).

Girouard, M., *The Victorian Country House* (Yale University Press, 1979).

Gore, J., ed., *Creevey* (John Murray, 1949).

Hall, S. C., *Baronial Halls*, vol. II (Chapman & Hall, 1848).

Hawes, F., *Henry Brougham* (Jonathan Cape, 1957).

Howcroft, G. B., 'George Shaw of St. Chad's, Saddleworth' (Saddleworth Historical Society).

Hudleston, C. R., 'The Brougham Family', *C.W.A.A.S Transactions* article XIV, pp. 131-168 (C.W.A.A.S., 1960).

Hudleston, C. R., 'The Birds of Bird's Nest', pts. I & II, Cumbria Family History Society nos. 32 and 33 (November 1984).

Hudleston, C. R., Boumphrey, R. S. and Hughes, J., 'An Armorial For Westmorland and Lonsdale', printed for the Lake District Museum Trust and Cumberland and Westmorland Antiquarian and Archaeological Society (1975).

Hughes, E., *North Country Life in the Eighteenth Century Vol. II, Cumberland and Westmorland 1700-1830* (Oxford University Press, 1965).

Hunter, A., Leaflet prepared on the visit to High Head Castle and Brougham Hall of the Association of Conservation Officers, 28 October, 1989 (Eden District Council Planning Department).

Hussey, C., 'Highhead Castle, Cumberland, The Seat of Major John W. Hills, M.P.', *Country Life* (15 October 1921).

Hutchinson, W., *History of Cumberland* (1794).

A. R. Jabez-Smith, 'Some Portraits at Dovenby Hall', *C.W.A.A.S Transactions* article XVIII, Series 2, vol. LXIV (C.W.A.A.S., 1963).

The Chevalier de Johnstone, *Memoirs of the Rebellion of 1745* (1822).

Kelly, *Directories of Cumberland and Westmorland* (1871, 1894, 1897, 1914, 1938).

Kidd, C. and Williamson, D., eds., *Debrett's Illustrated Peerage* (Macmillan, 1985).

'Life At Brougham Hall', 'Celebrity At Home' section, *World* (1891).

Mannex, P. J., *History, Topography and Directory of Westmorland And Lonsdale North of the Sands* (1849).

Mannex & Co., *Directory of Cumberland and Westmorland* (1851).

Marchand, L. A., ed., *Byron's Letters and Journals*, 11 vols. (John Murray, 1973-81).

Martindale, J. H., 'High Head Castle, Cumberland', 9 September 1910, article XXI, vol. 10, pp. 379-384 (C.W.A.A.S.).

Matthew, H. C. G., ed., *The Gladstone Diaries*, vol. 8, 1871-74 (Oxford University Press, 1982).

Maxwell, Sir H., ed., *The Creevey Papers* (John Murray, 1905).

Minshull, M. J., 'High Head Castle, Ivegill, Cumbria', brochure for the Brougham Hall Charitable Trust.

Neal, W. K. and Black, P. H. L., *Forsyth and Co. Patent Gunmakers* (G. Bell & Sons, 1974).

New, C. W., *The Life of Henry Brougham to 1830* (Oxford, 1961).

Mattin, C., 'Newington House', guide (Newington, Oxfordshire).

Nicholson, J. and Burn, R., *The History and Antiquities of The Counties of Westmorland and Cumberland* (1777).

Orbach, J., *Victorian Architecture in Britain: Blue Guide* (A. & C. Black and W. W. Norton, 1987).

Owen, H., *The Lowther Family* (Phillimore, 1990).

Parker, J., *King of Fools* (Futura Books, 1988).

Parson and White, *Directory of Cumberland and Westmorland* (1829).

Pawle, G., *The War and The Colonel Warden* (Harrap, 1963).

The Penrith Observer.

Pevsner, Sir Nikolaus, *Buildings of England: Cumberland and Westmorland* (1967).

Phillips, J. A. S., 'Reginald Phillips – A Forgotten Coachbuilder', Veteran and Vintage, vol. XV, no. 1, pp. 20-21 (September 1970).

Post Office London Directory (1865, 1869, 1878, 1886, 1900).

Rempel, R. A., *Arthur Balfour, Joseph Chamberlain and the Unionist Free Traders* (David & Charles and Archon Books, 1972).

R.I.B.A. Drawings Collection Catalogue.

R.I.B.A. Journal of Proceedings.

Rickman, T. M., 'The Late Richard Charles Hussey, F.S.A. Born 1806, Died 1887', *The R.I.B.A. Journal of Proceedings*, 3 February 1887.

Rivet, A. L. F. and Smith, Colin, *The Place-Names of Roman Britain* (Batsford, 1979).

Robertson, I., *France: Blue Guide* (Ernest Benn Ltd. and W. W. Norton & Co. Inc., 1984).

Robinson, J. M., *The Latest Country Houses* (Bodley Head, 1984).

Royal Commission on Historic Monuments (1936).

Sanders, C. R. and Fielding, K. J., eds., *The Collected Letters of Thomas and Jane Welsh Carlyle* (Duke University Press, North Carolina, 1976).

Scott, Sir Walter, *Tales of A Grandfather, being stories from the History of Scotland*, 3rd Ser., vol. III (Cadell and Co., 1830).

Seeck, O., ed., *Noticia Dignitatum. Accedunt Noticia urbis Constantinopolanae et laterculi provinciarum* (Berolini, Weidmann, Berlin, 1876; translation, Frankfurt, 1962).

A letter from George Shaw to James Dearden of The Orchard and Handle Hall, Lancs., *Gentleman's Magazine*, vol. XXIX, pp. 369-76 (April 1848).

Slater, *Royal National Commercial Directory and Topography of the Counties of Chester, Cumberland, Westmorland, Durham, Lancaster, Northumberland and York* (1848).

Smith, A. H., *The Place Names of Westmorland*, pts. I and II, vols. XLII and XLIII (English Place-Name Society, Cambridge University Press, 1967).

Snell, J., *Wetheriggs Country Pottery: 19th Century Industrial Monument*, pamphlet guide.

Stephen, Sir L., *Mausoleum Book*, introduction by Alan Bell (Clarendon Press, 1977).

Stewart, R., *Henry Brougham: His Public Career 1778-1868* (Bodley Head, 1986).

Hobart, Major-General Sir, P. C. S., *The Story of 79th Armoured Division October 1942-June 1945* (Hamburg, 1945).

Strong, R., Binney, M. and Harris, J., et al., *The Destruction of the Country House 1875-1975* (Thames & Hudson, 1975).

Tarr, L., *The History of the Carriage*, trans. Elizabeth Hoch (Vision Press, 1969)

Thomas, D., *Cochrane: Britannia's Last Sea-King* (Viking Press, 1978).

Thomas, M., 'A New Brougham', *Country Times and Landscape* (March 1989).

Thomas, M., 'New Hope For High Head', *Country Life* (2 June 1988).

Thomas, M., 'Brougham Hall: One man's crusade with help from the M.S.C. to rejuvenate a medieval castle', *Period Homes* (June 1988).

The Times.

Trevelyan, G. O., *The Life and Letters of Lord Macaulay* (first published, 1876), vols. 1 and 2 (Oxford University Press, 1978).

Tyler, D., *A History of Brougham Hall* (C. Terry, Ross Features International, 1988).

Walford, E. and Hardwicke, R., *The County Families of the United Kingdom* (1860, 1898).

Whellan, W., *The History and Topography of Cumberland and Westmorland* (1860).

Who Was Who (1916-28, 1929-40, 1951-60, 1961-70, 1971-80).

Who's Who of British Members of Parliament, vol. 1 (1832-85).

A. J. Youngson, *The Making of Classical Edinburgh* (Edinburgh University Press, 1966).

Ex info

Lord Hailsham, Radio Four, review of Robert Stewart's book *Henry Brougham: His Public Career 1778-1868* (1986).

Correspondence. Miss Gillian Furlong to Mr. Christopher Terry and others.

Dawn Tyler correspondence.

Mr. James R. Grisenthwaite, Toronto, Canada, letter to Mr. Christopher Terry, 3 August 1989.

Correspondence from Mr. Denis Perriam, Carlisle City Architect, to Mr. Christopher Terry and others.

Sir Anthony Stamer, Bt. Executive Director of the Bentley Club, letter to Mr. Phillips, 20 February 1970.

Mr. Eric Arnison, Mr. and Mrs. Walter Aylen, Prof. Gerald Aylmer, Caroline Bingham, Mr. Roger Bird, Michael, Lord Brougham, Mrs. Joseph and Mary Ballantine-Dykes, Major (retd.) V. T. Bridge, Dr. E. H. Burn (of Christ Church, Oxford), Dr. S. T. Chapman (of Penrith Museum), Mr. Geoff Crisp, Mr. James Cropper, The Dalemain Estate Office, Darlington Reference library, Mr. M. Dennett, (Hon. Archivist, Saddleworth Museum, Oldham), Mr. andLt. Col. J. J. Dingwall, D.S.O., Lt. Col. J. W. R. Dugmore, Cdr. (retd.) Dennis W. Edwards, Ms. Gillian Furlong, Mr. Anthony Galliers-Pratt, Dr. Kenneth Garlick, Mrs. Patricia Hamilton-Meikle, Mr. Anthony Hills, the late Mr. C. Roy Hudleston, Mr. Ulric Huggins, Mr. Andrew Humphries, Miss Sarah Johnston, Lord Kensington, Mr. W. Gordon Laycock, Mr. Michael Maclagan, Mr. Hugh Malet, Mr. F. Markham,Mr. Tom Marshall, Dr. Colin Matthews, Mr. Richard Mounsey, Professor J. Mordaunt Crook, Dr. Janet Myles, Mrs. Pluckrose, Mrs. Dorothy Snell, Dr. R. T. Spence, Mr. B. Stacey, Miss Marjorie (Peggy) Stacey, Mr. Christopher Terry, Mrs. Alison Terry, Mrs. Dawn Tyler, Miss Kim W. Woods, Mr. Peter Brougham Wyly.

List of Subscribers

Prof. Tim and Susan Breen
Mrs. C. Bretherton
Alex Broome
Peter Brougham Wyly
G. B. Brougham and C. P. Brougham
Michael, Lord Brougham
E. P. Brougham
P. Brougham
Kate Brougham
Christopher [Anthony Henry] Brougham
Gaynor Bryant
Mary Burkett and Mrs. D. Morgan
Derek Arnold
Paul Bedford
Michael Berry
Christopher Buxton
J. A. Cropper
A. M. Duxbury
Sir Charles Graham, Bt.
Lionel A. Helmsley
Ulric Huggins
Sarah Johnston
Daniel B. Johnston
Gordon Laycock
René Letton
R. F. Mounsey
R. Hall
Sheila J. Macpherson
Diana Brougham Macintosh
Judy Medrington
Dr. Meskenaite
Francis Noel-Baker
Mrs. Olga Peate
T. W. S. Marshall
Brigadier Tryon-Wilson
B. Stacey
Hugh, Lord Kensington
Hugh and Ann Lee
Keith Richmond
Dr. R. T. Spence
Peggy Stacey
Mrs. C. Terry
Christopher Terry
Dr. G. M. Thomas
Gordon Turnbull
Neville Whittaker
G. H. Winter
Alan Wood
Glen 'Rocky' Brougham
Mr. R. Gray
The Marquis of Anglesey
Mrs. M. L. Brougham
Lt. Col. J. J. Dingwall
D. P. Brougham
R. A. Brougham
Walter S. Aylen Q.C.
F. Goddard

Mike Jones
Dr. Rosalind Thomas
Jeremy Coleridge Hills
Geoff Lee-Martin
Mrs. Barbara Gernaey
The Earl of Carlisle, M.C.
Eric Hay
Jean Hubbert
Dr. Carol A. Brougham
Mrs. B. L. Applegate
Anthony L. Hills
H. L. Brougham
Peter Claydon
Roger Price
Roger Robson
Barrett Brougham
L. E. Brougham
Gary W. and Beverley C. Brougham
Mark Thomas
Mrs. Margaret Coombs (née Aylen)
Irwin Brougham
Philip Brougham

Australian Orders
Alan J. Brougham
Paul James Brougham
Mrs. Romola H. Waters
Mrs. Patricia C. Brougham
Mr. M. V. J. Brougham
Mr. Colin B. Healey
Mr. R. B. Healey
Mrs. Betty L. Coats
Mr. W. A. F. Brougham
Mr. D. N. Brougham
Mrs. P. L. Fuss
Mrs. K. L. Brougham
Mr. R. G. Brougham
Mr. H. H. Brougham
Mr. Graeme Healey
Mrs. C. M. Carr
Mrs. L. Bryant
Mrs. E. Brougham
Mr. L. F. Brougham
Mrs. Margaret Healey
Mr. Raymond Healey
Mr. R. J. Brougham
Miss M. C. Brougham
Mr. Trevor H. Brougham
Mrs. C. D. Sheardown
Mr. P. M. J. Brougham
Miss P. Brougham
Mrs. Marie Bubniw
Mrs. J. W. Brougham
Mr. W. R. Brougham
Mr. M. R. Brougham
Mr. H. M. Brougham
Mrs. Catherine Brougham
Mrs. G. Burns

Index

Compiled by Auriol Griffith Jones

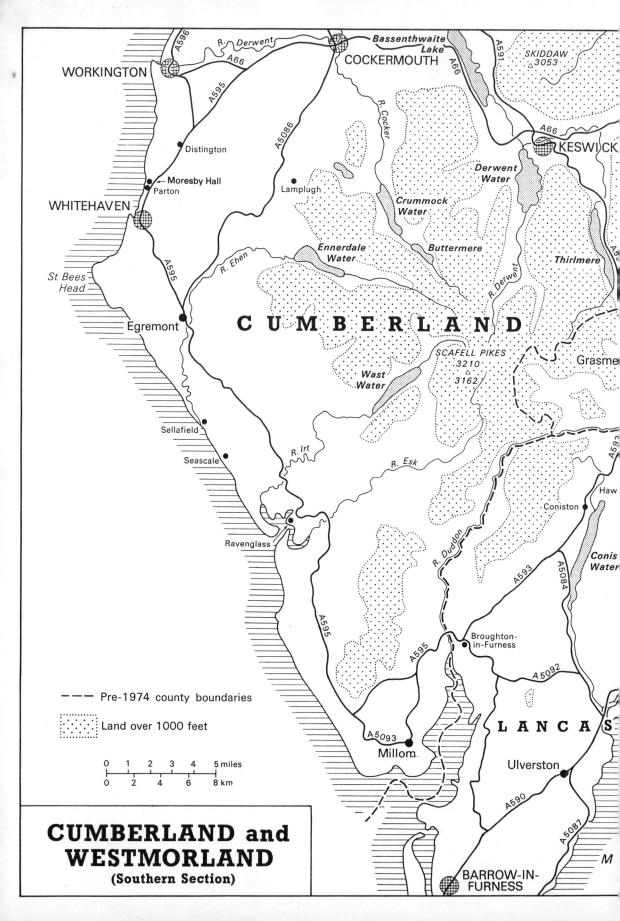

WORKINGTON

A596

A66 R. *Derwent*

Bassenthwaite Lake

COCKERMOUTH

A66

A591

SKIDDAW
△ 3053

A595

A5086

Distington

R. *Cocker*

KESWICK
A66

Derwent Water

Moresby Hall
Parton

Lamplugh

Crummock Water

WHITEHAVEN

Ennerdale Water

Buttermere

Thirlmere

R. *Ehen*

R. *Derwent*

St Bees Head

C U M B E R L A N D

Egremont

SCAFELL PIKES
3210
△
3162

Grasme

Wast Water

Sellafield

R. *Irt*

R. *Esk*

Seascale

Coniston

Haw

Ravenglass

R. *Duddon*

Conis Water

A593

A5084

A595

Broughton-in-Furness

A5092

--- Pre-1974 county boundaries

Land over 1000 feet

A595

L A N C A S

0 1 2 3 4 5 miles
0 2 4 6 8 km

A5093

Millom

Ulverston

A590

A5087

CUMBERLAND and WESTMORLAND
(Southern Section)

M

BARROW-IN-FURNESS